Beyond Reflective Practice

Reflective practice has moved from the margins to the mainstream of professional education. However, in this process, its radical potential has been subsumed by individualistic, rather than situated, understandings of practice. Presenting critical perspectives that challenge the current paradigm, this book aims to move beyond reflective practice. It proposes new conceptualisations and offers fresh approaches relevant across professions. Contributors include both academics and practitioners concerned with the training and development of professionals.

Definitions of reflection (which are often implicit) commonly focus on the individual's internal thought processes and responsibility for their actions. The individual – what they did, thought and felt – is emphasised with little recognition of context, power dynamics or ideological challenges. This book presents the work of practitioners, educators, academics and researchers who see this as problematic and are moving towards a more critical approach to reflective practice.

With an overview from the editors and fourteen chapters considering new conceptualisations, professional perspectives and new practices, *Beyond Reflective Practice* examines the new forms of professional reflective practice that are emerging. It examines in particular the relationships between reflective practitioners and those on whom they practise. It looks at the ways in which the world of professional work has changed and the ways in which professional practice needs to change to meet the needs of this new world. It will be relevant for those concerned with initial and ongoing professional learning, both in work and in educational contexts.

Helen Bradbury is Senior Lecturer at the University of Leeds, working in both education and healthcare. Helen worked in the NHS for 20 years as a hospital pharmacist before commencing her academic career.

Nick Frost is Professor of Social Work (children, childhood and families) at the Faculty of Health, Leeds Metropolitan University. Nick has published widely in the field of child and family social work, and worked for 15 years in local authority social work before he commenced his academic career.

Sue Kilminster is Principal Research Fellow in the Medical Education Unit at the University of Leeds. She has worked in vocational and professional education and research for over 20 years and was previously a nurse.

Miriam Zukas is Professor of Adult Education and the Director of the Lifelong Learning Institute at the University of Leeds. She has worked for the past 30 years with adult learners and with those who teach adults.

Beyond Reflective Practice

New approaches to professional lifelong learning

Edited by Helen Bradbury, Nick Frost,
Sue Kilminster and Miriam Zukas

Routledge
Taylor & Francis Group

LONDON AND NEW YORK

First published 2010
by Routledge
2 Park Square, Milton Park, Abingdon, Oxon, OX14 4RN

Simultaneously published in the USA and Canada
by Routledge
270 Madison Avenue, New York, NY 10016

Routledge is an imprint of the Taylor & Francis Group, an informa business

Transferred to Digital Printing 2010

Typeset in Garamond by
Taylor & Francis Books

British Library Cataloguing in Publication Data
A catalogue record for this book is available from the British Library

Library of Congress Cataloging in Publication Data
Beyond reflective practice : new approaches to professional lifelong learning /
edited by Helen Bradbury ... [et al.].
    p. cm.
Includes bibliographical references.
1. Continuing education. 2. Reflective learning. 3. Professional employees–
Education (Continuing education) I. Bradbury, Helen.
    LC5215.B5 2010
    374–dc22
                2009004479

ISBN10 0-415-46792-6 (hbk)
ISBN10 0-415-46793-4 (pbk)
ISBN10 0-203-87317-3 (ebk)

ISBN13 978-0-415-46792-6 (hbk)
ISBN13 978-0-415-46793-3 (pbk)
ISBN13 978-0-203-87317-5 (ebk)

Contents

Acknowledgements

We would like to thank Clair Atkinson and Pamela Irwin for their invaluable help with the manuscript. Thanks, as ever, to Jaswant Bhavra for all her ongoing support. Thanks to Fiona O'Neill for her contribution to Chapter 8.

List of contributors

Editors' biographical notes

Helen Bradbury is Senior Lecturer at the University of Leeds, working in both education and health care. Her research interests include clinical education generally, learning, health and life journeys, and inter-professional education. Helen worked in the NHS for 20 years as a hospital pharmacist before commencing her academic career.

Nick Frost is Professor of Social Work (Children, Childhood and Families) at the Faculty of Health, Leeds Metropolitan University. Nick has published widely in the field of child and family social work. Most recently he has written *Understanding Children's Social Care* (with Nigel Parton, Sage, 2009). Nick worked in local authority social work for 15 years before commencing his academic career.

Sue Kilminster is Principal Research Fellow in the Medical Education Unit at the University of Leeds. Her current research interests include transitions, supervision and work-based learning, policy-related research, assessment, inter-professional education and gender issues in medicine. She has worked in vocational and professional education and research for over 20 years and was previously a nurse.

Miriam Zukas is Professor of Adult Education and the Director of the Lifelong Learning Institute at the University of Leeds. She is also the editor of the journal *Studies in the Education of Adults*. Her research interests include adult education generally and academic identities, transitions from learning to work, and the development of clinical pedagogic identities more specifically.

Contributors' biographical notes

Stephen Billett is at Griffith University, Australia. He investigates learning through and for work. He publishes his work in journals, sole-authored books (*Learning through Work, Strategies for Effective Practice* and *Work, Change and Workers*) and edited volumes (*Work, Subjectivity and Learning* and *Emerging Perspectives of Work and Learning*). He is a member of seven editorial boards and is the Editor in Chief of *Vocations and Learning*.

David Boud is Professor of Adult Education at the University of Technology, Sydney. He is a Senior Fellow of the Australian Learning and Teaching Council. Recent books, with various others, include *Productive Reflection at Work, Learning for Changing Organisations, Rethinking Assessment in Higher Education: Learning for the Longer Term* and *Changing Practices of Doctoral Education* (all published by Routledge).

Geoffrey Chivers is Emeritus Professor of Professional Development in the Business School at Loughborough University. The main focus of his research has been post-experience learning and development across a wide range of professions, with recent papers published in the *Journal of European Industrial Training*. He has increasingly focused on informal learning at work as key to professional competence achievement. In 2005 he co-authored, with Graham Cheetham, *Professions, Competence and Informal Learning* (published by Edward Elgar).

Kate Collier is Senior Lecturer in Adult Education at the University of Technology, Sydney, Australia. She is Programme Director of a range of adult education courses. She began her career as a drama and theatre arts specialist but for the past 15 years has been involved in adult education in the tertiary sector both in Australia and the UK.

Ernest Dalton is the Director of Patient Teacher PR: consultant facilitator and evaluator with groups of health professionals and community organisations in the UK and the USA. He is also a writer and film maker, and is developing methods for framing and disseminating personal and institutional change in health care.

Jan Fook is Professor of Professional Practice Research and Director of the Inter-professional Institute, South West London Academic Network (Royal Holloway, University of London; St Georges, University of London; and Kingston University). She has worked mostly in the area of critical social work and critical reflection throughout her career. Her two most recent books are *Practising Critical Reflection* (with Fiona Gardner) and *Critical Reflection in Health and Social Care* (edited with Sue White and Fiona Gardner).

Janet Hargreaves is Associate Dean, Learning and Teaching at the University of Huddersfield. Her Doctor of Education thesis explored the concept of the 'good nurse', from which the chapter in this volume originated. Recent publications include: 'So how Do you Feel about that? Assessing Reflective Practice', *Nurse Education Today*, vol. 24, 2004.

Cheryl Hunt is Senior Lecturer in Professional Learning, and Director of the Professional Doctorates Programme in the Graduate School of Education, University of Exeter. She is an Executive Editor of *Teaching in Higher Education*. She has written extensively about the use and facilitation of critical reflective practice in professional education and is currently researching understandings of spirituality and their implications for professional practice.

Kate Karban is a Principal Lecturer in Mental Health at Leeds Metropolitan University. She has a background in mental-health social work and extensive experience of social work and mental-health education and training. Kate is currently involved in a British Council-funded, mental-health education project, working in collaboration with Chainama College of Health Sciences in Zambia. Recent research includes inter-professional learning and service evaluation.

Sue Knights and **Jane Sampson** were colleagues in the Faculty of Education, University of Technology, Sydney for over 20 years. Their research interests include self-directed learning, reflection and peer learning and they are now both working as independent consultants in learning and development. **Lois Meyer** taught with Susan Knights at UTS and is currently working as an Educational Development consultant in the School of Public Health and Community Medicine at the University of New South Wales.

Andrea McGoverin is Senior Teaching Fellow in Communication Skills (Patient Perspective) at the Medical Education Unit, School of Medicine, University of Leeds. She is a patient advocate, a presenter and a writer for children about long-term conditions and changing professional practice. Her research includes the role of learning in long-term conditions and the role of patients as teachers in medical and inter-professional learning.

Penny Morris is Senior Lecturer in Communication Skills at the Medical Education Unit, School of Medicine, University of Leeds. Her research interests include patient and community voices in professional learning; learning and long-term conditions; theoretical and methodological perspectives on communication in healthcare; and doctors in difficulty. She is co-author of the book *The Patient Doctor Consultation in Primary Care: Theory and Practice* and co-convenor of meetings about the 'Patient Voice'.

Jennifer Newton is currently an Australian Post-Doctoral Industry Fellow in the School of Nursing and Midwifery, Monash University, leading an Australian Research Council Linkage project on workplace learning. She has an extensive background in nursing gained both in the UK and Australia and is a proactive researcher in the field of clinical nurse education, reflective practice and practice development.

David Saltiel is a qualified social worker who has worked in a range of practice settings with children and families for many years as both a practitioner and as a manager. He is currently a Lecturer in Social Work in the School of Healthcare at the University of Leeds.

Sue Smith is the Director for the Centre of Excellence in Teaching and Learning for Enterprise at Leeds Metropolitan University. As a Principal Lecturer, she has been responsible for course design and has led on the Faculty of Health's inter-professional learning programme. She publishes in the fields of problem-based learning, inter-professional education and group working.

John Sweet is Clinical Associate Professor at the University of Warwick and has published on professional and inter-professional education situated in clinical dentistry; he works currently in educational development programmes for dental tutors. He advocates deepening reflective practices through appreciative inquiry, such as journaling and action learning. He claims these widen the development of the scholarship of learning, teaching and research in higher education.

Jools Symons is a Patient and Public Voices in Healthcare Education Development and Support Officer at the Medical Education Unit, School of Medicine, University of Leeds. She is also a carer advocate, and is developing ways of engaging patients, carers and the public in professional learning, including in communication teaching, medical-curriculum change and multi- and inter-professional education. She is researching the effects of public involvement, including 'Patient Learning Journeys'.

Linden West is Reader in Education at Canterbury Christ Church University. His books include *Beyond Fragments, Doctors on the Edge* and *Using Life History and Biographical Approaches in the Study of Adult and Lifelong Learning*. He is co-author of *Using Biographical Methods in Social Research* (Sage). He coordinates a European Biographical Research Network and is a qualified psychotherapist.

Introduction and overview

Sue Kilminster, Miriam Zukas, Helen Bradbury and Nick Frost

Background to the book

Across the professions, approaches to learning are often dominated by taken-for-granted assumptions about the processes of becoming and being a professional. The four editors of this book came together in order to examine and challenge some of these assumptions and some of the underpinning notions current in professional education. We have backgrounds in specific areas of professional learning (teacher education, medical and health-care education and social work education) and we are all concerned more generally with work and learning. Because our work crosses disciplinary and professional boundaries, we kept encountering contradictory understandings and practices within and across different arenas. We were interested in exploring these contradictions and tensions with others; and we therefore organised a series of one-day conferences for professionals from a wide range of backgrounds to engage critically with both theoretical and empirical research informing practice for professional learning. This book developed from the first conference, 'Professional lifelong learning: Beyond reflective practice', and presents the work of some of those concerned practitioners, educators, academics and researchers who are engaging in a variety of ways with a critical approach to reflective practice. As with approaches to learning in general, the authors within this book have different, sometimes contradictory, views and emphases but all offer critical perspectives and fresh insights on contemporary thinking in relation to reflective practice.

Reflection and reflective practice

Ideas about the importance of reflection in learning, particularly workplace learning, became prominent in the professional education literature in the 1980s. The most frequently cited source was Schön (1983), although others contributed to the zeitgeist, including Benner (1984), Boud, Keogh and Walker (1985), Brookfield (1987), Kemmis (1985), Kolb and Fry (1975) and Mezirow (1981). Polanyi's (1967) ideas about tacit knowledge – 'we know more than we can tell' (p. 4) – informed much of this emerging work on reflection. Although these authors were writing from different perspectives and within different contexts, they all suggested that practitioners could develop their work by thinking critically about their actions. As such, they offered support and academic justification for practitioners interested in critical praxis. Their work was relevant for those who were trying to challenge dominant professional paradigms across a number of professions but particularly in education, social care and some health-care professions. However, ideas about reflective practice – what it means, how practitioners can do it and, particularly, how they can show they are doing it – have moved away from those radical roots over the last twenty years

Although reflective practice was originally introduced as a way to address well-documented problems in professional practice, it was adapted by many health and social care professional educators and professional bodies as the accepted approach for the development of emerging and/or experienced professionals. In this sense, reflective practice moved quickly from the margins of educational and organisational theory to the mainstream of professional education and development practice. In the process, its radical potential was subsumed by individualistic, rather than situated, understandings of practice. This process of de-radicalisation was compounded by different understandings about reflection and reflective practice; societal tensions between professional autonomy and professional accountability; pressures for personal accountability and control; managerialism and audit cultures; and different understandings about learning. These influences all affect contemporary conceptualisations of reflective practice. They are outlined as themes in this Introduction and discussed in detail throughout the rest of the book.

The case of nursing demonstrates well the transmogrification of ideas. Nursing was the first health care profession to adopt notions about reflective practice and is probably still the profession where the ideas are most prevalent. During the 1980s, within the UK at least, nursing was engaged in a struggle for professional recognition and autonomy, most particularly from doctors (for example, Savage 1987). The struggle arose from a confluence of radical challenges including feminist and socialist perspectives on both women's position and the relationship of social inequalities, particularly poverty, to health. Some nurses, including the Radical Nurses Group, understood that nurses' position and practice were linked, that lack of professional autonomy limited patient care and that change would come by developing critical understandings which in turn would inform practice. From such a perspective, critical reflective practice had great potential for transformation. This was also recognised by more radical practitioners in nursing and other health and social professions. Unsurprisingly, proponents of such critical reflective practice met varying degrees of resistance.

Since then, there has been a shift away from such radical understandings and, in effect, a reversal in focus. Instead of reflection being the bedrock for the radical transformation of practice, instrumental approaches now predominate, both in the literature and in professional education and assessment. Definitions of reflection (which are often implicit) focus on the individual's internal thought processes and responsibility for their actions. The individual – what they did/thought/felt – is emphasised with little recognition of context, power dynamics or ideological challenge. Nor is there encouragement to critically evaluate professional practice such as health care and health-care delivery. In other words, there is little or no acknowledgement of the material reality in which the individual works. This individualistic focus on reflection is underpinned by the 'folk theory of learning' (Bereiter 2002) which assumes that learning is about putting content (attitudes, skills, knowledge) in minds. Within these restricted versions of reflective practice, although there might be some recognition of the embodiment of learning through the acknowledgement of emotion, nevertheless the place of workplace practices, cultures and power relations in learning is ignored.

The popularity of reflective practice in the education of professionals has also derived from public tensions between professional autonomy and professional accountability; these tensions have affected professional regulation, professional practices and professional education. One of the consequences for professional education, particularly in health care, has been the foregrounding of 'professionalism' (the behaviour and attitudes considered appropriate for a health-care professional) which is now taught and assessed. Reflective practice has been formalised by regulatory bodies as a way of developing the professionalism of both individual students, particularly through assessment, and practitioners through continuing professional development mechanisms. In addition, the growth of managerialism and the audit culture fuel demands for evidence, including the need for evidence to demonstrate reflective practice. Consequently, reflection is often used as a 'tool' for personal or professional development and students, and professionals are expected to produce some sort of written reflective record or portfolio (increasingly an electronic record). Conceptual debate is too frequently limited to assessment issues – how can one assess reflective practice? Furthermore, as has been recognised by many authors, the reflections themselves can be superficial and procedural, as if one were following a recipe compliantly, rather than questioning and challenging. Again the original idea of reflection as a tool for critical praxis is reversed and instead it becomes a tool for control and orthodoxy. This tension between reflection and reflective practice as emancipatory, both for the professional and their clients, and as an instrument of control, is developed in various chapters of this book.

Purpose of the book

Therefore this book, *Beyond Reflective Practice*, presents critical perspectives on the current paradigm, or even dogma, of reflective practice within much professional education. Our purpose is to challenge that dogma and critically to analyse and move beyond reflective practice. We believe that there is an urgent need to revisit the ideas of reflection and reflective practice in a systematic way for three reasons. First, previous challenges and critiques appear not to have been heard; second, it has become clear that the original conception does not take into account more complex forms of work and identity in general and the reconfiguration of the professional workplace in particular; third, the radical implications of the ideas of Schön and others have been somewhat diverted and we wish to reclaim them. The contributors advance this critique and try, in various ways, to develop more critical praxis in relation to reflection.

This book is different from the numerous texts which continue to be published describing reflective practice and making suggestions for its implementation, practice, assessment and so on. We have selected contributions which propose new conceptualisations of reflective practice and/or offer fresh critical perspectives. Even if they draw on one profession, all are relevant across professions, and some introduce new practices. Contributors include both academics and practitioners concerned with the training and development of professionals. We hope the collection will be relevant for those concerned with initial and ongoing learning, both in work and in educational contexts.

Organisation of the book

Any discussion of reflective practice is likely to be contextualised within one form of practice or another, one professional group or another. This professional contextualisation is important, as we shall show. But the broader contextual issues involving social, economic and cultural change, transforming professional/client relations. And organisational, policy and regulatory framing as well as globalisation, all contribute to a destabilisation of the conceptualisation of the professional, and ideas about what makes professional work distinctive. Within this broader context, our aim in this collection is critically to examine both the concept of reflective practice and its place in professional education.

We have organised the contributions into three overlapping parts, reflecting the main foci for moving beyond reflective practice. Our first part, 'Conceptual challenges', involves redefinitions and fresh conceptualisations of reflective practice, entailing new theoretical resources and critical insights. 'Professional perspectives', the second part, concentrates on current views of reflective practice through the lenses of specific professions. Our third, 'New practices', explores new ways of engaging with reflection and reflective practice in the context of both professional education and continuing professional development. Despite this artificial segregation, intended to offer the reader a quick guide to relevant material, there are many overarching themes. For example, we report on assessment issues in all three parts; empirical research informs many of the chapters; and our contributors draw on a wide range of theoretical resources, many of which are mutually exclusive. We have therefore introduced each of the three parts with a brief thematic analysis, high-lighting connections and disjunctions for our readers.

Below, we introduce each of the main chapters, drawing attention to some of their main findings.

Part I: Conceptual challenges

Nick Frost's opening chapter provides an overview for the rest of the book, reviewing changes over the last thirty years in the personal and public landscape in which professionals practice and reflect. His central argument is that changes in modern professionalism need to be understood in the context of wider social and global changes, specifically globalisation, informationalism, the emergence of the network society and managerialism in the context of the risk and audit society. Frost critiques what he calls the 'idealist' approach to reflection which assumes that professionals are able to create their own futures, and proposes instead a materialist approach to critical reflection which is located within this wider social and political context.

David Boud, our second contributor, is one of the best-known writers on reflective practice; from this erudite position, he interrogates the notions of reflection and reflective practice over the last twenty years. His critique suggests that whilst some applications of these ideas in courses distorted their original intentions and took an excessively instrumental approach to their use, they nevertheless provided useful framing devices to help con-ceptualise some important processes in professional learning. He argues that one of the reasons why these notions were readily accepted is because they shared an individualised view of learning with the very programmes in which they were used. He suggests that more recently this individualistic view of learning was challenged because of alternative conceptions that con-sider reflection within the context of settings which necessarily have more of a group or team-based work orientation. Boud poses three alternatives for the future: Should we reject earlier views of reflection? Should we rehabilitate them to capture their previous potential? Or should we move to new ways of regarding reflection that are more in keeping with what we know about the context of practice? He suggests that the pursuit of each of these directions together might be more worthwhile than an exclusive focus on any one.

As David Boud looks beyond reflective practice, so too does Jan Fook. She confronts the confusion between reflective practice and critical reflection, returning to the 'critical' aspect of reflection, rather than reflective practice more generally. Picking up from Boud, Fook examines theoretically how social and individual realms are linked. She begins with the individual in a social con-text, arguing that individual experience is a microcosm of the social. Social change is effected through changes in individuals' orientation – preferably towards an awareness of the political choices to be made in practice. Fook then con-cretises her theoretical position with an example of developing critical reflection with professionals on a Masters course. In this process, she redefines critical reflection as 'the ability to understand the social dimensions and political functions of experience and meaning making, and the ability to apply this understanding in working in social contexts'.

Whilst a materialist approach demands an understanding of the macro-context, the micro-context of the reflective workplace is highly relevant in moving beyond individualised versions of reflective practice. Furthermore, learning itself is central, although often ignored. Stephen Billett and Jenny Newton focus attention on both learning and the workplace. They propose a model of 'learning practice' which combines both individual and workplace elements. They argue that it is not enough to rely on individual epistemological acts such as personal reflection to understand 'learning practice'. Nor do the affordances in the professional setting such as workplace support suffice. Instead, both personal and institutional contributions need to work interdependently, both at an explanatory level and at the level of practice. Moreover, as work requirements, work conditions and workforce participation change, particular elements of this interdependent relationship may be accentuated. Billett and Newton emphasise the significance of this interdependence in remaking and changing practice, as well as its role in individuals' professional development. That is, they suggest that both workplace change and human development are products of relations between the individual and social, rather than one being posterior to the other.

Like Fook, Linden West draws on empirical examples to reassert the individual as the basis for critical reflection, basing this claim on his previous in-depth auto/biographical research into the lived experience of learning and working among professionals. His participants include doctors and trainee teachers, based in marginalised, inner-city communities in the UK. Like Frost, West highlights the significance of broader social questions, particularly the crisis of professionalism and of what counts as professional knowledge. He also suggests that the dominance of instrumentalism in professional education leads to the potential neglect of deeper forms of reflective learning and critical awareness. His central argument is that more holistic forms of understanding which combine self-knowledge with critical awareness are needed to develop more creative, effective and reflexive professionals. His research approach is, he suggests, a reflexive space for developing critical awareness and emotional insight alongside self-knowledge and deepening understanding of the other. West illuminates his argument with three case studies, concluding that auto/biographical approaches in professional lifelong learning can help build bridges between thoughts and feelings, self and the other, the social and the personal, the critical and the reflexive.

Part II: Professional perspectives

The chapters in this part all draw from specific professional perspectives, illuminating the arguments through the specificities of different professions and different policy contexts. Janet Hargreaves draws on her thirty-year history as a nurse and nurse educator, to reflect historically on the discourses within nursing (including that of reflective practice) which exert a powerful influence on the behaviour and practice of nurses. A number of gendered discourses about obedience, loyalty and vocation make up an image of the 'good nurse' which has its origins in the nineteenth century but can still be identified today. Her chapter gives a detailed analysis of the period 1945–55, and shows how nurses' self-conceptualisations were congruent with the prevailing discourses. However that traditional discourse is mediated in current practice with more contemporary discourses in which nurses are required not only to care 'for' (that is, practise surveillance and control) but to demonstrate their caring 'about' (that is, the emotional engagement of self). Thus nursing is a form of 'emotional labour' in which nurses draw upon their emotional selves (through reflective practice) to care for patients. Within this climate, Hargreaves concludes that discourses of emotional engagement, reflection and continuous self-improvement encourage people to see themselves as 'not good enough' and are thus a controlling rather than liberating force.

Following some of the earlier discussions about the need to go beyond individualised conceptualisations of reflection and reflective practice to take account of collaborative working and team working, Sue Knights, Lois Meyer and Jane Sampson's chapter focuses on team teaching as a way of enhancing professional learning in the academic workplace. Whilst it seems as if the process of planning, teaching and assessing together offers possibilities for rich collaborative reflection, they are concerned that the pitfalls and challenges should also be realistically portrayed. In their chapter they focus on the difficulties experienced in realising the potential for productive professional learning through reflective team-teaching partnerships. Drawing on data derived from a series of interviews and focus group discussions with tertiary teachers about their experiences of team teaching, they show how it is possible to achieve a functional level of collaboration, even if challenges such as trust might, ultimately, prevent collaborative reflection. This preliminary attempt to move beyond individualised conceptualisations of reflection and reflective practice throws up new problems and questions, even as it addresses old concerns.

To date, even the most challenging conceptual and empirical writing about reflective practice has failed fully to engage with the clients with whom professionals work. Penny Morris et al. redress this, positing that being a reflective practitioner is no longer enough to support new roles and relationships between professionals and the communities they serve. In the context of health care, they consider how we might refine and supplement reflective models with other theoretical approaches to highlight the value of participatory processes that put the patient at the centre of learning and practice. The authors outline changing models of the patient that capture a new health-care paradigm and examine related learning with patient voices that offers additional perspectives for professionals. They argue that this new paradigm requires a shift in perception for practitioners about their own role and that of patients and carers. Morris et al. draw on their knowledge and experience of bringing patient voices into medical and other health professional learning. They suggest that providing opportunities for health professionals to engage in learning with individuals who bring a patient perspective can be a powerful way of supporting professionals to become more patient centred in their practice, and to move beyond the limitations of reflective practice.

Geoffrey Chivers also redresses limitations in the work to date on reflective practice, this time by focusing on the broader learning and development of professional groups. He argues that reflective practice is only one of a range of ways in which professionals learn through informal processes. Drawing on previously published empirical findings derived from a survey with dentists, accountants, civil servants, surveyors, clergy and training professionals, Chivers claims that although many professionals can identify learning from reflection on practice, they are often equally aware of other more informal methods of learning which have not received nearly so much attention from researchers or practitioners in the field of initial or continuing professional development. He argues that these less-considered learning methods can be combined with reflective practice to produce powerful approaches to professional learning at every stage of the professional's career progression.

The final chapter in this part, by David Saltiel, reviews the status of reflective practice in relation particularly to social work. He finds much to celebrate: the valuing of experiential knowledge and creative practice; the counterweight to evidence-based practice; and the promotion of a vision of professionalism based on diversity and flexibility. But he is also concerned with the emergence of reflective practice as confessional, in the case of students, and as (Foucauldian) surveillance and control, in the case of practitioners. He argues that reflection should be considered as only one of a range of critical practices in order to avoid its mutation into a set of conforming and instrumental activities. Instead he advocates Barnett's move towards critical being – that is, engaging in critical reason, critical reflection and, most importantly, critical action.

Part III: New practices

Our final part moves beyond critique, (re)conceptualisation and context to consider new practices, new ways of engaging with reflection. The authors in this part cross boundaries and disciplines to bring fresh insights and inspiration to move beyond reflective practice. The first example from Kate Collier foregrounds the place of imagination and creativity in the reflection process. She mobilises ideas of the aesthetic and from theatre arts to show how they can be connected to the imaginative process of reflection. The concept of self-spectatorship enables her to highlight how putting action 'on stage', as it were, enables an individual to consider the 'action' as if one of the audience. This imaginative re-creation gives special meaning to the event. Collier describes how she tested these ideas and how she created processes for helping adult educators not only to reflect on their professional practice but to re-envision it and imagine how it could be changed. This reflective process involved visualisation techniques and the development of workplace case studies or 'scenarios'. Collier suggests that these new practices could offer a framework which valorises imagination and creativity in reflective practice.

Cheryl Hunt's chapter also explores relatively new terrain in relation to reflective practice: spirituality. Her contribution is based on a personal journey and takes its inspiration from two sources: reflections on the development of a module on reflective practice within a Masters degree, and discussion of issues arising from a seminar series entitled 'Researching spirituality as a dimension of lifelong learning'. She suggests that, especially for those who have a 'transpersonal orientation', questions about spirituality may be an integral element of reflective practice. Hunt proposes that *mythopoesis* and cooperative inquiry may be appropriate frameworks through which to address such questions. She argues that the implications of such questions should not be ignored in the context of professional lifelong learning – but that, in the current outcomes-driven rationality of much professional education, they may represent a step too far beyond the conventions of reflective practice.

Whilst many of the chapters so far have derived from work with uni-professional groups, Kate Karban and Sue Smith argue that, within health and social care, public concern, economic imperatives and the drive for a more flexible workforce have created an environment in which inter-professional working and learning is much needed, thus returning to a theme raised by Boud. Within this changing context, they suggest that it is possible to meet both organisational and individual obstacles to reflective practice by promoting reflection within teams and across professions. They illustrate how this might happen with reference to a programme involving nurses, social workers, dieticians, speech and language therapists, physiotherapists and occupational therapists. Multi-professional groups of pre-registration students meet regularly with reflective practice as both a discrete unit and a continuing theme throughout their shared curriculum. Karban and Smith conclude that such an approach is a significant challenge, not least because of the divergence between a critical examination of power relations with a focus on process and the technical–rational approach characterising much of the rest of the educational experience.

In the final chapter, John Sweet draws on new practices with dentists, an under-researched professional group. He also returns to one of the themes in this book – the suggestion that group reflection might be a better vehicle than individualised efforts. He supports this view with a comprehensive critique of what he calls reflective practice as individual incident analysis (RPIIA). His brief analysis of a study of group reflective practice with undergraduate dental students develops this group approach. Like Karban and Smith, Sweet warns that such collective approaches may foster disagreement and controversy, but that they may also help to resolve issues collectively and promote positive institutional change.

Part I

Conceptual challenges

Miriam Zukas, Helen Bradbury, Nick Frost and Sue Kilminster

Introduction

This book begins in familiar territory: many have already criticised the concepts of reflection and reflective practice, and the ways in which these concepts have been taken up by initial and continuing professional education. The contributors to the first part of the book collectively outline these main critiques, which are drawn on by many authors in later chapters. The critiques are summarised in the first section below. The authors then utilise a range of theoretical resources in order to explore alternative conceptualisations which either build on reflection and reflective practice and/or offer fresh conceptual tools for understanding professional learning and practice. These new conceptualisations are summarised in the second section below. Finally, in the third section, we summarise the ways in which the authors have expanded the focal points for reflection and reflective practice to take account of more complex contexts for and interpretations of professional learning and practice.

Critique of reflective practice to date

As David Boud outlines in his chapter, notions of reflection and reflective practice were quickly taken up by those involved in professional education from the late 1980s onwards. But Nick Frost suggests that what is striking is that, just as these ideas were gaining in popularity across a range of professions, a number of trends were developing which radically changed the ways in which professionals operated and were regarded in 'late modernity'. These included globalisation, informationalism and the evolution of a networked society. Whilst these all affect the contexts and conditions for professional practice, a fourth change, the rise of managerialism, risk and the audit society, changed the social contract with professionals, and therefore the ways in which professionals work today.

Whilst the working conditions for professionals have changed, so too have our understandings of reflection and reflective practice. The critiques might be divided into those which deal with the ideas themselves, and those which are concerned with the uses to which reflection and reflective practice have been put, particularly within professional education. Boud summarises those critiques which deal with the ideas themselves as follows. First, some criticise the notion of reflection as unclear and ask if, in the end, it is any different from thinking. Second, what might be called the critical critique asks whether reflection and reflective practice are, in and of themselves, 'good things' unless the reflection questions taken-for-granted assumptions and is critical (see Jane Fook's and Linden West's chapters for a development of this critique). Third, the idea of the individual professional, working as a separate being and engaging in individual reflection, is also critiqued. Some argue that professional work is characterised by team working and cross-professional collaboration and that the original notion of reflection does not take sufficient account of groups. However, Fook tempers this critique, arguing that we need to analyse carefully the relationship between the individual professional and the processes leading to changes in practice.

Others have suggested that the problems lie in the ways in which reflection is assumed to happen inside people's heads. Frost believes that some schools of reflective practice have marginalised the wider social context and are therefore what he calls 'idealist' in their approach – that is, they have understood reflection as something that happens subjectively in the head of the individual practitioner. Linden West also believes that this is a problem but his critique stems from an argument that many approaches are superficial and formulaic because they omit consideration of the anxieties and defences associated with learning and professional work. Stephen Billett and Jennifer Newton also reject the practitioner's head as the site for learning, arguing that learning arises as part of workplace practice, rather than separate from that practice. In contrast, Fook argues that there is a place for learning which is separate from the workplace – she believes that professionals need to be able to maintain their independence of a specific workplace setting and gives reasons for this such as the need to equip professionals with the ability to make sense of workplace cultures and organisational values.

Notwithstanding the critiques of reflection and reflective practice, contributors also question the ways in which such notions have been put to work in education and in continuing professional development. Boud suggests that one reason for the ready acceptance of these ideas within education lay in the individualised view of learning shared by those responsible for professional education. Like others throughout the book, he questions the assumed relationship between attempts to promote reflection and reflective practice itself, making the point that such interventions are often antithetical when they turn reflective processes into procedures or attempt to assess them. Like all the authors in this first part, he rejects a move on the part of some educators to proceduralise reflection through checklists and recipes of one kind or another. But he does not want to reject the concept altogether: he believes that reflection enables us to engage in making sense of experience in complex situations. However, he recommends a turn to practice, as do Billett and Newton.

Fresh conceptualisations

So far we have considered the general critiques proposed by contributors in this first part of the book. Now we turn to the ways in which each refines reflection and/or reflective practice, sometimes redefining, and sometimes proposing new forms of professional learning and engagement in practice.

West's development is drawn from three empirical studies with professionals where he explored, through a series of interviews over an extended period, what he calls auto/biographical forms of reflexive learning. Recognising that reflective practices may lack a critical edge (see the critique above), West offers the concept of 'really reflexive practice' in which 'criticality can be connected with feeling, self with the other, one biography and another'. The interviews with professionals offered a space for them to combine self-knowledge and critical awareness in more holistic forms of understanding such that they '[represented] a meeting point between historical and cultural forces and structuring processes, and struggles for agency, selfhood and integrity in a life'.

Fook's central concept is 'critical reflection', and the relationship between individual and social change. She suggests that the analysis of what is meant by 'critical' is crucial. For her, there are two aspects: one which focuses on unearthing deeper assumptions in order to bring about transformative change, and the other which is concerned with an analysis of power and power relations. However, unlike some versions of critical reflection (such as Freire's), Fook makes the point that social change has to be understood through individual action – 'individual experience may be seen as a microcosm of the social'. Thus critical reflection enables her to theorise how professional identity might be transformed and might, in turn, translate into new (or reaffirmed) professional practices.

Billett and Newton move away from all discussion of reflection and reflective practice to invent a new model of 'learning practice' to consider professional learning. They propose that we need to focus on learning in practice, rather than learning as an activity which takes place separate from practice. From this perspective, in order to promote learning, we need to consider on the one hand the affordances of the workplace for learning. This might include invitations to participate and to learn through workplace activities and engagement, including close and indirect forms of guidance. On the other hand, it will depend on the quality of an individual professional's participation in work (and learning). If professionals are engaged and learning intentionally, and the workplace provides opportunities to engage in new activities and to refine what has been learnt, with direct sources of knowledge and indirect guidance, then Billett and Newton's learning practice can be said to be operating effectively. In this way, learning and practice are integrated.

Boud too turns to practice in his refinement. He concentrates on the need to respond to a number of aspects of professional practice in the development of the concept of reflection. For example, like West, he recognises that practice is embodied; like Frost, he acknowledges the changing context of professional practice, although he focuses more on its collective nature than does Frost; and like Billett and Newton, he understands practice to be contextualised; but in addition he also recognises a new emphasis on multidisciplinary/trans-disciplinarity in practice and an emphasis on practice being co-produced with those with whom it is conducted. Taking all this into account, he introduces the notion of 'productive reflection' which is organisational rather than individual in intent; collective rather than individual in orientation; generative rather than instrumental in focus; connecting learning and work; involving multiple stakeholders and connecting players; and, most importantly, recognised as an open and unpredictable process which changes over time.

New terrains for reflection and reflective practice

These first five contributions not only suggest fresh or revitalised concepts to move beyond reflective practice. They move away (albeit in different directions) from the image of the professional as a decontextualised, asocial, rational and autonomous professional being to much more complex understandings of professional learning and practice. West challenges the process of reflection as an individualised activity by suggesting that the research process itself might afford new spaces for auto/biographical exploration and understanding. His psychodynamic perspective confronts assumptions about the rational professional, inviting deeper and more extended exploration than is usually understood by reflection. Fook insists on considering the individual in a social context, rather than as somehow independent of biographical and social concerns. Frost also resituates the professional, this time in a fast-moving social world in which issues of diversity, challenges to professional knowledge, and rapidly changing organisational practices and values all demand ongoing learning on the part of the professional.

Billett and Newton assert the interdependence between the individual and their workplaces both in terms of learning and in changing practice. They do not believe that reflection is sufficient to understand 'learning practice'. Nor do they believe that the workplace activities and settings should take priority. Instead, they make the case for an interdependent relationship. And in this turn to practice, Boud reminds us of other aspects which we need to take into account if we are to understand professional learning: team-based and/or collective approaches to work; relationships with clients and others with whom we co-produce our professional practice; and embodied practice itself, which has so often been neglected in favour of the isolated mind.

Chapter 1

Professionalism and social change

The implications of social change for the 'reflective practitioner'

Nick Frost

Introduction

This chapter aims to provide a wider social and political context for the chapters that follow. It argues that the space in which the modern professional both 'practises' and 'reflects' has been fundamentally restructured over the last thirty years, a period sometimes referred to as 'late modernity' (Parton 2006). The chapter outlines some of the important social changes that have taken place and analyses the implications for critical reflection in the late-modern era. The chapter draws on the experience of the 'human-service' professions in particular, although it is suggested that the analysis has implications throughout a wider range of professional work.

First of all it needs to be established that the environment in which the modern professional operates has of late been subject to rapid, persistent and fundamental change. It is argued here that as we live through the late-modern era we can reflect on four major forms of change in the wider social environment. These changes are identified as: globalisation, informationalism, networking and managerialism.

Once the case has been made that these trends are significant, it will be argued that social change has fundamental significance for the reflective professional practitioner. It will be argued that some schools of 'reflective practice' have become idealist in their approach. By this we mean that they have seen reflection as something that happens subjectively in the head of the individual practitioner, and thus the role of the wider social environment is underplayed. In contrast we argue here for a realist view of critical reflection – that is, that it should be grounded in the material social reality of professional practice.

Four major forms of social change

Initially the paper argues the case for the significance of wider social change for our understanding of professionalism.

Globalisation

Worldwide developments, often identified by the shorthand of globalisation, have had a profound impact on forms of culture, identity, economy and governance in late-modern societies. Giddens defines these changes as follows.

> Globalisation can thus be defined as the intensification of worldwide social relations which link distant localities in such a way that local happenings are shaped by events occurring many miles away and vice versa. This is a dialectical process because such local happenings may move in an obverse direction from the very distanciated relations that shape them. Local transformation is as much a part of globalisation as the lateral extension of social connections across time and space.
>
> (1991: 64)

These widespread social changes help to redefine the nature of professionalism as the professions confront changes arising from globalisation. As Giddens points out, time and space have been compressed in the period of globalisation. Thus we can communicate across the globe in real time, retrieve information from almost everywhere in the world and we may confront issues and challenges from many cultures within even one small neighbourhood of one city (Castells 1996).

Professionals therefore have to hold a worldwide reference point – we have to utilise the web, we may travel to conferences all over the world and we may have to understand cultures from diverse corners of the globe. As a consequence, quite literally, the space for reflection has been restructured and is global, diverse, changing and complex. This implies that reflection is a form of practice based in material reality – not simply an idealist form of reflection that simply goes on 'within the head' of the individual professional.

Informationalism

Perhaps the most profound change that has had an impact on contemporary professional practice has been the explosion in the availability and dissemination of information. Castells refers to contemporary society as an information society, where informationalism is: 'the attribute of a specific form of social organisation in which information generation, processing, and transmission become the fundamental sources of productivity and power' (Castells 1996: 21n).

The modern professional is surrounded by information – there has been an explosion in web-based information, professional journals, broadcast and printed information. Government, particularly in the UK, has been 'hyper-active' in producing new policy initiatives and guidance (see Fawcett et al. 2004). Handling the volume of information is a major challenge to the modern professional. As a result it becomes very difficult to feel comfortable with one's own sense of 'expertise', as there is always a new book we have not read, or a research report with which we are not really familiar. A recent Google search of 'reflective practice', for example, comes up with over half a million hits. We have to sift a wide range of diverse information. Charles Leadbeater critically reflects on the explosion of information as follows.

> More information is not better information. We are deluged by useless information. Our capacity to generate information far outstrips our ability to use it effectively. About 20 million words of technical information are published every day around the world. A fast reader, reading 1,000 words in three minutes, non-stop for eight hours, would need a month of solid reading to get through a single day's output. About 1,000 books are published each day around the world. There has been more telephone traffic in the world in the last seven years than in the rest of human history. More data will soon be carried over telephone lines than conversations. These floods of information make people anxious that they are missing out, being left behind.
>
> (2000: 42)

As Castells (1996) has argued, we are living in an 'information age' – where much of our time is spent collating, storing, digesting and producing information. The modern professional can feel that their major task in life has become handling information, rather than working with people. Whilst our claim to expertise, say in the 1960s, could feel firmly grounded in full and comprehensive research, this is a difficult claim to sustain today.

Further, the student, the patient, or the client we work with can be armed with information with which we might not be familiar – they have consulted the website we have not seen and read some research we are unfamiliar with. This profoundly shifts the location of power in the professional relationship. Bunting identifies three elements that have transformed the way individuals relate to state professionals: 'the end of deference, the information revolution and the rise of "consumer sovereignty"' (Bunting 2005: 139).

Before the advent of the world wide web it was much more likely that most information, say relating to an illness, would be located with the professional – now much information is held by the service user or patient, in a form unmediated by the professional. Thus 'the relationship', the core of many of the human professions, is restructured and changed in ways profoundly related to wider global change and the spread of informationalism.

The emergence of network society

Castells has also argued that modern Western societies are 'network' societies where individuals and organisations exist in a complex and ever-changing relationship to each other and where no-one can practise in isolation. Organisations and individuals have to be flexible to respond to the rapid pace of change we have already referred to, and this flexibility implies being involved in partnerships and networks.

This development of networking can be linked to the work of the sociocultural theorist Etienne Wenger and the key concept he developed with Jean Lave – 'communities of practice' (Lave and Wenger 1991, Wenger 1998). According to Wenger, learning in practice includes the following processes for the communities involved.

> Evolving forms of *mutual engagement*
> Understanding and tuning a *joint enterprise*
> Developing *repertoire, styles, and discourses.*
>
> (1998: 96)

The two theoretical concepts explored thus far – the network society and communities of practice – can assist us in understanding that the single, unitary professional or professional organisation can no longer exist in isolation. This leads to forms of professional expertise becoming increasing networked, integrated, or joined-up (Frost 2005), a development clearly linked to globalisation.

> A global (in the sense of transplanetary) social relation is one that (like an Internet chat room and certain communicable diseases) can link persons situated at any inhabitable points on the earth. Globalization involves reductions of barriers to such transworld social contacts. With globalization people become more able – physically, legally, linguistically, culturally and psychologically – to engage with each other wherever on Planet Earth they might be.
>
> (Scholte 2000: 59)

The new professional is therefore often a networked professional, having to cooperate and communicate with a wide range of colleagues within and outside their chosen profession. Again this reconstructs the space for reflection – it takes place in shared and networked situations.

Manageralism, risk and the audit society

The theorist Ulrich Beck has utilised the concept of 'the risk society' to argue that the emphasis on risk has led to demands that expert systems, run by professionals, have a key role in controlling and regulating risk. When risk is not effectively managed (for example, when a storm is not predicted or when a disease cannot be controlled), professionals and politicians are called to account. They are expected to predict, to control and to account for the wide range of risks that exist in the late-modern world. For professionals this might mean their actions being inquired into (for social workers after child-abuse deaths), criticised (for the police after false arrests), being subject to new systems of accountability (changes in registration as for GPs following the Shipman Inquiry) and calls for enhanced training (for the police following the findings of 'institutional racism').

The sum of these changes is to shift the terms of professional expertise. For a professional today to claim autonomy on the basis of their skills, knowledge or experience, sounds rather ridiculous. In a modern, complex society where each system is dependent on another there must be systems of mutual accountability. In everyday terms this is manifest in the daily complaints in the professional workplace about inspections, monitoring, league tables and specific initiatives such as the Research Assessment Exercise in the university system.

This audit approach to monitoring professional activity profoundly alters professionals' relations to their organisations. There is a shift from trust in the professional and their relative autonomy to an emphasis on measurement and managerialism. This can also have the effect of privileging a technicist, or 'what works' approach to policy that operates through adopting a seemingly neutral, 'technical' stance to professional practice, so effectively critiqued by Donald Schön (see Frost 2003).

Again such developments can be linked to globalisation. The changes linked to globalisation demand flexible ways of producing and relating to the consumer, but simultaneously demand standardisation and measurability. This places particular pressures on the professional to supply the 'personalised' service, whilst they are subject to audit, inspection and measurement.

The nature of these organisational changes are subject to bureaucratic forms of regulation and audit. The organisation has to perform in ways that can be inspected, audited and measured (Power 1997). The professional may experience an environment where their profession values and practices are 'trumped' by the requirements of inspection and audit.

Thus it is argued here that the growth of the 'risk society' (Beck) and the 'audit society' (Power) have reduced and restructured the space available for professional action, and thus arguably for professional reflection: perceptions of the role of professionals during the late-modern period have shifted and changed. This is a shift historically from professionals being trusted, self-regulating and held in high esteem, to being externally measured, regulated and often pilloried in the event of a tragedy or error. This in turn has a negative impact on the way that organisations operate which leads Power to argue that audit culture fails in two ways.

(a) The audit process becomes a world to itself, self-referentially creating auditable images of performance.

(b) Organizations are in effect *colonized* by an audit process which disseminates and implants the values which underlay and support its information demands. The audit process can be said to fail because its side-effects may actually undermine performance.

(Power 1997: 95)

The influence of the audit culture has been explored in a UK-based survey undertaken by the National Association of Head Teachers (NAHT). In a survey of the impact of inspections they report as follows.

63.5 per cent of the respondents felt that the impact on their school was at best neutral and at worst very unhelpful, with a large number of respondents (69.6 per cent) saying the effect on staff morale was unhelpful, or very unhelpful.

(National Association of Head Teachers 2008)

This also had a major impact on recruitment of a new generation of head teachers.

The most damning indictment of the current system is that 86.2 per cent of respondents felt that the impact of Ofsted inspections makes it less likely that potential candidates will be willing to apply for Headships. This weight of evidence (85.7 per cent) also applies to Estyn, the Welsh equivalent of Ofsted, that is felt to be less aggressive than the English version.

(National Association of Head Teachers 2008)

The Association argues that the whole audit regime generated a deep sense of insecurity.

On retention and security there is an overwhelming response with 85.9 per cent of respondents agreeing that inspection increases vulnerability and insecurity, which has a demonstrative effect on recruitment. As one deputy put it, 'I don't think I will apply for headship, because that will mean that I have to go though ten Ofsteds, and I am not prepared to do that.'

(National Association of Head Teachers 2008)

Thus we can see that audit regimes can seriously dislocate the relationship between the professional and their workplace. The impact on reflective practice is real and profound.

The impact on reflection

Thus far we have attempted to argue that the context of professional practice has changed fundamentally in the late-modern era. As a result, the role of and the space for critically reflective practice has also changed. In this final section we reflect on the impact of these changes on professional practice. What pressures and changes exist for the modern 'reflecting' professional in this emerging social environment? Five potential aspects of the impact on professionals are discussed in this chapter.

First, the modern professional often feels stressed and pressured. There are always targets to be met, papers to be read and waiting lists to be addressed. A recent UK survey of school head teachers found that 38 per cent of all those away from school sick were off with stress-related illness. We have seen a shift in the nature of work so that the professional has become 'a willing slave' (Bunting 2005). The professional has taken ownership of their role and organisational performance in such a way that they are willing to work whatever hours are necessary to demonstrate a high level of output. The sociologist Bauman explains how work has come to dominate the lives, not just of the poor but of the privileged.

> Workaholics with no fixed hours of work, preoccupied with the challenges of their jobs twenty four hours a day, seven days a week, may be found today not among slaves, but among the elite of the lucky and successful.
> (Bauman 1998: 34)

In the UK, 56 per cent of men report working over 40 hours per week, compared with 14 per cent of Swedish working males (Bishop 2004: 118). Bunting reports two specific cases of professional exhaustion and burn-out related to the demands of audit. An assistant director of social services reports being 'continually shattered' and a public sector chief executive who resigned states that, following a failure of his organisations to meet targets, the 'strains of the last five months have taken their toll' (Bunting 2005: 136).

Second, the modern professional feels less in charge of their own labour process. A concept such as 'professional autonomy' is today rarely referred to and seems to be clearly out of date. The modern professional has often to operate within a set of procedures and is instructed to change their priorities to fulfil an externally imposed agenda. The Research Assessment Exercise for an academic and the Ofsted Inspection for a teacher, provide examples of how new sets of 'professional' priorities are generated. Power argues that audit has the ability to restructure work life: 'The audit explosion has its roots in a programmatic restructuring of organisational life and a new "rationality of governance"' (Power 1997: 10).

Third, the modern professional feels the pressure of the 'risk society'. All the human professions are concerned by the questions 'What if something goes wrong?' 'What if the child on my caseload dies?' 'What if the student on my field trip is fatally injured?' Professionals are expected to foresee risk and to manage risk – when they do not, their skill and expertise will be challenged and sometimes subject to a public inquiry. Professionals are at the front line of late-modern society's ability to manage risk through the mobilisation of skill and expertise.

Fourth, as we have argued, the modern professional is audited, inspected and checked. These inspections might be regarded by the professional as misinformed, inaccurate and faulty – but they have profound implications for the future of professional work. The critical Ofsted report is difficult to move on from, the poor Research Assessment Exercise score has long-term funding implications. These regulatory regimes form a way of checking and monitoring professional practice and displace the role of trust and self-reflection traditionally undertaken by the individual professional: 'Existing structures of self-reflection on practice, which have traditionally been *ad hoc*, local and under control of practitioners themselves, have been harnessed to regulatory initiatives in the environment' (Power 1997: 114).

Fifth, the skill and expertise of the modern professional are constantly challenged and contested. The deference accorded to the teacher or police officer might be challenged by people they work with – who do not except a claim to expertise simply based on status or training. None of us would any longer base our expertise claim merely on qualifications or experience. Richard Sennet, the eminent American sociologist, has argued that quite the opposite is occurring – that potential trumps expertise and experience.

> The new order does not consider that the sheer passage of time necessary to accumulate skill gives a person standing and rights – value in a material sense; it views such claims based on the passage of time to represent yet another face of the evil of the old bureaucratic system, in which seniority rights froze institutions. The regime focuses on immediate capability.
>
> (Sennett 1998: 96)

Here we have some of the many challenges that face the modern professional. The list is probably endless – but the key argument here is that modern professionalism is changing and that professionalism is challenged by these changes.

The changing nature of the reflective practitioner

So what do these changes mean for professionalism and more centrally in this book for critical reflection?

First, the rapid pace of social change makes lifelong learning – in both the formal and informal senses – absolutely essential for professionals. As the world changes so rapidly thus professionals have to challenge and renew their expertise. A failure to do so will mean that professional knowledge and expertise will soon be out of date. Thus contemporary professionalism is necessarily a process of continuous change and reflection.

Second, in an increasingly globalised world, most human services professionals constantly confront diversity – in terms of social class, disability, sexuality, gender and ethnicity. These diversities are very challenging for professionals. Can professionals develop their reflection and practice so that they understand the wide range of diversity that confronts their practice? Examples would include a white police officer dealing with a 'mentally ill' African Caribbean person, or a white social worker assessing the parenting of a Bangladeshi mother. Such examples raise fundamental issues about skills, values and knowledge, and how these are deployed by professionals.

Third, handling the information explosion is a major challenge for all in our professional practice – Can we cope with the volume of e mails and the pace at which we are expected to respond? Do we have time to follow up journals and new research and so forth?

Fourth, challenging the organisational practices of our employer is a major challenge for the modern professional. We may feel deskilled by organisational practices and may disagree with a target-driven policy that diverges from our professional boundaries. This often leads to a disjunction between professional and organisational values.

The reflective-practitioner school is a wide church, as emerges throughout this book. It could be argued that we are all reflective practitioners now – and there is also a strong lobby for 'critical reflection'. This paper argues for critical reflection – but reflection that is grounded in the reality of modern social change. True critical 'reflection' cannot occur in a social vacuum and it is argued here that it is a mistake if reflection overemphasises the free space available for human choice and agency. The 'reflective practitioner' cannot become a free-floating practitioner separate from the constraints of the reality in which they practice.

The idealist approach to reflection can be seen in this approach to 'journaling' as a reflective tool, suggested by Rainer.

> The journal is a practical psychological tool that enables you to express feelings without inhibition, recognise and alter self-defeating habits of mind, and come to know and accept that self which is you. It is a sanctuary where all the disparate elements of life – feelings, thoughts, dreams, hopes, fear, fantasies, practicalities, worries, facts and intuitions – can merge to give you a sense of wholeness and coherence. It can help you understand your past, discover joy in the present, and create your own future.
> (National College for School Leadership 2004a: 17)

Wanaganayake, in a similar vein, argues that: 'leadership comes through one's life experiences especially as a child' (National College for School Leadership 2004b: 17).

These are examples of schools of thought that propose reflection as the way forward – but where instead of the focus on wider social factors that is proposed here, that focus is on 'the self' and 'one's life experiences'. In this context, reflection becomes something apart from the reality of professional practice where the individual professional can 'create [their] own future'.

Rather we propose a materialist approach to critical reflection. That is where reflection is not simply something that happens inside the head of the professional practitioner but occurs when that reflection actively engages with the material reality in which the professional works – a reality that we have argued is structured by globalisation, informationalism, the audit society and managerialism.

This is not, however, an argument for determinism. Whilst we have argued against the idealist position that you can 'create your own future', this should not be taken as arguing that we are all trapped in whatever material reality surrounds us. Etienne Wenger posits this debate as the tension between 'participation' and 'reification', arguing that we should not see them simply as opposites: 'Participation and reification transform their relation; they do not translate into each other. ... Participation and reification describe an interplay; they are not classificatory categories' (Wenger 1998: 68).

Thus the modern professional needs to engage both with their own professional skills and with the wider social, political and organisational context within which their work inevitably exists. This should form the basis of a truly critical reflective practice.

Chapter 2

Relocating reflection in the context of practice

David Boud

Introduction

Notions of reflection and reflective practice have become well established in professional education since the late 1980s. While some applications of these ideas in courses have distorted their original intentions and taken an excessively instrumental approach to their use, they have nevertheless provided useful framing devices to help conceptualise some important processes in professional learning. One of the reasons why they were readily accepted is because they shared an individualised view of learning with the very programmes in which they were used. In the 2000s we are, however, seeing a questioning of an overly individualistic view of learning previously associated with reflection, a focus on the nature of professional practice and an exploration of alternative conceptions that view reflection within the context of settings which necessarily have more of a group- or team-based work orientation. This chapter questions whether we should reject earlier views of reflection, rehabilitate them to capture their previous potential or move to new ways of regarding reflection that are more in keeping with what we know about the context of practice. It suggests that the pursuit of each of these directions together is needed. It goes on to explore features of reflection that are needed for contemporary and future professional practice, provide an illustration of a non-individualistic approach to reflection in organisations and identifies some issues that are still fully to be addressed.

The inclusion of elements labelled 'reflection' and 'reflective practice' have become commonplace in professional courses. Reflective practice is regarded as good practice – unreflective practice is certainly bad – and courses are supposed to promote the desirable features that are associated with reflection. These have become largely unquestioned assumptions. When they are considered in discussing courses, it is normally with regard to the activities associated with them – how they might be promoted. However, these activities may be either not effective in promoting reflection – they turn reflection into a procedures – or, in the case of assessment, may be antithetical to the notion of reflection. While reflection is considered an idealised good in professional practice, what it really consists of and how it can be learned are, surprisingly and with relatively few exceptions, not the subject of critical attention and empirical investigation. These criticisms are raised in the literature (e.g. Boud and Walker 1998; Brookfield 2000), but there has been relatively little follow – through in terms of teaching and learning practices, and an ambiguity about what operationally constitutes good reflective practice. There is also a considerable gap between strategies available and what occurs in any given course. In many cases, reflection turns out to be synonymous with writing about practical situations as if recording and thinking about what happened had simply been renamed reflection.

Alongside the particular problems of integrating ideas about reflection into courses, there has continued to be a more basic critique. Some of this is not new: the older philosophical position that the notion of reflection is unclear and, in any case, may not be different from thinking is still asserted. And some of those from a critical social theory perspective have often argued that the only variant of reflection that is significant is that of critical reflection and the fundamental questioning of taken-for-granted assumptions. The hard version of this position unfortunately establishes an inappropriate norm against which reflection is to be judged. And again, reflection has been criticised as being too individualistic a concept, as for example represented in the writings of Schön and others, and that in a world characterised by team working and cross-professional collaboration insufficient attention has been given to groups reflecting on common concerns – as distinct from the common practice of individual reflection in groups (Reynolds 1999; Reynolds and Vince 2004). There is merit in each of these positions, but none are sufficiently compelling to lead to a wholesale rejection of reflection as a generative idea. Ironically, it is the ambiguous nature of reflection that challenges some of the overly instrumental and banal ends to which it has been put.

This chapter suggests that we need to review the use of reflection for professional learning. A review will lead to the rejection of some activities that go under the guise of 'reflection' but cannot be justified in terms of any articulated view of the concept, the renewal or rehabilitation of some older ideas of reflection and reflective practice, and the development of some new directions to meet some pressing needs of the current world of practice. The direction taken in approaching this review is to suggest that the idea of reflection should be relocated in the context of practice and that the consequences of that relocation should be followed through into courses that prepare professionals.

Some earlier ideas

Most ideas of reflection relate to the questioning of experience. That is, the exploration of 'a state of perplexity, hesitation, doubt' (Dewey 1933), or 'inner discomforts' (Brookfield 1987), or 'disorienting dilemmas' (Mezirow

1990), or 'surprise, puzzlement, or confusion in a situation which he finds uncertain or unique' (Schön 1983). Although many years before Dewey was the person to bring reflection to the attention of those in education, serious discussion of reflection and reflective practice took root in professional education in the 1980s with a flurry of publications around this theme (e.g. Schön 1983, 1987; Boud, Keogh and Walker 1985). This was followed shortly thereafter with the taking up of these ideas in particular professional disciplines. They became inscribed into many professional courses, notably in teacher education, social work, nursing and health-related areas. These ideas were particularly well received in professions in which there was a particular emphasis on a personal interaction between a professional and a client. I suggest the reason for this is that such professions embody practice more obviously than others and that, even at the earliest stages of this kind of professional practice, there is no doubting that practice is more than the exercising of technical skills and knowledge. Practitioners in these areas were receptive to a notion of reflection that went beyond Dewey's (1933) emphasis on thinking to encompass feelings and emotions in practice settings.

The other reasons I suspect it was taken up so enthusiastically in professional courses are, firstly, because it fitted the individualistic culture of higher education and, secondly, because it bridged the work of the academy and practice when many professions relatively new to higher education were looking for ideas that grounded them in the world of practice but which also used a somewhat more conceptualised set of ideas than previously. It was a time when professions such as nursing had moved organisationally from a technical to a communicative view of training for practice, and needed practical ideas of a more constructivist and interpretive nature.

In 1998, David Walker and I examined what we saw then as common practices going under the banner of reflection (Boud and Walker 1998). We expressed concern that much of what we had regarded to be of value had been lost. This had occurred either through a misunderstanding of the ideas or by an over-literal interpretation that took invitations to engagement and turned them into rules for behaviour. What had been put into practice was often far from the ideas that we or Donald Schön, or indeed any of the advocates of reflection in the literature, would have wished to see. We identified problems including, amongst others, reflection as recipe following, reflection without learning, over intellectualising reflection and uncritical acceptance of learners' experiences.

In looking back now, it is tempting to see a connection between these problems and the teaching orientations of those people who were attempting to put reflection into practice. Prompted by Prosser and Trigwell's (1999) work on higher education teachers' conceptions of teaching, one suspects that those teachers experiencing the greatest difficulties (and probably not even being aware of these difficulties) were often of a technical orientation who saw reflection as part of an apparatus for instrumental learning. Reflection as articulated did not fit their model of knowledge and skill transmission and acquisition and, when prompted by colleagues who saw the value of a more holistic view of learning grounded in experience and conceptual change, took up some of the superficial features of reflective activity while leaving out the core. These problems were compounded of course by inappropriate assessment procedures such as the marking of raw reflective journals that had the effect of inhibiting the expression of any reflection by learners that might have been fostered through keeping a journal.

We can see various conceptions of reflection manifested teachers in their practice: a technical/instrumental view, an interpretive/constructivist view and a critical view. These give rise to quite different teaching and learning activities, each of which have unhelpfully been put in a single category and labelled 'reflection'. The literature contained extensive discussion of the second and third of these views of reflection. Indeed, there is little of a technical kind favourably reported, but if teachers are of an instrumental bent it was almost impossible for them to engage with the latter views and therefore they respond to reflection in the only way that exists in their conception of teaching and learning, that is, they adopt an entirely operational approach. They therefore constructed the strange practice of reflection by checklists, akin to 'painting by numbers'. They took the language of reflection – elements, stages, whatever – and turned these into procedures which they could identify as either being completed or not, as if we can ever tell when another person has reflected enough. An elusive and generative idea had been made functional. The language permeated professional schools, but it also gave reflection a bad name as colleagues saw what was occurring and decided, quite appropriately, that it was not for them.

Of course, we should perhaps not be too critical of this as it is also the fate of all educational ideas. They often arise in a particular context to address particular concerns. They are seductive because they enable us to name things we have a sense are important, without having fully thought through what was really important about them. They then get taken up and are used to label many things other than those for which their original proponents developed them. They also get disconnected with the theoretical or philosophical assumptions that underpinned them and they may be bandied around as a kind of educational fashion accessory. The appearance of engaging with them becomes more important than the educational work that they actually do. Regretfully, this can be seen in so many ideas in higher education: learner-centred approaches, problem-based learning, self-directed learning and so on.

So what can we take from this brief analysis? Firstly, that there are some aspects of the use of reflection that we should perhaps reject. That is, use in instrumental and entirely procedural settings and its use by teachers who have a transmission or knowledge acquisition view of learning. Secondly, it is important to focus on what reflection as previously conceived attends to, and not move beyond its legitimate scope in constructing personal knowledge.

That is, it is a means to engage in making sense of experience in situations that are rich and complex, and which do not lend themselves to being simplified by the use of concepts and frameworks that can be taught. This does not, however, mean that concepts and frameworks have no part to play in reflection. Quite the contrary, these are needed not to recall and regurgitate but to help prompt and make sense of the complexity of experience.

Changing awareness of practice

Such an analysis is insufficient to argue for a renewed focus on reflection. It is not just a matter of tidying up previous poor pedagogical practice. A fresh look at professional learning from initial preparation to ongoing expert practice is required. Is there still a place for reflection in this, and, if so, what should it be?

The place to start is in practice itself. There are now many studies of workplace practice in a range of settings and using a variety of research perspectives, and an increasing number of ways of conceptualising practice. Indeed, practice is becoming an important lens through which to study many phenomena and the *Practice Turn in Contemporary Theory* (Schatzki 2001) has been identified. This followed historically what we might call the *reflective turn in contemporary practice*. The reflective turn emphasised reflection and reflexivity, and moved discussions of practice beyond a technicised and competence-influenced discourse. The practice turn both gives new respect to and also problematises practice. It regards practice as a key unit of activity of all social phenomena; a focus that locates activities with those who enact them.

What is shared by many of the views of practice? Firstly, practice is necessarily *contextualised*. It does not exist apart from a particular setting, a community of activity and a set of social engagements. Unlike some aspects of academic knowledge, practice is always particular. Professional competencies and orientations are applied to particular concerns at particular times. It is not meaningful to discuss practice independently of the range of settings in which it occurs: when it is disaggregated from its settings it loses many of its features of practice.

Secondly, practice is *embodied* in the persons of practitioners. Practitioners enact practice with their whole person. Their practice involves a wide range of dispositions, motives, feelings and ideas of themselves, and it cannot be separated meaningfully from the person. This is not to say that attempts to make this separation do not occur, but they can only be successful to a very limited extent. Recognition of the embodiment of practice has profound consequences. It means that it cannot be considered independently of those who practice. It also means that to objectify practice is to fail to acknowledge its subjectivity. This is not to say particular elements of practice cannot be examined independently of practitioners, but it does mean that when these elements are combined into the complexity of any real life example of professional practice, this occurs through the practitioners themselves.

Although the mind cannot be separated from the body, higher education institutions sometimes operate as if they were only dealing with minds. As an illustration of one of many ways of thinking about this, we can look to the work of Hubert Dreyfus. Dreyfus and Dreyfus (2005) indicate stages through which someone moves from being unfamiliar with an area to being an experienced practitioner. His stages are: novice, advanced beginner, competence, proficiency, expertise, mastery, and practical wisdom. They draw attention to the importance of learning for the latter stages as these stages are often removed from consideration in initial professional education courses and an impoverished view of what is involved in learning a practice is used. For Dreyfus and Dreyfus, embodiment is central. They highlight the 'loss of the ability to recognize relevance' and that '[w]ithout involvement and presence we cannot acquire skills' (2001: 7). This leads them to be very critical of many uses of the Internet for learning and indeed any approach to learning that does not acknowledge that motives, commitment and actions are always involved.

Changing context of professional practice

It is not only the concept of practice that is evolving and becoming richer, but also the variety of settings in which professional practice takes place and the influences that impact on it. It was once assumed that practice continued more or less unchanged except for the influence of new knowledge and technology. These meant that the specifics of particular practices might change, but that the identity of the professional would not. This view is no longer valid and has not been so for some considerable time, but many programmes operate on the assumption that it is true.

The three major features of the changing context of professional practice are: firstly, those associated with its collective rather than individual nature; secondly, its multidisciplinary or often transdisciplinary character; and, thirdly, an increasing emphasis on practice being co-produced with those with whom it is conducted. It is rare for any practitioner now to work alone. Almost all work occurs in settings in which there are multiple players who need to cooperate closely with each other in order for them each to perform their own jobs. Professional courses have typically been designed on the assumption of individual practice. That is, the individual professional makes autonomous decisions and engages in their own practice uninfluenced by anyone other than occasionally senior colleagues. The defining feature of professions has been that they are collections of autonomous professionals who act together within their own profession to maintain standards of good practice. However, if we examine day-to-day activities in almost any area, they involve groups of people acting interdependently and these groups often contain participants from different professions or occupations. Autonomous practice is a dangerous idealisation because, by leaving out other practitioners within or outside one's own profession, an unrealistic assumption about what is involved in practice has been made. And actions taken on the basis of unrealistic assumptions can be risky.

Not only do practitioners work closely with others in traditional areas (such as hospitals, schools, law firms, etc.), but also professions themselves do not create the boundaries around most work in society today. Most large organisations in both the private and public sectors consist of people who may have trained in a particular profession or occupation, but they are mostly not engaged in that specialisation now. Most graduates do not undertake employment in areas immediately related to the subject of their degrees and those who do often migrate into other areas of work. High-level demanding work is not held together by professions or disciplines but by the nature of the work itself. Practitioners work in mixed settings that change over time, and in groups that are often formed and reformed for particular purposes related to whatever the organisation exists to do. These are not simply multidisciplinary groups, but transdisciplinary ones, whose knowledge is not helpfully framed by the traditional academic distinctions between subject matter (Gibbons et al. 1994).

One further change in professional practice that relates to our concerns is that of the changing relationship between professional and client (patient, student, customer, etc.). In many areas clients are being increasingly regarded as co-practitioners, involved in the co-production of knowledge about themselves and their own situation (Bovaird 2007, Dunston, Lee, Boud, Brodie and Chiarella 2009). That is, they contribute as actively to the interaction as the professional involved as they are personally implicated in the outcomes of the interaction. Examples of this are in the co-construction of health that occurs between a patient and a health practitioner, particularly in areas of primary care and acute conditions, the contributions to learning that students must make in working with teachers, and in the mutual problem solving that occurs between social workers and clients in case work. Not only are others party to professional practice, but it cannot occur effectively without them. While much professional practice of the past has been based on the assumption that the professional necessarily knows best, this is not a view that is sustainable in areas in which the client is an active subject.

Rethinking reflection: an illustration

Some of these features of practice are well established so, for example, Schön's descriptions of the reflective practitioner are rich in contextual detail. However, when we start to add to this the other elements we have discussed – embodiment, practice with others, transdisciplinarity and co-production – we see why our conceptions of reflection need to shift to encompass a wider range of practice than hitherto conceived. There are signs that this process is occurring and we are starting to see a new wave of writing about reflection that starts to engage with these issues (Reynolds and Vance 2004; Boud, Cressey and Docherty 2006). So far, this work has not taken up all of the issues considered here, but there is a fresh debate occurring about how we should think of reflection now.

The concept promoted in the book with which I was associated is that of productive reflection. Productive reflection, as an idea, picks up concerns about the need for new ways of considering reflection in workplaces that are not focused on the individual independent learner. However, it also engages with the context and purpose of work and, most importantly, with the imperative that reflection in such settings cannot be an individual act if it is to influence work that takes place with others.

The key features of productive reflection (Cressey and Boud 2006) can be summarised as follows.

1   *An organisational rather than an individual intent and a collective rather than individual orientation*
    The focus is not on individual interests, but on those of the purpose of the entity of which the practitioner is a part. Unlike earlier conceptions in which others were present in reflective activities solely to draw the attention of the individual to matters they had not taken account of and to ensure that they were not fooling themselves, the emphasis now is on reflection that leads to action with and for others and for the benefit of the work involved. It also involves shared interests of the group or wider entity.

2   *Reflection is necessarily contextualised within work; it connects learning and work*
    Reflective practices cannot be isolated from the context and organisational purposes for which they are used. These will necessarily differ from one situation to another. Work drives reflection and frames what is legitimate to do. Reflection connects work and learning and operates in the space between the two. It provides a link between knowing and producing and is a part of change processes. Productive reflection leads to interventions into work activity to change what is happening on the basis of insights into what has occurred previously. While individuals will often act, it is to organisational action that productive reflection is directed.

3   *It involves multiple stakeholders and connects players*
    The processes and outcomes of productive reflection are not confined to one group within an organisation. The group is a surrogate for what the organisation does: the heath-care team is there to provide appropriate care for the patients for whom it is responsible, not just to pursue its own learning interests. Each person has to take account of other perspectives if an outcome to satisfy all is to be sought; all need to find and operate on common ground.

4   *It has a generative rather than instrumental focus*

This is not a new feature of reflection as discussed above. It has always been the case, even though this has often been misunderstood. The notion of reflection aims to generate possibilities that can be appropriated, not to project manage a solution.

5   *It has a developmental character*
Productive reflection is part of a range of organisational practices designed to simultaneously contribute to solving organisational problems of today while equipping members of the organisation to be better able to deal with challenges that face them in the future. It does this through building confidence that those reflecting can act together in meaningful ways and develop their own repertoire of approaches to meet future challenges. It needs to nurture the group if it is to be sustainable.

6   *Reflection is an open, unpredictable process, it is dynamic and changes over time*
As is common with all approaches to reflection, it cannot be predicted where it will lead. It necessarily has unintended consequences. If organisations or groups knew where they were going, then productive reflection would not be needed. It deals with matters that do not have a ready solution and are not clearly formulated, and as such it cannot be controlled and managed as a routine process.

Implications of features of professional practice for reflection

The development of the idea of productive reflection was prompted by the need to locate reflective practice within organisations in which reflection was not *a priori* a feature. It necessarily had to shift reflection from an individual to a group focus. It provides one example of the changing emphasis of reflection. What then do the key features of practice and the changing nature of professional practice prompt us to consider?

Contextualisation

Practice always occurs in a particular setting and even if the type of activity is similar to that which occurs elsewhere, the practice and reflection on it is particular. The people involved vary, the influences of the organisation vary and power relations vary. This means that any standardised approach to reflection must be treated with great caution. What is appropriate in one set of conditions does not necessarily transfer to another. It is tempting to find a process of reflection that has worked well for others and import it into a new setting. Such importation of procedures needs to be treated with caution. Do they fit the different circumstances, different purposes, different people and different expectations?

The tailoring of reflection to suit local settings follows from a recognition of the importance of context. While models and strategies used by others are a good stimulus, reflection must be designed for context. It must take into account the particularities of the setting and accommodate the actual people involved and the practice that is being reflected upon.

Transdisciplinarity

The existence of transdisciplinary teams brings the issue of difference to the fore. When members of a group involved in reflection come from different backgrounds, different traditions, different cultures or different disciplines, it cannot be assumed that common assumptions will underpin the activity. Indeed, the notion of reflection and reflective practice might mean quite different things to different parties. Disciplines, whether they be formal academic disciplines, or less formal occupational traditions, encapsulate cultural practices that define what is and is not good work, what counts as appropriate outcomes and how tasks should be shaped to make them legitimate. When different members of a team come from different disciplines, they bring with them sets of assumptions about standards and what should be done in any situation. Reflection for each is framed differently and if they operate independently of each other, different incompatible outcomes may result.

The challenge for reflection of transciplinary work is that of creating common ground, which involves establishing agreed expectations of what the task is that is the object of reflection and what constitutes an appropriate outcome to their joint activity. Such a process is a demanding one as it involves the questioning of the taken-for-granted assumptions arising from the particular disciplinary backgrounds of the members of the group. They are not just learning a new way of operating with others; they are simultaneously unlearning some practices that have held them in good stead within their monocultural groups. Of course, one of the great benefits of groups that come from different disciplines working on problems that are transdiscipinary is that they can each draw on their traditions. Transdisciplinary reflective practice needs therefore to avoid a homogenisation of disciplines. There are considerable advantages in being able to step aside from one situation and view it from the perspective of another.

Embodiment

What does it mean to take the notion of embodied learning seriously, and how might this challenge some of our assumptions about learning for professional practice? An important feature of what is being referred to here as embodiment, is the notion of emotional engagement. Practitioners care about what they do. They have feelings and emotions about their professional work and these have an impact on what they do. They have a stake in what works and what does not work. They may resist new ideas no matter what the empirical base for them might be. These features point to the difficulty of rationalising and systematising reflection and requiring it of others.

Such systematisation can at times inhibit rather than prompt reflection as it does not engage with the affect. Volition is needed for reflection to be meaningful. Participants in reflective activities must, without coercion, choose to undertake reflection, because if they do not, they cannot effectively engage with the embodied nature of practice. They may be going through the motions of reflective procedures, but their bodies resist if it is not what they want to do. This means that the management of reflection by teachers in formal courses, through making it a required and assessed feature, is a particular challenge. Circumstances conducive to reflection need to be created. Obligations on students to deliver a particular product by a particular deadline are antithetical to the volitional character of reflection. They may lead to the production of work that is labelled reflective, but it would be hard to justify that reflection has been substantively taking place in such a situation.

How do we sufficiently account for the realities of practice in the activities that prepare learners for it, and what does this imply for what is highlighted in courses?

Co-production

How will we deal with reflection in the context of co-construction of knowledge when the partners in the process have radically different power positions and normal conditions for reflection are not obviously met? Is it possible to bracket the necessary imperative of operationalising reflection to ensure that a zealous emphasis on procedural requirements does not undermine the very processes we are trying to foster? Co-productive relationships commonly start from situations in which there are differences in knowledge between the parties, differences in skill and an imbalance of power – typically one side of a co-productive relationship has influenced the other.

In terms of reflection the most important consideration is: Will reflective activities be experienced as owned by all participants? Will they accommodate differences of position and power in the group? Most discussions of reflection assume parity of membership and symmetrical communication, but in work groups in particular this is rarely the case. There are some contexts in which reflection cannot be engaged, and others in which considerable planning to ensure all are involved needs to take place.

Bringing reflection into practice

These characteristics of practice: contextualisation, transdisciplinarity, embodiment and co-production each have their own implications for how reflection might be reconceptualised. However, as reflection itself is also a practice, these implications must be considered together. Reflection with groups of people for collective purposes involves high levels of commitment to the task, a willingness to be open to the ideas and experiences of others and, most important of all, a reasonable level of trust. Trust is not something that is or is not present, but it is built over time. Groups of strangers, outside therapeutic settings, need time working together, taking risks of disclosure, before they experience sufficient levels of trust for them to be able to engage usefully in collective reflective activity.

Conclusion

Reflection in professional practice is a way of thinking about productive work, not a strategy or technique. While it is premature to suggest that we need to move beyond reflection, we do need to move beyond older conceptions of reflective practice that are insufficiently rich to generate further work.

The realities of professional practice open up many challenges for reflection. There are still many situations in which individual reflection with others is an appropriate direction to take. However, we are seeing now the need to develop new ways of thinking about reflection that recognise the complexities and the relational qualities of practice. Is the notion of reflection sufficiently robust to sustain such further interrogation? I believe that it is, but I also suspect that the versions of it we have been using so far will need to be extended and the considerations alluded to above will need to be brought into our discussions. Reflection as we have been using it here is still primarily within the Deweyian tradition. What might fruitfully be considered are other more sociologically oriented traditions (e.g. Giddens 1991), related ideas associated with the practice turn (e.g. Schwandt 2005) and engagement with notions of reflexivity from a post-structural perspective (e.g. Fook 2002). As we move beyond the individual towards the social context then these need also to be brought into the repertoire. We need to find ways of rehabilitating some key aspects of reflection that have been eroded through unthinking use, while moving further to deal with these new issues. This is the challenge from professional practice that confronts us.

Chapter 3

Beyond reflective practice

Reworking the 'critical' in critical reflection

Jan Fook

Introduction

If we want to move 'beyond' reflective practice, what are some of the directions we need to be taking? In this chapter I look at this issue through the prism of critical reflection. I focus on the problem in two main ways: first, I revisit what the 'critical' in critical reflection means; and second, I address the potential for a collective focus, which forms one of the current concerns regarding the applicability of reflective practices in the workplace.

Why do we need to revisit an understanding of the 'critical' in critical reflection? First, there is a broad need to be clearer about what we mean when we talk about critical reflection and reflective practice. There is of course widespread recognition that critical reflection (and its close cousin, reflective practice) has widely divergent usages, spanning many different disciplines and intellectual traditions (Fook et al. 2006), and of course, popular usages (Moon 1999). On the one hand this may be a worthwhile and necessary underpinning for an inclusive set of practices and approaches, and indeed may be one of the very aspects of critical reflection which makes it widely appealing and applicable. On the other hand however, it does make it extraordinarily difficult to research and further develop the concept in more systematic ways (Woerkom et al. 2002). It is necessary I think to both include different understandings, but also work from some common basis of understanding, if we want to be able to refine and improve our practice of critical reflection.

One of my aims in this chapter therefore is to return to the idea of critical reflection, in particular revisiting the 'critical' aspect, in order to shed some further light on what this might mean in both theory and practice. I have chosen to narrow my discussion to critical reflection, rather than reflective practice more broadly, as this enables me to develop a particular theoretical framework in more depth. In addition, I think that as with any practice, the actual enactment of critical reflection may not necessarily match the theorising of it. In this paper, therefore, I want to try and see what might be learnt from its practice in order to enable further theorising of the idea. I do this first by elucidating my own theoretical framework for critical reflection, and by then presenting some detailed analysis of changes which have occurred for students in one of my critical reflection postgraduate programs. Spelling out some of the complexities of the process of changes and outcomes of critical reflection will I hope provide a basis for continued research. And in addition I hope this reworking might provide a clearer basis from which to better develop critical reflection as a process for both research and practice review, within and outside the workplace.

A second major trend in the current literature indicates calls for a more collective approach to critical reflection in the workplace (Reynolds and Vince 2004; Boud et al. 2006). These calls are based on the observations that most workplace learning literature 'sees reflection as an ability belonging to human subjects as individual learners, in principle detachable from social practices' (Elmholdt and Brinkman 2006: 170); and that in the educational literature, individual reflection is essentially focused on individual learning from personal experience (Boud 2006: 160). These arguments imply that the focus must either be individual or collective. I do think that in practice this has often been the case, but I do not want to risk the danger of overreacting by focusing solely instead on collective, social, or more organisational forms of reflection. Instead I want to argue for the need to revisit how the individual and social realms are linked. I want to take another look at the theoretical underpinnings which do link these realms, and to see what implications these might have for making the links in practice. I therefore want to revisit the notion of critical reflection, as practised individually, and redevelop its collective potential from this point of view. My focus will therefore also be on re-articulating a theoretical (and practice) framework for critical reflection which emphasises the *individual in social context*, and in particular what this might mean for changed practices within organisations. By analysing the detailed experience of the change process in critical reflection, and in particular focusing on the implications of this for the social contexts broadly (and organisations particularly) of the learners, I hope to further develop our understanding of critical reflection as a process which is neither inherently individual or collective, but instead one which is based irrevocably upon an understanding of the *individual in social context*. I argue that it is this integrated understanding which provides a sound way forward in developing better collective applications of critical reflection.

There are also sound reasons I think, especially in the field of professional lifelong learning, to maintain some kind of critical reflection learning process which takes individual experience as its starting point, and to link this with social contexts, rather than switching focus solely onto their collective application in these contexts.

First, many educators of practising professionals work independently of the workplaces in which learners are employed, and of course a good deal of their contribution to workplace learning is the ability to maintain and use this independent perspective in order to inform different approaches to organisational practice. It is important therefore that they see their students also as individuals, often seeking formal study because of their desire to learn independently of their own employment. In this sense, whilst I firmly believe that professional learning must be relevant to workplace context, I also think there is just as much call for people to develop a sense of their own professionalism, and professional practice, independent of the specific workplace setting. This is vital I think for professionals to develop a sense of integrity (Sullivan 1995), especially in the climate of current challenges to professionals. My focus in this chapter thus is on the social contexts of professional practice more broadly – this includes workplaces, but also professional cultures, social, political and cultural contexts.

Second, individuals are likely to change workplaces several times throughout their professional careers, or at least their workplaces will change around them. Therefore individuals need to learn ways of learning which are transferable between workplaces, in addition to actions which are context relevant.

Third, there is some evidence to suggest that it is characteristics of the individual worker, as opposed to characteristics of the workplace, which are more important as factors influencing critical reflective working behaviour (Woerkom et al. 2002: 378).

Fourth, workplace cultures can be very powerful, and also hidden in their operation. There is good educational reason to equip professionals with the ability to make sense of these, independent of their operation in specific contexts, so that they enter a new workplace alert to the operation of hidden, more fundamental organisational values.

Fifth, if the focus shifts too markedly from individual practice to organisational context, there is a danger that 'victim blaming' may be replaced by 'system blaming'. My contention is that neither individual nor organisation is 'to blame', but rather that both realms are constructed by each other. What is important is to better understand this co-construction, in order to make organisational changes which are meaningful at both individual and organisational levels. In this chapter, however, my focus primarily begins with personal experience, and the operation of the social and political dimensions within it.

I begin by revisiting the common understandings of the 'critical' theory of critical reflection and how this is enacted in the particular process of critical reflection that I use. I then present an analysis of some of the changes which occur in this process (from students in one of my postgraduate programs). I then rework my understanding of critical reflection in the light of this analysis. I finish by putting forward a preliminary model for how critical reflection might be used for practice review in an organisational context, based on this theoretical framework.

The theory of critical reflection

The reflective process in professional learning basically involves an examination of the assumptions implicit in practices. Not everyone of course distinguishes between reflection and critical reflection. However for those who do, there appear to be essentially two main understandings of what makes reflection critical. First, it may be critical because of its focus on unearthing deeper assumptions or 'presuppositions' (Mezirow 1991: 12). 'Critical', in this sense, is about the ability to be transformative, 'to involve and lead to some fundamental change in perspective' (Cranton 1996: 79–80). Second, it is critical because of its focus on power (Brookfield 1995: 6). In particular therefore, it is transformative because it focuses on dominant or hegemonic assumptions (Brookfield 2000: 126) which may influence our practice unwittingly. The two perspectives are not necessarily of course mutually exclusive, i.e. the deeper assumptions unearthed may, or may not, be about power. But of course what becomes clearer when we consider these two directions, is that what is considered 'fundamental', and of course how power is theorized, then become crucial to our understanding of the critical aspects of critical reflection.

For instance, we can further extend the above to encompass an awareness of how assumptions about the connection between oneself and social context/structure can function in powerful ways to maintain existing (often unequal) power relations, so that awareness of these assumptions can provide a platform for transformative action towards a more equitable society (e.g. Kondrat 1999; Fook 2002). These latter understandings are associated with a critical social theory tradition (Agger 1998; Brookfield 2005), and of course are related to earlier ideas of 'conscientization' (Alfrero 1972; Hart 1990) and other understandings of the ways in which critical theory can change people (Fay 1977).

Critical reflection, from the standpoint of this type of critical perspective, is reflection which enables an understanding of the way (socially dominant) assumptions may be socially restrictive, and thus enables new, more empowering ideas and practices. Critical reflection thus enables social change beginning at individual levels. Once individuals become aware of the hidden power of ideas they have absorbed unwittingly from their social contexts, they are then freed to make choices on their own terms. In this sense they are freed to change the operation of the social at the level of their personal experience.

However this basic view may be theorised more specifically in any number of ways, in any number of disciplines including philosophy, sociology and education, beginning with authors such as Socrates (Nussbaum 1997), through Dewey (1933), Freire (1972), Schön (1983), Habermas (1974), the critical theorists (Brookfield 2005), discourse analysts and those with an interest in narrative and linguistic construction (Taylor and White 2000), Foucault, feminism (Issit 2000), postmodernism (Fook 2002), Giddens (1991) and most latterly spirituality (Ghaye 2005). Therefore, depending on what other frameworks may be invoked, critical reflection may also primarily involve understanding, for example, how people engage with their social worlds and construct a sense of self (Giddens and reflexive modernity); how people make meaning from experience in order to guide action (Mezirow and adult education); how social structures and relations (including gendered ones) mediate and create personal experience; how language use and discourses construct personal meaning and identities; how people's fundamental values connect with professional and personal experience; and, more specifically, how professionals construct their knowledge and identities within a workplace context. None of these functions are of course mutually exclusive, but of course to some extent the type of learning that develops will partly depend on what frameworks are used to theorise the process, and of course what foci are considered important and how they are linked (Fook and Gardner 2007).

In this sense, for the purposes of critical reflection, individual experience may be seen as a microcosm of the social. This relies on an understanding of how knowledge and power are linked; how individuals participate in constructing knowledge (and therefore power); and how individuals act reflexively in their social worlds as agents, both constructing and responding to their environments. The critical reflection process provides a new awareness of the operation of the social in personal experience, thus enabling choices to be made anew. In the context of learning about professional practice, critical reflection is theorised as taking a focus on how the new individual control and changed personal/professional identity that results from this new understanding translates into professional practices (new or reaffirmed). Change is thus effected in the individual's social world through a change of individual orientation towards social ideologies/discourses and their effects on the individual.

In the next section I show how I have developed this theoretical framework into a practical process of undertaking critical reflection for the purposes of changing professional practices.

The process of critical reflection

In my own work I attempt to use a mixture of theoretical approaches: reflective practice; reflexivity; postmodernism (including a Foucauldian approach to power, notions of discourse and narrative); and critical social science, to comprise a broad two-stage process of critical reflection, primarily for professionals who wish to learn from practice (Fook 2004a and b; Fook and Gardner 2007). I use a mixture of theories as I find that different ways of understanding the process can help: they maximise the opportunities for different people to find a meaningful framework; they add some depth and richness to the process; and they better allow the exposure of different perspectives. The first stage focuses on developing a critical reflective analysis/awareness of practice through the exposure (unsettling or 'shaking up') of fundamental (dominant) assumptions and their sources; the second stage develops this awareness into possible practice strategies. By connecting changed awareness with changed practice, participants therefore develop their own practice theory. Both stages therefore focus on learning from practice; the first focuses on changed awarenesses and the second on changed practices. The whole process focuses on how these are linked and therefore enables more transferable learning. Further stages can be added for follow-up to enable initial changes to be sustained. When the process is used for more formal study (such as in postgraduate award programs), participants are asked to write formal assignments based on the above model, and also undertake subsequent stages in which they are asked to further develop the 'theory of practice' through research and/or experimentation in their workplaces.

In more informal continuing education settings, I normally conduct critical reflection in small groups (up to ten participants) over several sessions in which each participant presents a piece of practice for reflection in two stages: a reflective awareness stage and a linking with practice stage. The ultimate aim of the groups is to develop some changed practices as a result of reflections on fundamental (dominant) assumptions (i.e. to develop a theory of practice directly from one's own practice experience and incorporating one's desired values rather than those which are dominant). The process however functions in many different ways, according to the meaning of the specific incident which is raised for the person themselves. This will also depend on how it is theorised and understood, and of course on what types of fundamental assumption are unearthed and 'shaken up' for each person.

Participants bring a 'raw' written description of a critical (significant) incident from their practice. Group members help them reflect by using a set of questions derived from the above theoretical frameworks (e.g. 'What does your practice imply about ... ? What were you assuming when ... ? How did you influence the situation through your presence, perceptions, interpretations and assumptions? What were your beliefs about power and where did they come from? What perspectives are missing? What are your own constructions (especially binary categories)? What language patterns have you used and what do they imply? What is your own thinking and what is the result of power relations (e.g. gendered, cultural, structural).

The process is conducted within a deliberately reflective group culture which has been termed 'critical acceptance' (Fook and Askeland 2007; Fook and Gardner 2007): a climate which balances safety and challenge in order to maximise learning. The main purpose is to create an environment which enables a person to reflect and learn for themselves, including determining for themselves the thinking and practices they wish to develop (rather than being taught a predetermined framework of assumptions or values).

Analysis of the process

What actually happens in the change process? What changes are made and how are individual and social understandings linked and integrated by participants?

The following traces the processes of change and the outcomes for workplace practice, analysed from the written assignments of three postgraduate students. The students were enrolled in a Masters of Professional Practice Development at a university in Australia. This involved two subjects designed to teach the process of critical reflection, and to apply this learning in some way within their organisational context. They spanned a full year and involved two 5,000 word written assignments (one each at the end of each semester) which described and theorised student learning through the critical reflection process. With regard to the generic process outlined above, students undertook a series of stages of learning which went beyond the two preliminary stages. In the first semester they undertook stages one and two, and in the second semester they built upon this learning by formulating their 'theory of practice' into something which could be further researched in their organisation, with a view to implementing it in that context. Learning was continually processed through online journals (fortnightly) and class discussions (approximately monthly).

The three students were all social workers by background who worked in quite different organisations and roles. Cilla worked in a generic community health centre in a deputy manager role. Her initial incident involved designing a staff appraisal instrument sympathetic with feminist thinking. Tessa worked as head of a student unit, responsible for student placements in a large human services government bureaucracy. Her critical incident involved an angry confrontation with a colleague over a student's placement project. Anne was a team leader in a large government income security bureaucracy. She began with an incident from her personal life whilst on holiday overseas: her intervention in an angry argument between a hotel manager and a friend. I analysed the assignments thematically, looking for common themes regarding the nature and ordering of changes made.

The pattern of learning can be summarised as follows.

1   *A first level of assumptions is unearthed.* These assumptions may often be the 'safer' ones, i.e. those which are more easily identifiable and more acceptable as they fit closer with the person's stated theory. For instance, there were assumptions about power and gender, deriving from an explicit feminist framework. In Cilla's case, assumptions about power being equated with the possibility of abuse meant that Cilla constructed binaries of her work roles ('manager versus counsellor', or 'management philosophies versus narrative therapy'). For Tessa, there were clear binaries constructed regarding 'victim/perpetrator' (by definition, victims are powerless, perpetrators powerful, and therefore perpetrators/abusers cannot be powerless).

2   *These may move to another (deeper) level through further reflection.* Sometimes additional assumptions are unearthed which may appear unrelated to the earlier ones. Students, for instance, noted other assumptions, such as for Tessa, a concern with conformism (strong resistance to conformism); and for Anne, a concern with uncertainty, control and change which implied

a strong value on activity (and anxiety about inactivity), because activity implied control of change.

3   *'Breakthrough' connections are made.* Often these are made through the connection with a past (emotional) experience which integrates them and provides an overall meaning. In struggling to see which assumptions are more fundamental, it is often the realisation of connections with a personal experience (past or current) which allows connections to be made between all assumptions. In particular, it is often the emotional element of these experiences which provides a pointer as to their connected meaning.

For instance, Tessa reported remembering a powerful adolescent experience in which she had had a relationship with a young man contrary to the wishes of her parents. She began to experience this relationship as abusive at some point and made a firm decision to end it. From this she traced her strong value on the need to resist being made to conform. In her own mind she had constructed 'non-conforming' as resistance to control, and this was vital to her identity (personal and professional). Her fundamental assumptions therefore moved from being explicitly about power and victimhood, to being about the importance of not conforming, or resisting control. In Tessa's case, it might be said that the connection with her past experience enabled her to theorise her assumptions as being about her own identity formation, and the importance to her of being in control of this process.

Cilla experienced great anxiety at this point in the reflective process. She reported almost deciding to discontinue the course. She traced her anxiety to her childhood experiences of abuse. She realised that she had been using her feminist theory as a way of containing this anxiety (and a way of containing any tendency of her own to use power in an abusive way). This led her to explore the connections between the anxiety experienced from this early abuse, the anxiety she experienced through the critical reflection process, and anxiety in her workplace context. She realised she had equated anger with abuse, which led her to construct conflict (and therefore anger) as something to be avoided in the workplace. The connection for Cilla was about connecting similar emotions, and realising she had therefore equated the experiences associated with these emotions.

4   *This/these assumption/s are evaluated against current experience/values/assumptions (and also other people's opinions/experiences, literature).* Often the framing of the assumptions in the light of powerful experiences allows people to revisit the assumptions in a new light, and they are freed to examine them from different perspectives. It is almost as if understanding this thinking in the light of the context in which it developed allows people to be open to remaking their thinking in the light of different contexts. In other words, contextualising assumptions allows them to be further contextualised. But more than this, the impetus for this remaking

appears to involve a recognition of the political aspects of the emotion, i.e. the realisation that the emotional learning which has been taken from the experience itself performs political functions in their lives (i.e. is used as ideology to preserve a particular set of assumptions or actions).

Cilla reported being struck with two particular articles. One spoke about the connections between power and emotion in the workplace (Vince 2001) and the other about how enemies and allies are constructed in the workplace (Fook 2000). This led her to re-theorise her anxiety. She realised she had assumed that any anxiety triggered old fears about abuse, so she avoided any conflict in the workplace so that, she told herself, she would not risk being abusive towards others. But, she reasoned, anxiety can be caused by a variety of experiences (including the anxiety of any new learning). So, in fact, this avoidance of conflict was functioning to protect her as well. Therefore it also functioned as a use of her own power. Cilla wrote in her assignment, taking on Vince's (2001) views with some force, that 'emotion is political'!

Anne revisited her original critical incident, and decided that her value on activity, and professional leadership being about controlling change, was masking her own need to avoid the discomfort of uncertainty. She felt that her need to intervene was also a way of controlling uncertainty. Tessa decided that her theory of practice (assumptions about not conforming = resistance to control) was inadequate, as it was a reactionary stance, not necessarily strategic, and held the potential to be destructive if so closely tied to her own emotional needs.

5 *Old assumptions are then reframed as their desired theory of practice.* This may feel like a more 'freeing' formulation – one which may embrace the original fear/emotion and allow a reformulation of meaning. The reframing also involves turning the original issue/concern/set of assumptions into an actionable problem – something which can be researched and acted upon in the everyday workplace setting.

Anne decided that what she needed to do, rather than continue to avoid uncertainty, was to reframe her practice in more empowering ways. As a focus for further research on her practice, she decided to investigate: 'How can I practice powerfully in uncertainty?' For her this involved looking at how she might create an 'emotional scaffolding' that allowed her to contain uncertainty, to broaden her view of change into one of possibilities for opportunity.

Tessa decided to look at how she could reframe resistance as a positive thing. Her question then became one of investigating how resistance can be seen as identity making, and as therefore central to self-care in an organisation. In a sense she began to see making her own meaning (and therefore her fundamental theory of practice) as a form of 'identity politics': that the power to make one's own identity in the organisation is important to self-care.

In order for Cilla to further investigate her theory of practice, rather than focusing on how power might not be abusive, she reframed it in terms much closer to home: 'How can I exercise power to influence work relationships that are characterised by unresolved conflict?' Not only was this a more positive formulation, but it was also something which acknowledged the place of power in personal experience, and was framed in a way which allowed Cilla to research it directly from her own experience.

6   Changed practices which resulted.

More open to others and differences. All reported starting with being more open to different ways of communicating, of dealing with uncertainty, of resistance and identity making. In particular Cilla started by trying to create new environments which would allow for other people to communicate in ways that suited them. Tessa built multiple and different perspectives into her own understanding of resistance, so that it became 'resistance as creating the space within bureaucracy for complex/multiple/ contradictory perspectives, and the space for reinventing/negotiating identity'. She spent a lot of time having informal conversations with colleagues, and surprised herself at the multitude of different ways of resisting which she learnt about.

Multiple choices for action. All reported having a lot more options for ways to act, and to be more open to 'experimenting'. For instance, Anne was able to deconstruct the idea of uncertainty, so that she was able to prepare for a confrontational interview by separating what remains constant, and what is new or unknown. She was able to draw on past experiences and clarify boundaries which allayed her anxiety in conducting the interview. Cilla reported many more ways to discuss issues with her co-manager, and different tools for supervision to use with her supervisee.

More empowered stance. All reported feeling more 'active', often accompanied by a sense of relief, of being released from past restrictive thinking. For example, Anne spoke of feeling enabled to 'embrace uncertainty', to move towards controlling the structure rather than being controlled by it. She reported discussing a plan for a new program with a colleague, and surprising herself by asking him to think of it 'without the structure'.

An 'other' focus. All spoke of different relationships with co-workers, particularly Cilla, who experienced previously fraught relationships as more fun and supportive, and of having a breakthrough with a supervision relationship in which only four sessions managed to produce what the previous three years had not (a focus on clinical skills). She also made a conscious decision to factor in her own constructions of other people in relating to them. Anne spoke in particular of developing 'new ideas about how to share knowledge in a community of learners' and 'how to create a learning culture'.

Overall the process seemed to involve a complex interplay of reflecting on specific personal experiences, filtering out different sets of assumptions, and again using the prism of personal experiences, particularly the emotional element, to distil some fundamental meaning (theory of practice) which connects the disparate assumptions. Sometimes part of this fundamental meaning involves the awareness of the importance of the past experiences in identity formation, or in emotional politics. This fundamental meaning is then scrutinised against current contexts (literature, current experiences, other perspectives) and remade in ways which seem more appropriate in these contexts. This remaking involves turning the fundamental meaning (theory of practice) into an issue which is researchable and actionable in the current workplace context.

Implications for further theorising critical reflection

On the face of it, this process appears little different from the changes which it is claimed are made through reflection more generally. For instance, it is similar to Boud et al.'s (1985) outline of the broad process of learning from experience which is involved in reflection: (1) a return to experience; (2) attending to feelings; and (3) re-evaluating experience. There is also similarity with the broad learning in reflective practice in that there is clearly a move from Model 1 to Model 2 thinking (Argyris and Schön 1974) and both single and double loop learning take place (Argyris and Schön 1996). For instance, there was general recognition of how social contexts such as professional ideologies (assumptions about change and activity), workplace cultures (assumptions about organisational conformity), or cultural contexts (value on feminist approaches) might have influenced fundamental assumptions. However what is interesting is that these awarenesses do not figure large in the written accounts of the students. We will return to this further on. In terms of critical social science perspectives, we do see a move towards unearthing more fundamental assumptions regarding power, and a transformation in the way these are evaluated and reworked in line with current experiences. There is a recognition of the social origin of some of these assumptions (in that they originated from other theories about power, abuse, leadership and control), a sense of the restrictiveness of this thinking, and a sense of empowerment with more awareness and individual choice in reworking these (Fook and Askeland 2006).

However there are also some aspects which require further scrutiny, and raise further questions to be examined. For instance, there are many levels and types of assumption raised, many of them complex, and without clear relationships between them. Some are clearly more fundamental (from a cognitive and logical perspective) than others. Others may seem to have an origin deep in personalised experience, but also connect with the social context and position of the person. What criteria do we use to decide which assumptions are more fundamental than others? And how do we know when we have reached an appropriate level of fundamentality? Whilst there have been some useful schemas posed in respect of different levels of assumption (e.g. Mezirow 1998), it appears sometimes as if differentiating levels does still not allow meaning to be made of their connections. In the learning process generated through our course, it seemed as if meaning could only be made of apparently unrelated assumptions through reconnection with personal experiences.

A second issue centres around an apparent trend in the above accounts of change. Students tended to start with assumptions which were gleaned from their social context of beliefs about professional practice (because this was their espoused theory), but seemed almost irrevocably, in the reflective process, to delve into the personal meaning of these. On the face of it, this runs counter to conventional critical theory in that the learning process is presumably primarily about arriving at a social understanding. However it almost seemed that this personal level was more unsettling for these students. This may have had something to do with the professional background of the students as social workers – maybe they had already been educated with some social and critical awareness? It was perhaps that they needed to rework their understanding of their own socially critical views in the further light of personal experiences. But does this also suggest that (deep) meaning may only be made (for some people) through further connection with personal experiences? This indicates, I think, a need to revisit and further research the nature of the connections between personal and social realms. It is perhaps not so easy to divorce the realms from each other, either in experience, in learning and in action. What are the complexities of the relationships between personal meaning and collective social changes? A critical awareness which results from a process of critical reflection may, in this sense, be much more complex than simply deriving a better understanding of the operation of social ideologies in personal experience; this is in some senses the traditional linear view of learning we take from our understanding of consciousness raising (Hart 1990; Fook 2004a); it might involve freeing from these in order to act in more collective ways. It may involve an integrated understanding of how these social ideologies are also constantly remade personally in ways which sometimes run counter to intended collective changes. This perhaps suggests that personal experience may be one prism through which social meaning is made in a critical reflection process.

And what is the place of emotion? It was almost as if emotion not only triggered learning issues, but acted as the impetus and motivation for finding meaning and continuing reflection. Whilst most major writers on critical reflection acknowledge the importance of emotions in learning (Boud et al. 1985; Mezirow et al. 1990; Mezirow 1991, 1994, 1997, 1998, 2000; Brookfield 1995), what exactly does this mean in social terms? Do we need to factor a social theory of emotions more explicitly into our theory of critical reflection? Many writers have developed the use of psychodynamic or psychoanalytic theory (e.g. Vince 2001; Obholzer and Roberts 1994) in relation to organisations. There are related attempts to develop a relational perspective on reflective practice, which emphasises the role of containment of anxiety (Ruch 2005a, b). In addition there are social constructionist views of emotion in organisations (e.g. Fineman 2003) and the concept of emotional labour (Hochschild 1979). However I wonder whether we may need some more sophisticated understanding of the complex interplay of personally and organisationally experienced emotions incorporated into critically reflective learning. This would at the very least involve having a better understanding of how the emotional aspects of professional experience, both negative and positive, contribute to the making of professional identities and professional practices in particular workplace contexts. For instance, Olesen (2001) posits that professional learning and personal development are intertwined – the subjective side of work can be understood and theorised through an examination of workers' life histories. In this sense professional practice can also be understood as made in workplace context along with professional identity. How does emotional work underpin notions of professionalism (Smith and Kleinman 1989)? We might, for instance, understand critical reflection as involving a more complex understanding of how the social management of emotion (through internalized assumptions) impacts on notions of professional identity (Shields 2005) and related practices. And of course we need to develop the direct links between emotional experience and power: the ideological role of emotions in preserving power relations at individual and social levels.

It is also important to point out that although the critical reflection process discussed here is primarily focused on personal learning from personal experiences, it nevertheless yields concrete results and changes in relation to other people, and to organizational practices. For instance much literature claims various benefits and outcomes of critical reflection including: better informed practice; self-awareness and emotional support; more inclusive and emancipatory practice; and improved professionalism, collegiality and organizational learning (Fook and Gardner 2007: 143).

Conclusion

In summary then, I think there are several main points we need to reiterate in order to further develop our understanding of critical reflection. These articulate some more ways in which personal and social realms are integrated in experience. Critical reflection therefore needs to incorporate:

1   *An understanding of the importance of personal experience to provide a meaningful framework for disparate assumptions.* 'A meaningful framework' is understood here in a fairly specific sense as providing connections between apparently unrelated assumptions so that their relative importance can be understood. This process also functions to help people decide what assumptions are of fundamental importance to them. This effectively

extends our understanding of the role of personal experience in critically reflective learning. In this sense not only is critical reflection a process of learning *from* experience (Boud et al. 1985), but it is also a process which may depend on experience for deeper learning at the assumptive level.

2   An understanding of the remaking of power as personal (in addition to the remaking of the 'personal as political'). This includes an understanding of how professional knowledge is used politically in one's own experiences. The 'politics of personal experience' is therefore important, particularly in identity making (personal and professional), re the role of emotions in preserving personal ideologies, and in the broader recognition and incorporation of the role of emotion.

3   The foregoing point also involves a more complex understanding of emotion as an integral part of experience and therefore with personal, cultural, social and political aspects, with particular implications for the making of professional identities and practices.

4   A more complex understanding of how personal and social experiences are integrated, and indeed necessary for meaningful action in the collective realm:

   (a) Personal experience may need to be recognised and validated in order to effect broader collective/social changes from this reflection (Fook 2004a).

   (b) An important part of personal empowerment may involve a sense of reflexivity and agency (Fook 2004a) – this enables both the motivation, vision and energy for collective actions.

   (c) A view that the 'personal' and 'social', rather then being different realms, are simply different perspectives. One way of looking at personal experience is simply as a microcosm of the social, and that, in fact, for individuals, the social realm cannot be meaningfully understood except through the prism of personal experience.

In reworking a theory of critical reflection, I would now articulate critical reflection as involving the *ability to understand the social dimensions and political functions of experience and meaning making, and the ability to apply this understanding in working in social contexts*. Let us compare this with a quote from Argyris and Schön (1996: xxii) regarding organisational learning. This may be seen as learning about 'the political conditions under which individuals can function as agents of organisational action'. From my perspective then, what the above concept of critical reflection allows, is to add a sense of the internalised and personally experienced political conditions. What personal meaning is made by individuals, of the political conditions in their organisation? And how can the understanding of this be used to make changes in organisational practices? Asking these sorts of question allows us to further develop the notion of the 'critical' in critical reflection as a tool for organisational learning and change.

Acknowledgement

A version of this chapter has already been published in the online resource materials with J. Fook and F. Gardner (2007) *Practising Critical Reflection: A Resource Handbook*, Maidenhead: Open University Press.

Chapter 4

A learning practice

Conceptualising professional lifelong learning for the health-care sector

Stephen Billett and Jennifer Newton

Introduction – A learning practice

This chapter proposes and elaborates a model of lifelong professional learning referred to as a 'learning practice' and illustrated through its application to the health-care sector. A learning practice comprises a duality between the contributions to learning provided by engaging in everyday work activities in professional work settings and how professionals elect to engage in and learn through these activities. It emphasises the significance of the learning potential and outcomes that can be secured through everyday professional practice and throughout professionals' working lives. This potential includes the agentic and critical engagement by professionals as learners with what is available to or afforded them through their workplace. In all, the potential of a learning practice will be best realised through the enactment of supportive practices in these work settings and effortful engagement by learners. In doing so, this model offers bases for directing effort and resources to support initial and ongoing learning, and the reshaping of work practices and work culture. The concept of learning practice has its origins in a submission to a commission overseeing the reform of an Australian health care system (Billett 2006a). Premised on the concept of workplace participatory practices (Billett 2002: 457–81), the model's core elements comprise the contributions to learning occurring through engagement in everyday professional work activities and professional workers engagement in and learning through their everyday practice. It comprises a duality: on the one hand, what workplace affords workers in the form of invitations to participate in and learn through engagement with workplace activities and interactions, including close and indirect forms of guidance, and, on the other hand, the quality of individual professionals' participation in their work and learning as exercised by their intentionality, agency and interests. While this model of practice-based learning is applicable to all kinds of work and worker, it seems particularly fitting for health-care professionals whose work carries expectations of continual engagement in self-initiated and directed lifelong learning. That is, it fits the expectation that professional workers will be agentic in their work and learning.

Although presented here as an ideal, this model of lifelong professional learning is founded on empirical research on learning through work. It was developed as a response to growing concerns about developing and maintaining workers' capacities for effective work practice through their work and throughout their working lives, including their need to respond to constant changes in work requirements. It is premised on the idea that most of learning throughout working life arises through practice, including responding to transformations in workplace and occupational requirements. Earlier research identified a range of factors that support or promote individuals' learning through their work, and also factors that stand to limit that learning (e.g. Billett 2001): the strengths and weaknesses of learning through practice. Subsequently, the efficacy of workplace interventions (i.e. guided learning, workplace curriculum) in enhancing learning through practice, including overcoming limitations, were appraised. This research indicates the potential of workplace pedagogies, and prospects for their enactment are best realised through workplaces that afford opportunities to engage in learning through work, and that provide progressive opportunities to engage in new activities and refine what has been learnt through opportunities to practise (i.e. a workplace curriculum). In addition to providing an environment that afforded sources of knowledge that were observable and could be engaged with, the direct guidance of more expert practitioners provides a key source of working knowledge. The latter is especially helpful when the knowledge to be learnt cannot be accessed by discovery learning alone (i.e. trial and error). Moreover, individuals' intentionality and engagement – their agentic approach to learning and work – is held to be central to the development and exercise of effective personal epistemologies that support learning for working life (Billett, Smith and Barker 2005: 291–237). Collectively, these evolving and separate contributions are synthesised into a model of professional learning throughout working life that is presented here as an ideal: a learning practice.

Professional lifelong learning

As foreshadowed, the concept of a learning practice addresses the core focuses for this volume by positioning professionals' learning centrally within the exercise of their practice. However, it cautions that it is not sufficient to rely alone upon either individual epistemological acts (e.g. personal reflection) or the affordances of the professional work setting (e.g. workplace support). Indeed, personal reflection has recently been critiqued with Schön's (1983, 1987) two main concepts: reflection-on-action and reflection-in-action being held to fail to account for how individuals reflect and contemplate future possibilities, and how those possibilities might be achieved. Thus, this projective dimension is held to reduce the potential for learning and improvement (Wilson 2008: 177–84). By accentuating the interdependence between the personal and institutional contributions to learning, the learning practice concept emphasises that both are needed to secure effective learning throughout professional life. Yet, it is the active engagement in learning by professionals that can most effectively bring together the personal and social contributions to that learning, which acknowledges reflection and reflexivity that seem fitted to professionals' ongoing need for proactivity in their work and learning.

Privileged here, then, is the nature, focus and intentionality of individuals' active learning efforts (i.e. their personal epistemology). This epistemology goes beyond conceptions of critical reflection as enacted moments of intentional learning, to embrace a more ongoing and ubiquitous form of proactive professional learning. Moreover, consistent with the dualistic concept advanced here, what constitutes productive reflection will most likely be assisted through interaction, direct or otherwise, with more experienced practitioners. Learning, as Boud et al. (1993: 8) suggest, 'builds on and flows from experience: no matter what external prompts to learning there might be ... learning can only occur if the experience of the learner is engaged'. However, as work requirements, work practices and workforce participation change, particular elements of this interdependent relationship may be required to be accentuated (Billett 2006c: 1). For instance, older workers (i.e. those over 45 years) or those who are disabled may have to rely more upon their own personal epistemology and agency (Church and Luciano 2005) than the affordances of their workplaces in securing and maintaining effective workplace competence because of employers' preferences for supporting younger workers, most markedly in their expenditure on the development of well-educated younger workers (Bishop 1997: 19–87).

The theoretical salience of a learning practice is its explanatory power to elaborate the development of workers' working knowledge through a consideration of both personal and social contributions to that knowing and knowledge and the relations between the two (e.g. Bhaskar 1998; Gergen 1994; Giddens 1991; Valsiner 2000). It emphasises the interdependence between the social and personal contributions not only in individuals' professional development, but also in the ongoing process of remaking and changing of occupational practices. This remaking arises through responses to the continual and new challenges that occupations, such as those within health care, need to address in response to particular problems, circumstances and situations that constitute the actual enactment of professional practice. In this way, both workplace change and human development are held to be a product of relations between the individual and social, not one being posterior to the other.

Key concepts and practices for a learning practice

There are probably no easy solutions to developing and sustaining professional capacities, particularly in large-scale workplaces such as health-care facilities, given the scope and diversity of occupations that are deployed within them. However, there are practices and processes that can be enacted in these workplaces that can assist securing ongoing professional development. Many of these are about guiding learning in workplaces and developing work practices that include a focus on promoting and assisting learning as part of everyday work practice. The key and salient claim here is that, regardless of whatever structural changes and additional training programmes are enacted, without the establishment and enactment of systems, values and processes to maintain and enhance the learning and further development of practices within workplaces, the proposed changes will not be realised. The concept proposed here is workforce development through enacting and maintaining a learning practice; an approach that has benefits for those practitioners who are engaged in learning, those practitioners who assist in the learning process (e.g. mentors, experienced practitioners, preceptors), health-care organisations (e.g. health-care institution) and their clients. Importantly, the kinds of learning practices proposed here are to be conducted in workplaces and as part of everyday professional work. These circumstances provide access to authentic experiences and direct and indirect guidance in ways that are generative of rich professional knowledge.

As noted, it is imperative for any reform or restructuring of an organisation and its work practices to be accompanied by ongoing work-based processes that support and guide both practitioners' learning about and the remaking of professional practices in ways that are consistent with the intended institutional changes and desired personal development. Organisational restructures, new work arrangements and training programmes will be insufficient unless the everyday activities and learning required to understand and enact these changes are enabled. This guidance for practitioners is essential because, as foreshadowed, health practitioners are constantly engaged in processes of learning that are shaped and influenced by the activities they undertake and interactions in which they participate (Anderson 1993; Rogoff 1990; Van Lehn 1989). Consequently, it is the quality of their engagement with these activities that shapes not only how they implement new practices, strategies, norms and values, but also what they learn through this enactment (Sheehan et al. 2005). Therefore, more than simply enacting work tasks, the cognitive processes engaged when undertaking goal-directed activities and everyday work activities also generate a legacy in terms of learning. As Rogoff and Lave (1984) put it, activity structures cognition. Much of the learning secured through everyday work activities comprises the reinforcement, refining and honing of what is already known about or is being practised through undertaking activities which are similar to those previously learnt (Billett 2001). Therefore, the kinds of practice they encounter in their everyday work will, in different ways, have a legacy: their learning (Scribner 1985). Moreover, when health practitioners engage in new activities, such as those brought about by changes to their work activities or the organisation of their work, individuals will develop new knowledge or ways of under-standing and doing tasks. Both the everyday activities and novel tasks of practitioners, therefore, comprise the basis for ongoing learning and the development for the conduct of their work (Anderson 1982; Lave 1993).

As proposed, individuals learn continually through their work and also engage in the ongoing process of remaking their work practices (Billett 2001; Fuller and Unwin 2002). This everyday learning is very helpful in terms of personal and organisational development, because workers are actively engaged in learning and reshaping their practice (Billett, Smith and Barker 2005). So, there is no need to make ongoing learning occur in practice settings: it will happen regardless. However, not all that learning and remaking of practice is effective or appropriately focused. Bad habits, dangerous short cuts, inappropriate procedures and attitudes can be learnt as well as those attributes that support effective practice for employees and their work units (Billett 2001). Yet, and importantly, no matter what structural and organisational changes, external training or initial preparation occur, the day-to-day experiences of work are key sources of learning and remaking practice (Anderson 1993; Rogoff 1990, 2003). It is these learning experiences, and how they are construed and constructed by workers, that will ultimately shape whether these reforms and the work practices that support them will be realised. Consequently, without appropriate guidance and organisation, there can be no confidence that the ongoing learning occurring through work and its impacts upon work activities will achieve outcomes that are in the individual's or organisation's goals (Billett 2001). Therefore, this model of professional learning comprises a series of contributions to learning that include the following:

- *Guiding practice.* The guidance provided to workers by more experienced practitioners assists both the specific and strategic decision making associated with that practice and its development, including career trajectories.
- *Workplace support.* Identifying and organising the means for assisting and monitoring individuals' progression through workplace activities as they progressively develop the skills required for competent performance.
- Organising a *'workplace curriculum'* or a learning curriculum that identifies the sequencing and pathways of activities in workplaces that individuals progress along in order to develop further their workplace competences.
- The use of specific *guided learning strategies* to assist the development of procedural capacities (i.e. knowing how) that cannot be learnt through discovery alone, further developing understanding (i.e. knowing that) and the kinds of values and attitudes required for securing effective practice.

The key focus here is on *workforce development through practice.* But this does not necessarily exclude training programmes, particularly where the programmes offer the optimal experience for learning new knowledge that cannot be secured through practice alone. However, whenever these programmes are enacted, there is a need to actively integrate the activities and learning from those programmes with practice-based activities to assist their benefits being realised in practice. These four concepts of learning practice are discussed in the next section using examples from current research that investigate the development of nurses' work as a learning practice in a major health-care facility in Australia (Newton et al. 2007). While each of these contributions represents affordances, in the form of support provided by the health-care setting, the active engagement and participation by health-care workers is also essential. So, beyond the exercise of support for learning from the workplace will be the agency of the learners.

Developing a learning practice within a health-care workplace

The concept of, procedures for and strategies that together comprise the model of a learning practice arise from a programme of enquiry into how workers across a range of industries learn through their work, and how that learning might be advanced. The findings of this programme are informing how such learning might be best ordered in the health care sector (Newton et al. 2007). The proposal here is intended to provide the basis for a practice-based model of ongoing professional learning in these health-care settings.

Guiding practice

The guidance provided by more experienced practitioners may well be essential to assist both specific skill development and strategic decision making associated with health practice and its development, including accommodating career trajectories. This guidance includes the workplace mentoring role in which the more experienced worker (e.g. preceptor, specialist) acts as a guide to less experienced workers in a particular field and/or circumstance of health work (e.g. particular ward, clinic, etc.). An example of such guidance identified through the nursing research project is as follows. Toni is a newly qualified registered nurse undertaking a graduate programme. She is on the first placement of her graduate programme and has a preceptor (i.e. an experienced registered nurse) assigned to guide her learning. In the following interview extract, Toni shares what would be considered an exemplar of guiding practice, where the wisdom of the more experienced nurse provides assistance to the novice.

> I had a really bad shift this one afternoon at Ward A, by about 10 o'clock[pm], that's when I started writing my notes and she finished up there and she stayed back with me. I couldn't even think to write my notes,

and she just went through everything with me, what had happened, what I should document and she stayed back and then she made sure I was OK to go home because you know when you're upset and it was about a half-hour drive home and she was really good. She was not just about supporting me with learning, but just making sure that I was OK to go home and that. She explained to me that it was a good idea to come back the next day and because that shift was just a learning experience. And then the next day you probably have the same patients and you can learn from that and then kind of continue on with the progress of the actual patient.

This guidance includes providing localised and contextual advice which informs strategic decision making for what constitutes effective nursing practice. It also emphasises that productive reflection extends to understanding and appraising the value of particular contributions to learning. For instance, understanding the circumstances of the local population and their health-care requirements, to treatment prospects for the support of treatments is likely to differ across communities served by health-system services (e.g. between metropolitan, regional, remote, indigenous and rural communities). The experienced practitioner may not always be a supervisor or a more senior nurse or a medical officer, but rather someone from whom health workers who are new to the workplace or situation may need to seek advice. Yet, evident in the quote above is the engagement of the learner with the guide. This illustrates that the process of guided learning is not just transmission of knowledge, but includes the openness of and engagement by the learner. Of course, there are power relations and dependencies, but individuals' learning will ultimately be premised on how they appropriate or learn from what they encounter and experience in health-care settings.

Specific forms of guidance can have particular pertinence for learners at different stages of their development. Being new to a workplace, particularly for a student, can be daunting, and having the support of a variety of members of the health-care team in guiding the direction of students' practice through the provision of experiences offers an invaluable learning experience. For instance, Leeny, a second-year undergraduate nursing student, having just completed her first acute care clinical placement, recounts her experience.

> I thought it was fantastic in my ward. We got to interact with occupational therapists, the receptionist, the doctors and the pharmacist. ... We got to see that multidisciplinary team and be a part of it as a student that was very encouraging. It really opened my eyes as to how important it is to work as a team.

The process of appropriation arising through productive engagement and reflection is illustrated here. This arose because the student felt invited to engage, was supported in that engagement, and then secured important insights and came to appreciate the positive and supportive values underpinning the experience. In these ways, guidance by more experienced co-workers can assist in developing the kinds of capacity required for expert performance. However, it comprises a reciprocal process of participation by both the guide and the learner.

Workplace learning support

This is defined as identifying and organising the means for assisting and monitoring individuals' progression through workplace activities in developing the skills required for competent performance. In other words, understanding the readiness of the health workers to progress to subsequent tasks, planning and monitoring their advancement and organising specific guided learning when and where appropriate (Billett 2000: 272–85, 2001). For instance, each time a new task is to be performed, consideration should be given to involving staff who would benefit from participating in and learning through engaging in that task. Three salient elements of learning practice enacted here are the organisation of a practice-based curriculum, pedagogic opportunities and the use of guided learning strategies. This kind of support can be useful when learning a new task. Yet, and as above, beyond what is afforded in terms of workplace support is the agency of the learner in appraising the worth of and engaging with that support. As a third-year undergraduate student, Sally shares one of the learning sources she is able to draw on in the health-care workplace, and her interview extract reveals the importance of the invitational quality of the workplace, as well as her taking up of that invitation.

> Sometimes the doctors will let you watch a procedure and will explain things and even physiotherapists and dieticians … they are not the main sources but they do give you extra learning material. I'm always interested in learning a new skill and if the preceptor (the registered nurse) makes me feel happy that I'm there and gets me to do these new skills then it is more motivating too that they want me to be there.

This extract illustrates how workplace learning support can be secured through the effortful and appreciative engagement by the learner with opportunities that arise and are afforded through everyday work activities in the health-care setting.

Organising and enacting a practice-based curriculum

For health practitioners engaged in learning new tasks or work roles, it is helpful to identify what a 'practice-based curriculum' might be, identifying the sequencing and pathway of health-care activities that individuals should progress along in order to develop workplace competence (Lave 1990; Billett 2006b). Usually, this pathway of activities involves commencing with engaging in tasks of low accountability and then moving towards more critical aspects of the role. It includes the movement by health-care workers from being totally guided and monitored in undertaking these tasks, to being able to perform them without direct supervision. This kind of practice-based curriculum is commonly exercised in hospital wards and is constituted by, for example, the sequencing of activities that nurses participate in and the scope of workplace tasks they engage in as they move towards being able to perform a greater range of nursing tasks independently. For instance, Ellie is a third-year undergraduate nursing student completing her final clinical placement for the Bachelor of Nursing. Throughout the six-week placement she has been supported by her preceptor (a registered nurse) working the same shift roster. Having the same nurse for this period of time has enabled Ellie to develop a degree of independence in her work. This has been through a process of negotiation and trust.

> The first few days are always they [the preceptor] watch you do everything and they say 'don't do anything unless you tell me', so I would say 'I am going to refill the burette for the intravenous therapy' and the preceptor would say 'okay go ahead'. I'd say 'I'm going to do a finger prick on this child because there is a slip in the front of their folder for one' and the preceptor would say, 'okay go ahead' and then after it was all done and the notes were done and everything was checked, she said I could just do it on my own.

This example illustrates how learners are able to progress through activities of greater accountability under the careful monitoring of a more experienced co-worker. As with the other elements of the learning practice, the enactment of the learning curriculum is more than the provision of activities and support, it also includes the extent that the worker-learner engages with what is provided. It is this kind of sequencing of experiences and engagement with these experiences that constitutes progression along the practice-based curriculum.

Pedagogic opportunities

Beyond the learning opportunities of ongoing engagement in both new and familiar work, some experiences will provide potentially rich pedagogic opportunities, and these are worth identifying and utilising fully. For instance, the handover sessions used by teams of nurses at the change of shifts has long been acknowledged as offering particularly helpful insights into nursing practices and can provide rich learning purposes for practitioners at different levels of competence and with different specialisms. For instance, in discussing what contributes to her learning during her first clinical rotation in her graduate nurse programme, Clare describes the learning experience that can be afforded during a handover.

> You will go and hand over your patients and the nurse-in-charge ends up telling you more than you tell them. I find that really helpful and they are just continuously giving you education and support as you go along.

Novice nurses engage in these meetings to understand the particular conditions of patients and their management, along with the range of conditions and treatments in a particular ward. More experienced student nurses can make judgements about the kinds of treatment and the progress of the patients, whereas more advanced nurses can engage in actual deliberations about the efficacy of the proposed treatments, for instance. Again, beyond what is afforded (e.g. presence at handovers and engagement with other nurses) are the ways in which nurses can elect to engage with what is experienced. The same experience can lead to quite distinct learning outcomes, depending on the nurses' level of knowledge and understanding and also on their interest in engaging with the patients' cases. Preparatory work might maximise the experiences; for instance, novice nurses might be given the task of organising patients' medications, thereby becoming familiar with a range of pharmaceuticals, dosages and means of administration. Yet, some prior opportunities to learn to identify the prescribed pharmaceuticals from the available range in the drugs cart may enrich this learning experience. Of course, the worth of such preparatory work will be dependent upon the engagement by learners with such activities. Potentially rich pedagogic opportunities such as these are freely available in supporting practice-based learning. As such, they need to be identified and utilised fully. Moreover, they can be enhanced by making them richly teachable moments (Bailey, Hughes and Moore 2004).

Guided learning strategies

Specific guided learning strategies have been identified as being useful in assisting the development of procedural capacities (i.e. knowledge how), understanding (i.e. knowledge that) and, across both, the kinds of values and attitudes required for effective practice (Billett 2000, 2001). These strategies include the use of modelling and coaching; for instance, to develop procedural capacities and the use of questioning, explanation, etc. for developing understanding in workplace settings. They have been trialled in workplaces of different kinds across industry sectors. Their use requires some preparation and has been shown to be easily adopted by those who have enjoyed the benefits of professional training, which has, in turn, generated a rich understanding of the concepts and procedures that they use in their practice (Billett 2001). The selection of appropriate strategies sits well within a model that supports the use of more experienced professional practitioners to assist those who are less experienced in a particular area of practice. For example, Clare, who had just completed her first semester's clinical placement as a third-year under-graduate student nurse, experienced such support. She describes how a good preceptor guided her learning in undertaking two new clinical skills.

> I find it helpful and interesting when you are doing things like taking blood or doing an ECG, what I find helpful is a good preceptor when I do the skill for the first time that I can be shown it and then I do it and that someone [the preceptor] is with me that makes a big difference.

Here, the collaborative qualities of learning specific procedures are illustrated through the reciprocal process of modelling and demonstrations followed by approximations of the modelled activity by the learner. So, guidance focuses on the activities of the learners, and is therefore premised on their taking up of this opportunity. Toni, during her third-year clinical placements, undertook a rotation in the operating theatre. Having learnt about surgery and theatre during her lectures at university, she stated that she 'wanted to go and see everything being done'. Toni was fortunate that this placement provided her with a hands-on approach which was enhanced by her enthusiasm.

> I worked with a scrub nurse, an anaesthetic nurse and a recovery nurse and they were all really interesting ... and even the doctors and the anaesthetist ... because I seemed so eager about it, they just put me in positions and were like, 'okay you can help me intubate then' and I'm like 'what do I do?' and I just helped them and all that kind of thing. ... It was somewhere I had never been before ... that is why I kind of just asked lots of questions and they kind of put me in the spot. It got to a point in theatre where the doctors pulled out some of the bowel and said 'I think is it an intussusception' this is what it looks like and he pulled it and I am like 'whoa'.

This is an illustration of the exercise of the learner's agency, of engagement with partners and activities, and conscious and effortful participation in professional practice. Yet here agency is also exercised by the more experi-enced co-worker in the guidance she provides to the student nurse. As a registered nurse, Margaret, who takes on the role of a preceptor, shares her understanding of what this role entails, which succinctly encapsulates the inherent meaning of guided learning strategies.

> I don't necessarily try and teach them, oh this drug does that and the side effects are that ... my role is more this is how you be a nurse.

In these ways, the provision for enacting the curriculum practices and peda-gogic strategies that underpin the learning practice have the potential to be well-supported within health-care settings. It is acknowledged and understood that the health-sector workforce can be hierarchical and, like most workplaces, subject to contested relations. Nevertheless, the relatively high level of education and preparation, the presence of professional values, traditions of providing learning support for health-care staff (e.g. preceptorship, internship) and concerns about professional practice all provide a strong foundation to enact support focused on effective learning and practice. The potential benefits suggest that these strengths are worthwhile being built upon to overcome the limitations that might arise from hierarchical and contested relations.

In all there is a range of potential benefits arising from the enactment and sustaining of a learning practice within health-care settings. These include: (a) utilising and building upon the ongoing work and learning processes engaged in by health-sector workers; (b) maintaining a focus on effective practice; (c) developing capacities required for the health system, including appropriate values and dispositions for practice; (d) enhancing the status and retention for the experienced practitioners providing support to learners; (e) effective initial training in clinical and other settings through workplace learning support; (f) potentially enhancing retention rates and a sense of work identity through supportive learning processes; and (g) inherent succession preparation. These potential benefits address important needs of health workers, their work practices, health-care organisations and their patients.

So the prospects offered through a learning practice as an ideal is to assist workforce development through supporting initial and ongoing development of skills within health-care workplaces as a component of everyday work activity by health-care workers. There are benefits likely to go beyond initial skill development because they apply equally to maintaining and extending existing work competence throughout working life. This can occur in at least two ways: firstly, participation by experienced practitioners in work activities and interactions in ways that develop further the novice nurses' understanding of procedures for, and dispositions associated with, effective nursing; secondly, there are likely to be benefits from the direct role played by experienced practitioners in supporting less-experienced counterparts in terms of the development of their own professional capacities and sense of self as a nursing practitioner.

Developing the capacities for a learning practice

Many aspects of the developmental processes outlined above should be straightforward for many practitioners, because of their rich experiences of practice and the current activities assisting skill development in health-care workplaces. However, these kinds of process may require some preparation and capacity building. Perhaps, a key conceptual change for many is to understand the potency of their own practice and that of others as a rich source of learning support (Billett 2002). A workforce largely comprising tertiary- and higher-educated individuals may not always fully appreciate that rich and legitimate learning can occur outside education institutions.

There will also be a requirement for some specific skill development. This would focus on the kinds of process (e.g. guided learning strategies) used by health workers in their practice to assist others to learn; health workers should also understand how they, as learners, might best engage in the process of their own development, albeit through assisting others or being assisted themselves. Opportunities may arise for skill development at induction processes, meetings and also specific educational interventions to develop these capacities (e.g. short courses). The promotion of such practices is most likely to be supported when they are part of the workers' job descriptions and there is time available to fulfil the roles (Billett 2003). Including the guiding of others' learning in duty statements and the role of professional practice might well provide a foundation for changing practice that can be monitored and developed through staff-management processes.

Different kinds of reward are likely to be helpful for buoying health workers' participation in supporting and participating in their workplaces as rich learning environments. For some, this reward will be from the enhanced sense of self and professional identity as a result of both learning and assisting others to learn. However, it might also be necessary, for some categories of health workers, to organise for practice-based learning to be assessed and formally recognised, and linked to their career progression. In particular, lower-paid and lower-status health workers, for whom there are limited educational programmes and/or recognition but often considerable costs incurred in securing recognised qualifications, may not reap an appropriate return. Consequently, assessment and recognition processes, as well as certification, might be required for these kinds of worker.

The above represent a set of conditions through which learning practices might be developed across health-sector workplaces, and there is much that is already in place to assist such development. However, there are factors that can limit the achievement of the full potential of workplaces to become sites of learning practice. For instance, most health workplaces, like other workplaces, are hierarchical and contested. Therefore, the degree to which these hierarchies and contestations play out are likely to inhibit the possibility of developing effective learning environments. Certainly, in the health-care setting recent studies highlight an embedded nature and culture in nursing of 'getting the work done' that impacts on the learning environment (Newton and McKenna 2007; Maben et al. 2006). Reluctance to share information and work interactions constrained by suspicion are unlikely to be positive environments for constructive learning and developing practice. The support for particular cliques, factions or affiliates within a workplace may inhibit the sharing of knowledge and support across cohorts. Certainly, if there is negativity and stifling hierarchies, these will inevitably continue to be perpetuated unless there is a change in how work is undertaken and practice remade. This is why the processes proposed here are so important.

Towards a learning practice

Here, a scheme for promoting learning through and for health practice is proposed as an ideal: a learning practice. The health sector is relatively well-positioned to enact a learning practice and, thereby, secure effective learning experiences because of the relatively high level of education its practitioners enjoy, the sense of professional practice and purpose, and the goals towards which health practitioners are directed. These qualities stand as foundations for enacting processes focused upon developing and sustaining effective professional practice. These conditions are probably more available in most health workplace settings than in many other workplace settings. Of course, there are limitations and barriers in any situation or scheme to realise this potential. The enactment of power and interests in ways that make workplaces non-invitational through affordances that limit participation and guidance and seek to restrict participation can nullify all the potential of such sites of practice and learning. However, the enactment of professional values and practices that support learning in health-care settings, including those that can transcend interdisciplinary and cross-disciplinary fields, can do much to secure effective learning. In conclusion, processes of workplace-based learning can be organised to guide health-sector workers' learning towards the key goals desired for enhancing personal professional and organisational practices.

Acknowledgement

The authors acknowledge the support provided by the Australian Research Council who funded the investigation referred to here and to the contributions of the nurses and student nurses in that project.

Chapter 5

Really reflexive practice
Auto/biographical research and struggles for a critical reflexivity

Linden West

I know there are connections in life and there are ... narratives ... woven together in ways that we ... don't always understand ... and if that means what I think it does [it is] a hugely ... beneficial thing to do to draw people's biographies together, because understanding the way that things are woven together and the connectedness of it ... can help enormously in the drawing together of programmes for individuals and coping with things that aren't working very well at the time. ... It is a brilliant process.

> (A participant in a teacher education programme called Teach First, based in 'challenging' London schools).

Introduction

This chapter stems from in depth auto/biographical research into the lived experience of learning and working among various professionals, including doctors and trainee teachers based in marginalised, inner-city communities in the UK. The research is related to the crisis of professionalism and of what counts as professional knowledge, as well as to the dominance of highly instrumentalist imperatives in professional education, to the potential neglect of deeper forms of reflective learning and critical awareness. Ironically, the research itself provided a reflexive space in which emotional insight could develop alongside critical awareness, self-knowledge with a deepening understanding of the other. The basic argument is that reflective practice in professional preparation and development can be superficial and formulaic, while more holistic forms of understanding, which combine self-knowledge with critical awareness, are needed in becoming a more creative, effective and reflexive professional.

Despite the pervasive mantra of reflective practice as being essential in medicine, health care, education and other settings, this, to repeat, can be superficial and formulaic, encouraging compliance, even cynicism, rather than awareness and radical questioning. Yet it is also suggested that reflective practice of a sustained, more holistic kind is essential in building critical forms of insight into self and the other. Really reflexive practice, which includes engaging with the auto/biographical dimensions of professional interactions, can provoke profound questioning of taken for granted norms in working contexts.

There is, of course, a long-standing belief in the importance of reflective practice in developing the artistry, alongside the 'science', of professional work (Schön 1987). But reflective practice has also been seen to discourage critical interrogation of the way things are or might be, locked as such practice can be in servicing the needs of the present or in consolidating the status quo, rather than questioning it (Fook 2002, Furlong 2000). The debate about reflective practice connects with the wider crisis of trust in professionals and their knowledge base among policy makers, across the Anglo-Saxon world and more widely (Chan, Fisher and Rubenson 2007; Furlong 2000). The belief that professionals necessarily act with responsibility in relation to those they serve no longer holds, while the relative autonomy of the professions and their training has been under intense assault from government and its agencies for some time (Furlong 2000). Governments have chosen to intervene and shape professional educational programmes and practice as part of the 'modernisation' of human services, under rhetoric of standards and accountability (West 2001; Chan, Fisher and Rubenson 2007). This applies to relatively high-status professions such as medicine as well as the 'softer', 'lower-status' ones such as teaching, health care and social work. A culture of audit and managerialist prescription, rather than professionally led improvement, is the order of the day.

Medicine is a case in point. Doctors seem unhappy about the increasing prescription surrounding their role and surveillance of performance (Smith 2001: 1073–74). The pressure for accountability and the low trust of policy makers (as well as their wish to control expenditure) find expression in ubiquitous clinical protocols, monitoring of performance and compulsory continuing professional development, alongside the drive for more evidence-based practice. If reflective practice is trumpeted, at least in general practice, as important, this, for some, can appear an unconvincing mantra in a context of work intensification, meeting targets and performance indicators. Doctors' morale and motivation can suffer, while primary care, in the words of doctors themselves, can be 'a very unreflective work setting', with practitioners becoming 'brutalised early on in their careers' leading them to 'adopt mechanical work practices' (Burton and Launer 2003: 10–13). Despite the introduction of sociological, psychological and, to an extent, narrative forms of understanding in the professional curriculum, critical and emotional forms of learning – including locating professional practice in a broader culturally and socially aware critique – may remain marginal in medical culture (West 2001; Sinclair 1997).

There may be similar tendencies among teachers, although the historical context is different, given the lower status of the profession. Central government agencies, rather than higher-education institutions, in the UK increasingly prescribe the teacher-education curriculum (as they have done in the classroom). Belief in a professionally led, context-sensitive development perspective on teachers and teaching has dissipated among policy makers. Furlong (2005) argues that professionalism has diminished almost to vanishing point as teachers become like technicians, delivering curricula according to prescribed criteria, in specified ways. Interestingly, while Furlong considers reflective practice to be important, in reconfiguring professional knowledge and in challenging deprofessionalising tendencies, he turns, in the main, to critical theory for some salvation; to the idea that good practice lies in challenging the tacit, unconsidered assumptions of everyday life via more open and dialogical relationships and forms of communication. Reflective practice can, of course, lack a critical edge, yet, as will be illustrated, it can also be a means to deeper forms of critical as well as self-understanding. It depends on how personal experience and the nature of reflexivity are perceived. Engaging with biographical experience, in professional as well as personal contexts, may be considered an escape from questioning dominant assumptions. Or it can also be considered, in the spirit of C. Wright Mills and feminism, as representing a meeting point between historical and cultural forces and structuring processes, and struggles for agency, selfhood and integrity in a life (Wright Mills 1959 and 1970; Merrill and West 2008; Dominicé 2000). Feminism, especially, has also taught how the personal, or for that matter the professional, is highly political terrain, and that we can learn to use our experience to build more confident and knowledgeable senses of agency alongside psychological insight (Merrill and West 2008).

The present chapter is also informed by psychodynamic perspectives, from which vantage point reflective practice can appear psychologically superficial, with limited attention paid to the anxiety at the heart of learning and professional work, and the associated defences against thinking for self that experience can evoke (Salzberger-Wittenberg et al. 1999; Froggat 2002). The place of emotions, and learning about and from them, in teacher education, for instance, as well as in medical training, remains uncertain, despite a longstanding interest in reflective practice and the emotional experience of becoming and being a teacher (Atkinson and Claxton 2000; Hayes 2003: 153–71; Stephenson 1995: 309–18; Malderez et al. 2005; Fabbri, Melacarne and Striano 2008).

Similar observations have been made about the training and professional development of health-care and social-work practitioners. Froggett (2002) argues that the language of feeling and relationship in diverse professional contexts, including programmes for social and health workers, has been impoverished. The extent to which social workers and others on the ground are able, under pressures of work intensification, and externally imposed standards, protocols and audit, to question their human practice, in more open-ended, exploratory ways, is increasingly constrained (Chamberlayne et al. 2004). Moreover, certain kinds of knowledge are privileged: what is easily evidenced or expressed in measurable outcomes, as against what is more diffuse, biographical, subjective, interpretative, emotionally embedded as well as potentially critical. Under the mantra of evidence-based practice, harder more quantitative 'scientific' and 'objective' evidence is emphasised rather than what is 'personal' and subjective.

I want to use evidence from three studies – of family doctors, trainee teachers and of different professionals working in programmes like Sure Start (designed to offer services and support to hard-pressed families in economically marginal communities and modelled on the USA's Head Start programme (West and Carlson 2007)) – to suggest how auto/biographical forms of reflexive learning offer potentially rich ways of thinking about how criticality can be connected with feeling, self with the other, and one biography and another (West 2001). For reasons of space, attention is mainly paid to doctors and teacher trainees. Engaging with the personal and biographical, it is suggested, can be a source of profound learning, which includes challenging everyday assumptions and the ideologies that may underpin them.

The research design

The methodology is shaped by the wider turn to biographical, life history and/or narrative research in the study of professionals, including in medicine, primary care, social work and teaching (Chamberlayne et al. 2004). Biographical approaches derive, in part, from the social constructivist idea – reaching back to symbolic interactionism and the Chicago School – that the social is not simply internalised but is actively experienced and given meaning, which can help change it. Psychodynamic insights are proving influential among some biographical researchers, with attention paid to the role of unconscious factors in learning and professional life as well as in research (Froggett 2002; Hollway and Jefferson 2000; Roper 2003: 20–32). A highly interactionist notion of professional practice lies at the heart of this research, with unconscious factors, such as anxiety and resistance to learning, considered (Chamberlayne et al. 2004). The 'auto/biographical' perspective challenges the idea of the detached, objective biographer of others' lives, and the notion that a researcher's (or professional's) history, identity (including gendered, raced, classed and sexual dimensions) and power, play little or no part in shaping the other and their story. Liz Stanley writes, instead, of an 'intertextuality' at the core of biography (and by extension professional practice), which has been suppressed in supposedly 'objective' accounts of others' lives. This is part of preserving a kind of de facto claim for biography as science: a process producing 'the truth,' and nothing but the truth about its subject (Stanley 1992).

The first study was of twenty-five GPs, mostly based in inner London (West 2001). The aim was to illuminate how they manage their work and learning in the context of a changing health-care system and in difficult and potentially draining inner-city environments. The research lasted four years, involving six cycles of interviews with most doctors, each interview lasting upwards of two hours. Transcripts and tapes were used to establish themes and to consider their meaning and significance, collaboratively, over time. The study progressed towards a profoundly 'auto/biographical' as well as iterative learning process, in which I was a learner too, including interrogating gender, masculinity and the management of emotionality in my own life as a psychotherapist as well as an academic (West 2001). The second study was of trainee teachers in a new teacher-education programme called Teach First, based in difficult London schools. Teach First recruits the 'brightest and best' graduates from 'elite' universities into what is a business-led, mainly schools-based, training. A discourse of leadership infuses the programme. Unlike many previous initiatives in improving educational opportunities for marginalised groups – in which solutions were seen to lie in recruiting more teachers from such groups – the rhetoric of Teach First is one of leadership from the brightest and best, providing the yeast for a modernising agenda (Hutchings 2007). The experiences of seventeen graduates in a first cohort were chronicled via five cycles of in-depth interviews over the two years of the programme. A third piece of research, referred to briefly, is of professionals operating in family 'support' and learning programmes, such as Sure Start, also located in economically marginalised communities (West and Carlson 2006: 359–80, 2007).

It should be emphasised that rapport and attentive listening were at the heart of these process, building on the traditions of feminist epistemology. This depends, in part, on the capacity of researchers to feel, identify and empathise with their subjects. It has to do with creating a good enough transitional space in which people's anxieties diminish, relationships strengthen, and curiosity towards experience, in all its dimensions, and the capacity to think about it, grows (Winnicott 1971). Themes emerged inductively over time and were subject to interrogation. Stories we tell as professionals or more widely can be partial, defensive and even illusory, born, for instance, out of an unconscious anxiety about our capacity to cope with difficult experience or for fear of what researchers or colleagues think (Hollway and Jefferson 2000).

Some case studies

I want to use individual case studies to illustrate how really reflexive practice can serve to understand and challenge self, practice and received wisdom. A metaphor of 'on the edge' developed in the study of GPs (West 2001). The fragmented, neglected condition of the inner city, and its mounting crisis of social exclusion, escalating problems of mental health, growing alienation as well as increasing inequalities in health care and life chances, fuelled the metaphor. There are high levels of mental illness (according to an important report, one in three families in inner-city areas has someone suffering from mental illness (LSE 2006)), alongside more unplanned pregnancies, substance abuse, and higher mortality rates relative to national averages. Two thirds of asylum seekers and refugees in England and Wales arrive and settle in London. There are large numbers of people sleeping rough, squatters and hostel dwellers, as well as a major problem with HIV. Doctors can feel 'on the edge' working in such contexts: the morale of many doctors appears poor and the incidence of stress, alcoholism and mental-health problems, as well as suicide, is on the increase (West 2001; Salinsky and Sackin 2000; Launer 2002; Burton and Launer 2003).

There is an absence or closure, as some see it – under pressures to perform and process patients – of suitable spaces in which doctors can be open and learn from the messiness of practice and their own disturbed feelings. Balint groups, for instance – specifically designed to enable doctors to explore the affective side of their work, and drawing on psychodynamic insights as a basis for learning – are in decline (Salinsky and Sackin 2000; West 2001; Burton and Launer 2003). There seems a continuing tendency in medical education to disparage the subjective aspects of learning and experience, alongside sociological perspectives: these can be dismissed as anecdote rather than hard, 'robust', 'scientific' evidence. The gaze of a positivistic natural-science paradigm and objectivism remains strong (Sinclair 1997). Struggles for self-knowledge, and critical insight in the profession can, culturally speaking, get marginalised. Moreover, writing about the effects of greater accountability and weeding out the unacceptable in medical practice, Salinsky and Sackin (2000: 44) conclude that the study of interpersonal issues, especially the doctor–patient relationship, is in danger of going to the bottom of the pile, while 'the archaic system of junior doctor training in medical schools means that many students become less person centred and lose their humanitarian ideals'. As Burton and Launer (2003) have observed, GPs have to deal with difficult, demanding and expanding workloads, without guidance. 'Unreflectiveness', they argue, 'has become institutionalised ... and the contrast between the neediness of doctors and the myth they are so highly trained, is great' (2003: 9).

The starting point for the research was an experiment with self-directed learning (SDL) groups, designed to create space for GPs to consider, reflectively, 'critical incidents' with selected patients, which might cause anxiety. These could include an unexpected death, or a doctor feeling inadequate and even disturbed by a patient with sexual or other emotional problems. Space was to be given to the doctor's fears and anxieties as well as to consider different management options. Each group consisted of about eight doctors, was confidential, and led by a skilled facilitator. The idea was to create, like Balint groups, a learning rather than a blame culture, where GPs could be more open about their feelings and muddles, and seek to learn from these without fear of blame or inadequacy. I was invited to evaluate the groups, which provided the basis for the more extended study.

Dr Daniel Cohen (all the names are pseudonyms) was a doctor participating in an SDL group and felt himself to be an outsider in medicine.

> I don't believe in what the mainstream believes in. ... I am ... often appalled by the discourse, ... the whole set of assumptions about the nature of reality, about ... the doctor's power and ... sexist and racist ... ideas and ... the collusion around that. ... I feel profoundly alienated. ... Like mining a seam of gold called the medical fact ... from a pile of shit, ... the patient's ... life, ... a way of talking about patients as if the patient isn't there.

Daniel experienced a major crisis of career some eight years previously. He was unhappy at work, he said, while vocational education, of whatever kind, seemed incapable of meeting his needs. Being a doctor forced him to ask basic questions of himself, at many levels, as he engaged with patients asking questions of themselves. There was no neat distinction between the questions patients asked: 'Who am I?' or 'Where do I come from?' or 'Why do I have the kind of problems that I think I have?' or even 'What is good?' and those of the doctor, he said. There was a seamless web, he insisted, connecting their struggles to his. Daniel used psychotherapy and experiential groups to consider issues in his personal and professional life; he revisited questions about his family history and identity. He was the child of refugees from Nazism, which led him, like many others, into a caring profession. The desire to heal, he thought, was primarily directed at self. He was brought up, he told me, with the experience of Nazism and fleeing persecution, but the emotional dimensions of this were rarely talked about in his family. He was driven by a need to succeed and never to complain or rebel. What right had he to complain about anything, given what his family had been through? He described himself as having been outwardly successful but inwardly distressed.

There was, he said, continuing suspicion of subjective and emotional learning in medical culture, or, for that matter, of critical perspectives in what was a practically orientated profession. Yet such understanding was at the core, he came to appreciate, of becoming a better, more authentic doctor; the science needed to be connected with other ways of knowing. He told a story of a Somali woman refugee who came to his surgery.

> A mother and five children, father may have been killed in the war there, ... [the] children with a huge range of problems from asthma to epilepsy. ... The mother ... brought me a present for Christmas. ... I was immensely moved because it was a really strong symbol that we were providing ... a secure base ... and that she identified me as one white British person in authority who she can trust. ... We ended up having the most extraordinary conversation about Darwinian evolution in relation to why her children were getting asthma and eczema here when children didn't get it in Somalia.

He found himself, as he put it, having a grown-up conversation with this mother and she was transformed 'from being an exotic stereotype into an intelligent equal'. This was part of a process of her becoming a person again: 'That she could actually have what I would guess is her first conversation with somebody British which wasn't just about immediate needs, about housing or benefits, or prescriptions and that sort of stuff but actually recreate her as an equal adult'. He realised, in telling the story, that he was connecting his own history with the patient's, for the first time. A GP, in his family narrative, had provided a secure base for his parents and other relatives fleeing from persecution.

> I think it is in a way always coming back to the business of a personal search, actually trying to find out what life is about and what you should be making of it and having others there who listen and encourage.

This was a form of auto/biographical, reflexive learning that transcended the dualities of the personal and professional, self and the other, thinking and feeling, culture and interiority.

Daniel, like others in the study, was sceptical about aspects of formal professional education. It was not that the science or technical understanding was unimportant, but that they needed to be integrated into a more holistic appreciation of the work. He placed changing relationships and a reflexive, questioning, emotionally open culture in his own surgery (where he worked with diverse colleagues) at the heart of learning to be a doctor. Two colleagues, a therapist, a new partner and having young children were woven into his learning narrative. The journey towards greater insight into emotional life – of self and patients – was one, in fact, we shared in the research, as two professional men, in what became a profoundly auto/biographical, reflexive experience (West 2001). GPs, Daniel concluded, were situated between the truth discourse of the mainstream, and the uncertainties and messiness of whole people and whole problems. A subversive synthesis was required, taking what was essential from the medical model and locating this within a person, narrative-centred but also culturally sensitive, fuelled by a commitment to social justice.

Teacher education

There are strong parallels in the trainee-teacher research. Teach First is a relatively new programme, which recruits people, as noted, from among the 'brightest and best' graduates from 'elite' universities. Teach First draws on New Labour's desire to secure private-sector involvement in public-sector education, and, more widely, as a way of improving provision. Business could specifically assist struggling secondary schools by recruiting the very best teachers – defined in terms of academic achievement – based on a similar programme in the USA. If business did not know how to deal with kids, they did know how to recruit 'bright graduates', it was stated, and how to motivate them (Wigdortz 2003).

Participants worked towards qualified teacher status (QTS) in their first year. During that year, following attendance at a summer institute, there were six days for subject studies and 'individualised training and support', partly based on keeping a reflective journal and drawing on fortnightly visits from tutors. A final short summer institute was to be held, where participants completed their training requirements and prepared for a probationary year. In the probationary year, trainees enrolled on a Foundations of Leadership course run at Imperial College London. They were allocated a business mentor and could choose either to stay in teaching or opt for a different career: a prospect made more alluring by the top companies endorsing the project and providing mentors, and thus potential access to alternative, very 'desirable' occupations.

The struggles of particular trainees to learn, and teach, in more confident and authentic ways – in contexts that could produce confusion and turmoil – echoed the doctors' themes. Feelings of vulnerability, and of a need to learn about self and how best to engage with pupils and their difficulties, came to the fore. The trainees were engaged in transitional processes themselves, as young adults and putative professionals, which evoked anxiety about the capacity to cope or to be good enough. These experiences were in marked contrast to what could be the one-dimensional leadership of change rhetoric of the programme. Questions about the role of schools, as well as of themselves, surfaced, in the context of hard-pressed, multicultural communities in which family problems as well as cultural tensions spilled over into school. The difficulties of inner-city communities were no abstract entities.

Yet there could be cynicism towards the formal learning associated with achieving QTS. 'Jumping, sometimes cynically, through hoops', as one participant put it, including the hoop of reflective practice. It was often easier, it was said, to anticipate the answer required rather than engaging with the complexity of experience. Participants talked of being encouraged, on occasions, to tick the boxes relating to standards and learning outcomes, rather than to take the process too seriously. At the same time, the trainees raised fundamental concerns about the lack of a clear, structured relationship between their experiences – around racism, for instance, in the classroom, or the educational values of particular schools – and the formal, more theoretical aspects of the training. Learning from experience, for whatever reason, in any deeper psychosocial sense, was neglected.

Anna: a case in point

Anna was a language and humanities graduate from an 'elite' university who was placed in a business academy. Her narrative developed over two years, encompassing moments of anxiety, vulnerability, frustration, anger, muddle and self-doubt, alongside resilience and progress. There was evidence of a complex interplay between self and the culture of the programme; and of a strong dynamic between past and present relationships, embracing her family and the academy. Emotions ran high in the first interview, following an especially fraught teaching assessment. Anna felt she had let herself down.

> Well, it is interesting actually because ... I am in the thick of it at the moment. ... I had my ... assessment. ... and my paper work was OK and everything, but my, the lesson that the assessors observed was abysmal, ... it felt like a lesson in November, ... that I hadn't progressed at all, and my reaction ... when something goes wrong in those sorts of situations, and I really hope that professionally this changes, is to get very upset and I cried with my assessor for about 45 minutes after the lesson. ... And at the time I thought god thank god that there is a woman because at that time I felt very much, I don't know why, I think I just ... but I cried for a while after that.

Anna felt she had let herself down in the context of a class in which she had worked hard to build enthusiasm. She talked, at length, of feeling unsupported in the academy, despite claims from management that this was a supportive, stimulating environment. Anna expanded on this theme, in a second interview, six months later.

> There is a tension ... and the management are very concerned to be the cutting edge of education. There is, the sort of restructuring of the way it works, I am not sure that we talked about it last time, but the fact that there was no middle management. There is no sort of heads of department, and heads of year. ... It is there are six management plus all the other teachers and that has sort of been, apparently it has been kind of taken from business structures. It is the sort of cutting edge of what people think education should be now, but there is a tension there with the people who are on the ground, the everyday teachers who are. ... finding it hard to deliver what they want. It is hard to deliver what people want on a daily basis ... and I am not sure ... they recognise how hard it is to deliver, especially in a community that is fairly switched off from education.

Teaching, she added, did not come naturally to her, which she needed to think about. She talked of academic success but this was accompanied by uncertainty about who she was and wanted to be. She was struggling, she said, with a difficult family history – including her parent's divorce – and a need to make the right career choice, for self. The sense of family, she thought, was strong at present because teaching ran in the family, alongside difficult relationships.

> With my dad, very depressed although he recovered quite quickly, I think. … He became disaffected with teaching as some teachers do sort of 20 years into it, or whatever. … It got better and over those two years things got better and now they have got a friendship. … As a 12 year old I distinctly remember going out for dinner or lunch or something with my dad, and saying to him, "I am old enough now, get divorced. I am old enough, sort it out."

Her mother and father decided to divorce, and Anna felt the need to help with family difficulties, partly by being successful. She was also anxious about getting things wrong. Yet her family and its values were also a resource in finding a growing sense of vocation. She was passionate about some of the children and committed to a wider social and spiritual purpose in education. She was concerned about the business values in the academy and in Teach First. Her mentor, she said, had been a high-flying stockbroker who lived for little else other than work. Yet in the first mentoring session, time was taken with the mentor confiding in Anna over her failures in relationships, including with her mother. She, Anna, was used to listening to family troubles.

Teaching, Anna decided, was not to be her long-term career. Her passion lay elsewhere and she was planning to work abroad. Yet she was caught up in various school initiatives, including helping the academy explore how to make money from curriculum materials. She was, in these terms, a Teach First success. Yet she described the whole project as 'slightly flashy'. Like aspects of the academy, 'where all is not what it seems and there is a gulf between teachers and management'. But Anna wanted to work with management too, recognising their faults and the difficulties of business sponsorship – with people wanting quick financial returns – and she sought to contribute to the well being of the academy as well as the children. This, she concluded, stemmed from her Christian values, rather than those of Teach First.

Despite academic success and of doing well in the academy, her narrative was riddled with vulnerability and anxiety. Her strong spiritual identity helped her keeping on, she said. But learning to be a teacher involved needing to get everything right, which included getting things right in the interview. She was anxious about what I thought (I interviewed Anna on my own), not least given her ambivalence towards Teach First. She was constantly looking after people, she said, born of a mix of religious conviction and family history. However, Teach First had offered some transitional space, if at times difficult, to work on who she was and might want to be.

Rupal

Rupal's placement was in a mixed secondary school with 40 per cent of the students eligible for free school meals. Educational attainment was poor. The thing that attracted Rupal to the school, she said, was the diversity of cultures represented by the pupils, who frequently needed support with English as an additional language. She felt ethnic minority pupils could benefit from the presence of an Asian teacher, acting as a role model. She initially embraced Teach First because it projected enthusiasm and a chance to 'offer a ray of hope'. To an extent, she willingly took on the mantle of leadership that Teach First projected onto its participants.

> We are the top, some of the top. ... We've gone to some good universities ... you know, educated very well and it was just yes you could see there was some very smart people there, we are top graduates, we are doing something good, we are trying to put something back in to like the community, into ... other peoples' lives, we are going to touch hundreds of peoples lives.

However, the rhetoric of leadership brought pressures, including a fear of not living up to high expectations, echoing themes across her life. 'I've always tried to do everything that I can, I always pile on too much and then like drown under everything'. She tried hard with particular pupils.

> There's so much I want to give to them. ... I am an Asian girl and I am getting somewhere. ... There's ... a couple of really bad kids ... but most of them are really nice people just looking for attention, they've all got problems ... and they just want someone to care for them. ... It's very difficult. ... One black guy he's just a nightmare, he's got so much attitude. ... My Year 10 ... [are] just hell, ... just taking the piss, ... they are really pushing me as hard as they can. ... A lot of time I end up ... just going round sorting out behaviour problems. ... Discussions, ... I couldn't do that because they don't respect me and it's learning how to do that.

Anxieties increased as the placement proceeded, intensified by problems in her private life. She talked of 'leading a double life' and the 'challenge' of being part of an ethnic minority culture while also embracing London and its hedonistic side. She reflected on a difficult family history, of losing a sister to terminal illness, and being an anchor to her parents, one of whom had a severe disability. She was forced to grow up early, she said, and had needed to earn money while doing her degree. The challenge was to reconcile different parts of her life and to feel better as a teacher. She was aware that teaching asked a lot and that 'I work hard and play hard'. She knew her public self had to appear competent even if this was built on a fragile base. But it was hard to keep up appearances and she turned to counselling for help.

She began, over the first year, to articulate more of what she saw as the weaknesses of teacher education. She talked of the meaninglessness of 'standards' when there was little or no space to explore and interrogate what they meant in the specific context of her classroom: 'doing all this portfolio stuff, making sure you have met each standard, to me is nothing'. She became disenchanted with doing assignments and craved, sometimes desperately, forms of knowledge that could be applied day to day. Disruptive classrooms, including racism, dug deeply into her. She could empathise with young Asian pupils and they with her, she said, but felt undermined by racist behaviour from white and black boys in her class. She thought there was insufficient support or time to think about this, or about racism and the role of schools in general in multicultural environments. Ironically, the research provided much-needed space, she felt, to consider her experiences of learning to be a teacher.

> It was good to see them [the transcripts]. ... I think there are times before that we have spoken and I remember coming out it feeling as if I had managed to reflect and actually think something new, because I spent quite a lot of time in the last two months ... reflecting on what I am doing here, ... the whole point of it. ... I think that the Teach Firsters who haven't had this opportunity ... have probably missed out in the sense that if I hadn't this then I would have just been stuck in the school not having any one else to discuss anything with.

Families, professionals and their learning

This section draws on research involving professionals in family support and learning programmes, which sought to chronicle and illuminate the meaning and impact of particular interventions through their eyes (as well as those of parents). Two projects, in particular, were successful in creating what was termed 'sustaining space', especially for mothers, in difficult contexts, as well as some transactional space for new forms of active citizenship by engaging parents in the management of projects, in advocacy work and in questioning the design and delivery of many public services (West and Carlson 2006: 359–80; West 2007).

We asked parents about the factors enabling them to take risks and to claim some of the space provided by projects for their own agendas. The role and personalities of particular workers were seen as essential: 'like good parents really'. We explored these processes with the health-care and social workers, speech and language therapists and Early Year's educators concerned. They told stories of their own learning, and how they frequently drew on personal experiences of marginality, and even abuse, in their own lives, to work effectively with families. Crucially, in such programmes, while there was pressure to meet, as speedily as possible, diverse targets – increased breast feeding, cessation of smoking, etc. – there was some space, compared to their previous work in the mainstream agencies, for reflective practice. They were encouraged to consider what they were doing and why, and how things might be done differently, including from psychodynamic perspectives. There was some supervision – as a form of facilitated learning in relation to live issues – where anxieties could be contained and processed, to an extent. The research was important in its encouragement to engage, reflexively, with difficult experiences, such as domestic violence, and conflicts between the professionals' own values and the deficit models of people and communities that can pervade perspectives from on high. A speech therapist, despite pressures, chronicled, for instance, a shift from a medical model of practice to more of a collaborative, holistic approach, working more dialogically with diverse professionals and families (West and Carlson 2007).

Conclusion

Research, in other words, can provide space for really reflexive learning: for a mix of thinking about self, the other and work, set in a social and ideological context; and for more holistic forms of learning, in which more nuanced understanding of self in relationship can develop alongside questioning everyday assumptions, in dialogue with others. This was important for many of the professionals in the research, given decreasing space in formal training or the workplace for feelings as well as thoughts. We are given glimpses in these narratives of possibilities as well as constraints. The research illuminates some of the problems of reflective practice when used as an assessment tool, in reductionist and technicist ways (Boud 2007). The struggle to be a better professional, bound up as this is with the kind of person we are, and can get lost. The research echoes the insights of writers such as Stephen Brookfield that creating critically reflective practitioners depends on interrogating experience through different but interconnected lenses: autobiography and the experience of the other, and theory with deeper forms of dialogical engagement with colleagues (Brookfield 1995).

The reflexive criticality that auto/biographical approaches can encourage are being applied in some training contexts (in the training of adult educators, guidance workers, and professionals in doctorate programmes, for instance), and there is evidence of them providing a powerful learning tool while also enhancing the experiences of service users (Chamberlayne et al. 2004; Dominicé 2000; Edwards, Reid, West and Law 2003; Hunt and West 2006: 160–77; Reid 2008). Some of this work has been influenced by feminism and psychoanalysis, as well as biography, in which the personal is conceived as profoundly social, while anxiety is fundamental to learning, thinking, transitions and imaginative endeavour, at all levels. In good training situations, instead of being overwhelmed by anxiety or denying its existence, trainers recognise this as a legitimate part of experience and utilise everyone's adult capacities, as well as their own auto/biographical awareness, to manage the problem (Salzberger-Wittenberg et al. 1999). Such psychological insights can be neglected among those committed to reasserting professionalism and building more self-confident and questioning professional cultures. The personal can get split from the social, and the critical from more intimate and emotional dimensions of life and learning (see, for instance, Furlong 2000: 15–31). Opportunities for really reflexive practice – grounded in hermeneutics as well as emancipatory values – can get lost as other agendas shape, or seek to shape, contemporary professional lifeworlds.

Part II

Professional perspectives

Helen Bradbury, Sue Kilminster, Nick Frost and Miriam Zukas

In this part we present some specific professional contexts and perspectives which illuminate the overarching themes discussed elsewhere in the book. In particular, this part provides examples and critiques of the predominant instrumental approaches to reflection discussed in the previous part. Across the professions, exhortations and demands for reflection can be found at the levels of policy, regulation, education and training, as well as practice. Failure to demonstrate appropriate reflective practice can have serious implications for both practising and training professionals because reflection is explicitly linked to continuing professional development (CPD) by professional bodies and is an assessed part of undergraduate education as well as pre- and post-registration training.

For example, the continuing professional development frameworks of the Royal Pharmaceutical Society of Great Britain (2008) and the Royal College of General Practitioners (2008a) suggest that practitioners should reflect on their practice as a way to identify their 'learning needs'. The Nursing and Midwifery Council (2008) states that practitioners should reflect on the way in which learning has informed and influenced their work. Some professional and regulatory bodies list the activities which promote reflection; the Royal College of General Practitioners suggests these include critical incidents, appraisal and personal learning diaries. Undertaking and recording appropriate and sufficient CPD is a required part of continuing professional registration and will be required as part of a revalidation portfolio, at least in some professions (Royal College of General Practitioners 2008b). Reflection is not defined in these frameworks although it is cast as integral to CPD, which is necessary for continuing professional registration. These professional frameworks are demonstrating exactly what David Boud suggested in the previous part – they turn reflection into a procedure and make the assumption that professionals have an understanding of what reflection is.

The same process is evident in most undergraduate and pre- and post-registration education where reflection is assessed through such formats as reflective diaries, portfolios and learning logs. There is little clarity about what reflection is – for instance, the Foundation Training Programme documents (that is, the documents on the training for doctors in their first two years of professional practice) suggest that portfolios should support reflective practice but do not explain it (Foundation Programme 2008). Throughout these documents there is an assumption that trainees and trainers have an understanding about reflection and reflective practice. At the practice level, reflection can affect career progression and pay for allied health professionals, pharmacists and nurses. Career progression and pay levels are determined by the development review process together with the *NHS Knowledge and Skills Framework* (Department of Health 2008c). Practitioners' reflections on practice and learning are expected to inform the development review process.

Reflection and reflective practice are not sufficiently defined or explained by the professional, regulatory and training bodies. However, it is evident that the ways in which they conceptualise reflective practice are linked to the ways in which practice is conceptualised: individual understandings about learning and reflection often ignore workplace practices and cultures, and current theoretical understandings about learning as situated and relational. Across the professions, reflection is seen as the responsibility of the individual and is assessed as such. No longer is reflection conceptualised as emancipatory but it is used as an instrument of control. This is particularly evident in the linkages to CPD and revalidation.

There are contrasting levels and perceptions of criticality in this part. Janet Hargreaves and David Saltiel make strong arguments in their contributions: that reflection and reflective practice are used as instruments to control practitioners. Susan Knights, Lois Meyer and Jane Sampson, and Penny Morris et al. take a different view and argue that, by adopting particular perspectives about reflection, it can be emancipatory for individual practitioners and inform more radical perspectives. Other forms of learning can be connected with professional practice, and in his work with dentists, accountants, the civil service, charter surveyors and clerics, Geoffrey Chivers argues that, in these professions at least, informed learning can be combined with reflective practice.

Chapter 6

Voices from the past

Professional discourse and reflective practice

Janet Hargreaves

Introduction

In this chapter I intend to present and defend an argument about reflection and reflective practice that I have been exploring and developing for a long time. I have been a nurse for over thirty years; coming into an educational role in the late 1980s, my career could be said to run parallel with the development of reflective practice within the health professions. I, like Cheryl Hunt in her chapter, enthusiastically designed and ran modules using refection as a medium for learning about professional practice in the 1980s and 1990s; I have made my limited contributions to the literature in this area and have been forced to reflect much more deeply and critically about my own practice as a result of doctoral study. My argument is as follows.

Firstly, that professional practice is subject to a discourse, or a number of over-lapping discourses, that exerts a powerful influence over our practice and its articulation. Secondly, that reflection, or reflective practice, is now so embedded into our regulations, learning and teaching strategies, and our assessment – particularly assessment of fitness to practice – as to be indivisible from that practice. From this I conclude that the embodied nature of the professional discourse distorts the ways in which reflection and reflective practice are processed so that they tend to negative rather than positive outcomes. Many of the chapters in this book (e.g. Cheryl Hunt's and David Boud's) are a testament to the challenges that are being made to this situation. However, I suggest that unless we understand, identify and shift the discourse, we will struggle to change practice. In order to defend this argument I will draw on the literature, my thesis and my own personal reflective journey.

As a doctoral student I was interested in reflective practice, in particular the relationship between how professionalism was presented in academic and practice settings. Having a background in health-care ethics I was inclined to ask questions like, 'Why do we do this?' and 'Is this a good thing to do?' In doing so I became puzzled and frustrated by the apparent inability of nursing and nurses to change, despite quite radical developments in curriculum design and professional organisation.

Streuburt and Carpenter (1999) suggest that, amongst other things, historical research may be useful because something from the past may help with understanding the present or the future. This is very relevant to me as the performance of the collected health professions is seen as pivotal to managing the new 'modernised' NHS, and I am in a position of responsibility with regard to health professionals' education. Taking this to heart, my focus became the history of hospital-based adult nursing from 1945–55, specifically exploring the discourse around education and the ways in which 'good' nursing was described and talked about. Seemingly regardless of the sex of the nurse, a number of gendered discourses around obedience, loyalty and vocation made up an image of the 'good nurse' in the post-Second World War period. In order to conduct this research, the literature drew me back a further 100 years to the emergence of nursing as an occupational group in the nineteenth century as the discourse formed then seemed to exert a powerful influence on the contemporary behaviour and practice of nurses.

Whilst the research underpinning this chapter was conducted with nurses, I do not have any evidence that there is anything particularly unique or special about nursing as an occupational group; thus this argument may have a wider application.

Discourse as a starting point

Many conceptual frameworks have been used to structure investigations into nursing: an early and very comprehensive study by Abel Smith (1960) is grounded in social and health policy; Dingwall et al. (1988) focus on socio-economic policy; Summers (1988) and Starns (2000), taking the First and Second World Wars, respectively, present a convincing argument for the pervasive influence of the military in nursing's development; and Hallam (2000) offers a fascinating study of the way that nursing's image is manipulated and presented in literature and film. In addition, gender and class are significant influences which might suggest that a feminist approach was more appropriate (Davies 1995). However, I was interested in the ways in which nursing understood itself, so, taking Hallam's (2000) three voices, 'autobiographical', 'professional' and 'public', the chapter focuses on the discourses that emerged from my data.

Many authors (see, for example, Sawicki 1991; Usher et al. 1997; Cheek 2000) argue for the pervasive and controlling effect of discourse. Cheek suggests that:

> Discourses create discursive frameworks which order reality in a certain way. They both enable and constrain the production of knowledge in that they allow for certain ways of thinking whilst excluding others.
>
> (Cheek 2000: 23)

Having identified the importance of discourse, Michel Foucault was chosen as a guide. In the *History of sexuality* Foucault (1979) proposes a dominant, powerful discourse about sex and sexuality. Of particular relevance to the development of nursing in the nineteenth century is his focus on the concept of family. Initially a middle-class and upper-class preoccupation, Foucault argues that from around the 1830s the middle-class family model came to be seen as the 'indispensable instrument of political control, economic regulation for the subjugation of the urban proletariat' (Foucault 1979: 122).

Hospital-based nursing with its emphasis on control and order thrived within this discourse. Hospital development, particularly of the 'voluntary' hospitals which were funded by local subscriptions (Abel Smith 1964), was modelled on the middle-class family household, imported wholesale by the reforming new matrons. Thus the physician or surgeon was in charge with a 'good' strong woman in the role of matron to oversee the routine (Abel Smith 1960). A strict hierarchy existed below this, where each more junior grade of nurse was more controlled by the grade above. It appears that good nurses, like good women, knew their place within this model and strove to maintain it.

The rise of capitalism and the growth of military power in the nineteenth century, of which hospital-based care is just one element, would not have been possible without the control of the working population as a key component of the economy. Foucault's (1979) argument is that the family model was the medium though which such powerful control was achieved.

It should be no surprise therefore that much of the literature presents the discourse on the growth of nursing in the nineteenth century as one in which middle-class women imposed their (superior) values on working-class people for the good of the nation. Jane Brooks, for example, researches the role of the special probationer (these were more wealthy women who could afford to pay for their training and were often coached from the outset to be ward sisters and matrons): 'These women (elite, middle-class nurses) could inculcate the working class recruits without becoming polluted by them, in much the same way that middle-class women could undertake '"rescue" work with prostitutes without becoming contaminated' (Brooks 2001: 14).

However, this does not fully explain the way that discourses around nursing developed. Foucault's notion is that discourse is not simply top-down power, but permeates at all levels of society (Hoy 1986). This allows for a more holistic view which acknowledges the much more complex class divisions, power relationships and disciplines within nursing. Each grade of nurse within the hierarchy exerts a level of surveillance on the others and self-regulation becomes inculcated into professional identity.

Further elements of discourse identified by Foucault include gaps and silences, resistance, control and finally 'bio power'. That is the regulation and control of the body, power over the individual body and over sexuality, and thus ultimately power over life and death. Ways in which bio power works as a professional discourse can be seen in the way that cleanliness becomes the 'science of hygiene', promoted by Florence Nightingale (1992) and much discussed in early nursing texts (see, for example, Ashdown 1934). In addition Sawicki states:

> Bio power was without question an indisputable element of the development of capitalism. The latter would not have been possible without the controlled insertion of bodies into the machinery of production and the adjustment of the phenomena of population to the economic process.
>
> (Sawicki 1991: 140)

This resonates strongly with both the literature and my own data. Nurses no longer simply watched over patients, but are described by Maggs (1985) as managing time and controlling illness, much in the way that factories in the Industrial Revolution managed the process of production.

All of this was a revelation to me. My own reflective practice, and the practice I had encouraged with my students, tended to focus on the 'here and now' of professional encounters. I had not really given much thought to unpicking what might lie behind.

The good nurse

It became clear to me that exploring discourse offered an insightful framework though which to better understand nursing and nurse education. This was borne out, as my data illustrated every aspect of discourse as presented by Foucault. In addition to the review of the literature which identified the discourses shaping nursing through the period 1850–1950, three data sets were collected and analysed: a full life history of a single nursing career from 1932–74, interviews with nine retired nurses regarding their training between 1945 and 1955 and documentary analysis of two journals (the *Nursing Times* and the *Nursing Mirror*) for the same period.

Analysis of this data led me to conclude that the way nurses from the 1940s and 1950s talked about nursing revealed the ambiguity that existed between the reality of their situation – giving intimate physical care to people who were not their kin – and the expectation that they were pure/incorruptible. Taken together, the findings suggested that the way in which good nursing was talked about in the post-Second World War period was derived from discourses originating many years earlier around 'woman' and 'middle class', so that:

- femininity must be conveyed but without any overt sexuality;
- motherly caring must be conveyed but without any apparent emotional engagement;

- masculine/military attributes such as discipline, punctuality and emotional distance must be developed without the nurse becoming masculine;
- an intimate understanding of the physical self must be conveyed without any apparent acknowledgement of the implications of such knowledge, or its relationship to emotional and sexual self.

The chapter goes on to illustrate these tensions by drawing on a selection of the data.

The nurses talked about themselves as girls rather than women.

> March 1948, my mother took me in a taxi and left me at the door and I was absolutely an innocent abroad, I had never worn make up, never left home, straight from school.

This was typical of their memories of themselves as they entered nursing, but despite this they had a very subtle understanding of the expectations of their new status as nurses.

> You may have hit on something there I mean some of us were wild! (laughter) but I think we probably all came from let's say more or less the right background so we would not have got tarted up I mean when we went out we might have worn a bit of lipstick but eye shadow just wasn't ... (trails off to silence).

This reminiscence was made with humour and reflects their childish innocence. However the fine line between wearing lipstick and eye shadow as a demarcation of respectability is just one of many examples of their clear understanding that the aspiration of nursing to be a middle-class female occupation required much of their femininity to be hidden. This quote also serves to illustrate the ways that gaps and silences work in the discourse along with phrases used when avoiding discussions around boyfriends – 'you never thought of ... you would not have dreamed of'. These silences hint at a hidden but implicit sexual self which has no place in the overt discourse around good nursing. As all but one of my nurses married, mostly within months of completing their training, this apparent lack of self-awareness is patently not true!

A lack of understanding of these 'rules' could lead to almost certain dismissal.

> Women were being called up, she was an actress, or she would have liked to have been, so she was sent to a munitions factory, but she decided she would like to do nursing – she 'heard the call' (laughter) very dramatic! We all arrived at PTS[1] we all had our hats on, well her hat was a particularly soggy one, she arrives like this with all her make-up on – very glamorous, and was promptly sent to get washed and when

she came back – every eyebrow, everything went – this pale completely naked face – she did not last long! (laughs).

Pre-training school allowed nurses to learn to wear the uniform correctly and to practice cleaning and cleanliness which were very important within the ward routine.

It was a hard slog [on the wards], and we used to mop the floors and everything like that. ... and the sterilisers and that were either brass or copper and they would have to be perfect, and it had to be spotless, all the urinals were glass and had to be without stains.

Words like 'spotless' and 'stain free' occur regularly within the data, visible 'dirt' indicating contamination and lack of control over an unpredictable, disease-ridden environment. Despite engaging in this cleaning work, nurses were expected to always look clean themselves. The meticulous detail of this was captured in one nurse's recollection of the ritual of apron changes.

And of course we went on the ward at 7.30 and at 9.15 and 10.15 had two apron breaks where you went for a cup of tea and changed your apron from the dirty work so you came back on again with a clean apron so your dress was never actually in contact with the patient – [they] had a big bib and came right round and were starched.

The uniform was a source of undisguised pride for all the nurses I met and wearing it correctly was clearly very important. It seemed to act as a metaphor for 'moral cleanliness' as well as enabling physical cleanliness. In uniform they were no longer just young women but nurses. It gave emotional and physical protection, status and esteem, 'hid' their individuality and presented an outward declaration of their allegiance to the hospital rules. In uniform they could be 'close' to patients performing the motherly nurturing acts of washing, feeding and protecting, whist remaining 'distant' as a fellow human being. On reflection, this illusion of closeness resonates with my own nurse training in the 1970s when it was made clear to us that 'getting too close' to patients was personally dangerous and professionally deviant.

In this post-Second World War period of my research the importance of the uniform appeared to verge on obsession, with one nurse being publicly reprimanded for coming on duty with her sprained ankle in plaster – not because she was unfit to be on duty, but because the plaster meant that she could not wear the regulation shoe and stocking correctly on that leg!

Unquestioning obedience was essential to the smooth running of the hospital system. A particular reminiscence left me reflecting on how skilfully the education system inculcated this into the recruits:

> We were taught how to do them [injections] with oranges and then to inject ourselves and then each other with sterile water – this would not be allowed now – we used to have to pass Ryles[2] tubes! We used to have to pass them on each other – if you think about health and safety.

Doing an injection and passing a Ryles tube both take a steady hand and a fair degree of self-confidence; both techniques if done incorrectly can cause quite serious damage. Thus the new recruits were 'tested' in the safe environment of the nursing school, passing this stage before they were allowed to practise on patients. In addition, both activities require the nurse to inflict pain and discomfort on the patient, thus they run counter to any romantic images of nursing which the new recruits may have arrived with.

Clearly student nurses who did not have the courage to perform these activities in the safety of the classroom were unlikely to succeed in practice and so this was an important practical test. However, exposing the student to such procedures was equally important as another effective filtering process. Agreeing to perform these tasks on a fellow student and allowing an inexperienced person to do it to you would happen only in a situation where there was an absolute obligation to obedience and no opportunity to refuse. If a recruit was unable to both do and experience such procedures, it signalled either weakness or deviance.

Having passed the many social and practical tests set in the pre-training school the young recruits spent the next three years rotating through day- and night-duty nursing experiences and living in the nurses' home. For those who thrived, the hospital routine controlled everything including the patient's day. As I was analysing the data I kept returning to one particular reminiscence, reflecting on what it meant to me and to my research.

> Yes they were long hours, the nursing was a very physical job, we did so much more for patients and they were in hospital longer, we did everything for them, bathed them, absolutely everything, they were expected to be this patient in this bed, which really for me was easy because that was how I saw life being very ordered, the pillow opening had to be away from the door and the lockers had to be tidy. I was a very well-disciplined nurse I do not find it easy to work where beds are untidy and people sit on the beds – [you] cannot take away the skill of making a patient comfortable and putting the patient first, we cut their nails, we shaved them, we did everything for them.

I did not detect any tension between competing concepts in listening to this memory. The nurse appeared confident and proud of this as a positive and unremarkable assertion of her identity and role as a nurse at that time and her continued identification with this as an example of good nursing. The person – 'this patient in this bed' – is expected to conform to having every activity of his or her life controlled, from nail cutting to the juxtaposition of pillow, bed and locker. The patient is beholden to the nurse for the performance of all bodily functions and can only perform these in the ritualised ways permitted within the hospital, to which the nurse is the gatekeeper. Even personal untidiness is not allowed as this will disrupt the orderly view of the ward; and yet the nurse declares that this is illustrative of nursing's goal of 'making a patient comfortable and putting the patient first'.

It appears that this fragmented, or task-oriented approach to the patients' day meant that patients were simultaneously the precise object of the orderly routine and as individuals totally irrelevant. The regulation of human existence was the work of the nurse; her role to ensure that the patient's physical needs are attended to, not as natural functions but as nursing procedures. The combination of the apprenticeship model of training and living in the nurses' home meant that these values were reinforced at every turn.

The women I interviewed seemed to have achieved their complex and confusing metamorphosis into nurses despite their youth, innocence and limited life experience. On the one hand they displayed the apparently innate womanly ability to 'care' and quickly acquire nursing skills, but on the other they knew that if they displayed weakness, became emotionally or sexually involved with their patients or revealed too much of their individuality they would be singled out as unsuitable.

They appeared not to learn to nurse, but became nurses and in doing so accepted an alteration and suppression of self. This is manifested in the subjugation to the hospital routine and to the acceptance of a position of power over each individual patient's daily routine, whist having no power over decision making in policy or practice. Nurses, in line with Foucault's (1991) concepts of disciplinary control, did the 'work' of surveillance and control over individual patients and over their illnesses, whilst simultaneously doing the same for themselves and their profession in the same way that mothers do with their families within society.

Listening to the nurses talk and then reading their transcripts, left me reflecting on the strangely dated discourse that was being presented. This was echoed in the analysis of the nursing press at the time. For example, when the Royal College of Nursing commissioned the Horder Report which declared that 'the training of nurses in this country could be developed into one of the great national education movements for women' (Horder Committee 1943: 5), it was met with vitriolic dismissal in letters from ordinary nurses as well as editorials and papers by educational leaders.

The characterisation of the 'good nurse' that I felt I had identified in the 1945–55 period seemed to typify the philanthropic women described by Brooks (2001) of the late-nineteenth and early-twentieth centuries. These women engaged in Christian work supporting the sick poor and formed the early ranks of nursing pioneers such as Florence Nightingale (Woodman-Smith 1950) and Sister Dora (Manton 1971). However they seem strangely dated when applied to 17- and 18-year-old grammar school girls in the post-Second World War period.

From blind obedience to reflective practice

These findings suggested that the nurses' self-conceptualisation, emotional distance and absolute obedience are entirely congruent with the discourse. Furthermore, that the apprenticeship system, combined with the 'raw materials' of the recruits and the hospital-based care system, effectively nurtured this discourse well beyond its useful lifespan.

Reflecting on these findings may have relevance for current professional practice and education. Whilst nursing may have some unique character-istics, much of the socialising into the professional role is shared by other health professionals, social workers and teachers. All seem to be permanently locked into a situation where practice, education and policy struggle to coexist, and current practice is always open to criticism for being either out of date or too radical.

The initial training for many 'caring' professions within the UK, for example, social work, teaching and health visiting moved into higher edu-cation long before nursing, as did many of the allied health professions. Despite these differences, it is now expected that all health and social-care professionals are educated in higher education. I would like to argue that one of the major, significant developments of professional discourse that has been enabled by this transformation is the emergence of reflective practice as the process through which professionals are expected to mediate their learning and personal development.

Whilst its origins are much earlier, reflection and reflective practice were introduced to the professional discourse in the 1980s through the seminal work of people such as Schön (1983) and Boud et al. (1985). In nursing, extensive phenomenological research (see, for example, Benner 1984; Benner et al. 1996 and Macleod 1996) has confirmed reflective practice as a feature of expert (and thus good) nursing. This offers a wonderful, radical antidote to the unquestioning obedience of the past. Reflection offers a supportive model for thinking about what we are doing and why, and a strategy for improvement.

It is therefore inevitable that reflection became embedded into the learning and teaching ethos of professionally regulated courses. Whilst many authors (see, for example, Burns and Schultz 2008) have expressed doubts regarding the wisdom of formally assessing reflection, the currently favoured 'alignment' model of curriculum development (Biggs 2003) makes it extremely difficult to make the development of reflective skills a core element of the curriculum design without it being overtly assessed. Despite my own reservations regarding the ethics of assessing student reflections (Hargreaves 1997: 223–28, 2004: 196–201), even I would struggle to envision a curriculum where reflection was central to the learning strategy but absent in the design of assessment.

So as we have moved from the hospital-based apprenticeships of the post-Second World War era to the higher-education courses at present, reflection has become the process through which students' engage with their understanding of themselves and their practice. Alongside this, professionals are now expected to have a very different relationship with the people they care for.

Within one generation there has been a complete reversal of the emotional expectations of professional people. The gaps and silences in the discourse I explored showed how nurses had learned to embrace a situation in which they did not get too close to patients, focused only on the physical manifestations of their patients' needs and did not acknowledge their own weaknesses; although I trained many years later that expectation remained. This contrasts remarkably with the current professional literature on caring and emotional labour.

The change in emphasis regarding 'care' can be dated in the literature from the 1960s and suggests that caring *for* (i.e. surveillance and control) is no longer sufficient and that caring *about* (i.e. emotional engagement of self) is an essential part of professional care (examples of this extensive literature are Noddings 1964; Benner and Wrubel 1989; Swanson 1991). Nursing is described as 'emotional labour' (James 1989: 15–42; Smith 1992) in which there is an expectation that nurses draw upon their emotional selves in order to care for patients.

Taken together with reflective practice, all these concepts contribute to a current discourse in which the emotional engagement of self (an expectation that one understands, cares about and overtly expresses empathy with the social and psychological needs of the patient), the imperative for continuous self-reflection and for academic improvement are embedded in educational programmes and the literature. Two quotes serve to illustrate this change. Firstly, one taken from the 1946 probationers' notes for St George's, London, hospital (cited in Rivett 2006).

> She must be observant and possess a real power of noting all details about her patient. She must be promptly obedient and respect hospital etiquette. ... A nurse's manner to her patient should be dignified, friendly and gentle, but no terms of endearment must be used. She should surround herself with mystery for her patient and never discuss her own private affairs.

By contrast Johns (2004: 3) describes reflection as

> being mindful of self, either within or after experience, as if a window through which the practitioner can view and focus self within the context of a particular experience in order to confront, understand and move towards resolving contradiction between one's vision and one's actual practice. [In which his vision is to] ease suffering and nurture growth through the health-illness experience.

The first paragraph of the quote relates to nursing exclusively, whereas Johns writes for an audience of any practising professional. Clearly expectations have changed greatly from one in which the worker creates a barrier between his/herself and the patient and the second in which nothing less than total engagement is acceptable.

The research underpinning this chapter suggests that throughout nursing's development the dominant discourse has reinforced a distorted view of womanhood where the 'desirable' aspects were promoted and the undesirable suppressed. Amongst the desirable aspects were obedience and loyalty as well hiding, or suppressing, one's own thoughts and feelings. From this I think it can be argued that 'caring about' and emotional labour are moderated in nursing through the dominant discourse around 'altered womanhood' outlined earlier. Consequently, the imperative that nurses embrace and positively use their emotional selves in their practice may be just as controlling as being required to suppress it.

At this point the reader may feel I am overstating my argument – I don't think so. One of the questions I asked the older nurses I interviewed was what they thought being a 'good' nurse meant in their time. This either puzzled them – they struggled to find a vocabulary – or they laughed and said that they never ever felt, or were encouraged to feel, that they were good enough. Forty years later, my experience of asking practitioners to recount a critical incident illustrative of their practice yielded wave upon wave of negative memories (for example, 'my worst shift', 'the baby died', 'the doctors were wrong but no one stood up to them'). Given the freedom to reflect about themselves and their practice, few practitioners recount instances which portray themselves or their colleagues in a positive light. In my experience, this phenomenon seems to transcend the gender of the writer and may cross professional boundaries too.

In the study period, nursing discourse mirrored the dominant (gendered) discourses of the day, expecting nurses to be unquestioningly obedient and to have respect for the authority of the medical staff, matron and the hospital. My reflections lead me to believe that professionals today are equally coerced into obedience by emotional manipulation and the tyranny of being required to 'care' in systems which, despite the rhetoric of current policy, are no more people centred than in the past. Furthermore, for nurses, in the past the stressful environment in practice was tempered by the protective buffer offered by living in the nurses' home; they had no need to worry about laundry, bills, food or shelter and had a ready-made, close-knit group of people with whom to share their experiences. None of these privileges exist for nurses today, and there is evidence that poor morale is prevalent as can be seen in research on bullying (Randle 2003a: 395–401), poor self-esteem (Randle 2003b: 51–60) and burnout (Deary et al. 2003: 71–81).

Reflection, reflective practice and the use of one's emotional self in caring do not have to be a tyranny. Benner (1984) and Benner et al. (1996) both demonstrate forcibly how reflection on practice can be a positive, life-affirming process, which highlights expertise and good professional care. In this volume David Boud suggests relocating reflection in practice, and Cheryl Hunt refers to the need for 'unfettered places' in which to be free to reflect. However, the continuing discourse within nursing specifically and possibly also in other 'caring' professions is suspicious of any activity that is not controlled and measured. The overriding discourse encourages practitioners to identify what they have done wrong and to see themselves as failing, rather than build on and celebrate their strengths.

Conclusion

The research on which this chapter is based was initiated following frustration at sustained criticism of nurse education for producing the wrong sort of nurse. The findings suggest that nursing is subject to powerful discourses which are predicated on values of service and obedience, and an adaptation of more general discourses around womanhood. The suggestion from the findings is that reflective practice absorbs the discourse (which is slow to change) and resists attempts to challenge its central assumptions. Furthermore, this phenomenon is unlikely to be exclusive to nursing.

Policy directives which tell practitioners what they should do and how it should be done, including the requirement to demonstrate reflective practice, seem unlikely to yield the changes required unless there is a massive paradigm shift. Professional, lifelong learning needs to have a much clearer vision of what is needed to bring about change and to have realistic expectations of the extent to which this threatens the central discourses that control practitioners. Most professions would claim that the move to a higher-education setting with its philosophy of giving practitioners knowledge and confidence means that its members are no longer simply obedient but are ready to be professionally accountable. However, the bulk of professional practice is still learned through placements with supervision from qualified educators in a real practice situation. The control over moulding the character and behaviour of students that this creates will tend to override any theoretical model which the students have been presented within an academic setting. Bolting an academic education onto what is, in practice if not in name, an apprentice system is unlikely to yield the radical change that successive governments and education leaders' desire.

It therefore seems reasonable to assume that the discourse that students are exposed to during their practice experience will exert a disproportionate influence on their experience and socialisation into the norms of their profession. Understanding this discourse, and the tensions it creates for students who are torn between the real and espoused experience of practice, is essential if professional educators are to effectively support their reflection and improve practice.

Notes

1 Pre-training school.
2 A 'Ryles' tube is a thin plastic tube passed through the nose into the stomach, in order to drain the stomach contents and to 'rest' the gastrointestinal tract. Having one passed is very uncomfortable, and carries the danger of aspiration pneumonia if the tube is inadvertently passed into the lung by mistake.

Chapter 7

'It's all right for you two, you obviously like each other'

Recognising challenges in pursuing collaborative professional learning through team teaching

Sue Knights, Lois Meyer and Jane Sampson

Introduction

The possibility of enhancing professional learning in the academic workplace through the practice of collaborative peer reflection has been explored in various ways and in a range of educational contexts in the past decade (Knights and Sampson 1995; Martin and Double 1998; Crow and Smith 2005; Knights, Meyer and Sampson 2007). One approach often promoted as enabling this practice of collaborative reflection and professional development for both experienced and less experienced academics is that of team teaching. It offers opportunities for developing understanding about teaching and learning in the same way that working alongside colleagues in research teams helps academics to deepen their understanding of research. Whilst sharing a strong personal commitment to the process of team teaching and the possibilities it offers for concurrently stimulating the classroom learning of university students and the professional learning of their academic teachers, the authors of this paper are concerned that the challenges should also be realistically portrayed.

In this chapter we raise some of the common difficulties experienced in realising the potential for productive professional learning through reflective team-teaching partnerships. Data obtained from a series of interviews and focus-group discussions with tertiary teachers about their experiences of team teaching are used to illustrate some dimensions of the complexity of collaboration.

Team teaching as a vehicle for collaborative reflection

Reflection is something that academics may engage in almost unconsciously as they are involved in the teaching process and from time to time more consciously through conversations with colleagues. Whilst informal conversations about teaching can lead to useful reflection, the addition of some form of agreed structure appears to make the conversation more likely to lead to insight and professional learning. One form of structure is the observation of one colleague by another, followed by feedback and discussion (Jarzabkowski and Bone 1998; Martin and Double 1998; Cosh 1998).

Discussion with a colleague who has been invited to observe the teaching session adds a valuable additional dimension to informal individual reflection as Crow and Smith suggest: 'The process of engaging in a critical dialogue about one's practice is important not only in opening up one's reflections to public scrutiny but also, we would argue, in providing an ideal forum for collaborative learning' (Crow and Smith 2005: 493).

Although the feedback of an invited observer may often lead to productive reflection, the nature of the relationship is likely to be occasional and places the observer at a distance from the practitioner. This can be contrasted with the partnership required by the team-teaching process when the relationship is not one of practitioner and observer but one of colleagues sharing equal responsibility for the teaching and learning outcomes. We suggest that working together on the planning, teaching and assessment of an academic programme and being together in the classroom with students over an extended period of time offer the possibility for even richer collaborative reflection (Knights and Sampson 1995; Knights, Meyer and Sampson 2007).

However, even within the team-teaching approach there may be varying degrees of richness in the collaborative reflection and subsequent learning, dependent on issues such as the nature of the team relationships and the challenges present within team teaching itself. Head's analysis of the process of collaboration and his distinction between 'functional' and 'effective' collaboration provide a useful aid to understanding the complexity of the process of moving from one level of collaboration to another (Head 2003).

Head argues that collaboration is multidimensional, and 'at its simplest level' comprises a range of closely related acts such as coordinating, consulting, communicating and cooperating (Head 2003: 51). All these need to be achieved at a satisfactory level simply to allow the team teaching to work at a functional level. To move beyond this to 'effective collaboration' (Head 2003: 51), there needs to be a mutual commitment not just to planning but to dialogue in which all elements of the teaching are up for question (Knights, Meyer and Sampson 2007).

Issues and challenges in team teaching

Comments such as the one in the title of this chapter remind us that team-teaching relationships are not automatically harmonious. The quotation in the title comes from a participant in one of our workshops about team teaching who felt that our own enthusiasm for the process was overly influenced by our personal friendship and that we were underestimating the difficulties that can arise.

We acknowledge that using team teaching as a basis for collaborative professional learning is likely to be easier if there is an existing positive working relationship. However we believe that this is not an essential pre-requisite and that colleagues can build a productive team-teaching relationship by making a commitment to working collaboratively and recognising the challenges that are likely to arise.

One of the more familiar difficulties is the need for additional time for joint planning and reflection. Other issues relate to the complexity of the collaborative process in the nature of working collegially, such as the feeling of vulnerability arising from differing levels of experience or professional status, or different levels of familiarity with the programme. Other challenges arise when a team-teaching situation is not freely chosen by colleagues but dictated by an organisational need to balance subject expertise. All these factors contribute to the challenges of developing a strong relationship as team teachers and in turn affect the nature of the collaborative reflection and the learning resulting from it.

In the next section of the chapter we discuss some of these issues and the challenges they may present to achieving productive professional learning through reflective team teaching.

Time constraints

An obvious starting point is the issue of time. Head's discussion of the depth of dialogue that needs to occur when a subject is taught by a team rather than by a single lecturer illustrates why finding time for this is a challenging process (Head 2003). His list includes the purpose of the teaching task, its value and derivation, the dimensions of the task, agreed strategies for engaging with the task and overcoming difficulties, criteria for assessing the success of the task and a shared understanding of the relevance of the current task for future learning. When thinking about this range of issues it is easy to see why most team teaching remains at a *functional* level of collaboration and often consists of allocating different aspects of the programme to different members of the team. Even this level requires time and effort on the part of the team members to make sure the course functions. Moving into deeper issues may provide opportunities for deeper professional sharing and learning but it is certain to make far more demands in terms of time.

A comment from one of the interviewees in our study illustrates the influence of time constraints on the level of collaboration entered into. In this case the team-teaching partners were particularly stressed for time, and they were working with existing course materials that had been developed by one of them but not the other.

> We actually physically met with the materials and went through them, did our lesson plans and went through the materials. ... Doing it on the day didn't leave much scope for devising anything particularly new, or junking what we might plan as the result of the discussion, coming up with something new, it was limited.

This was contrasted with a previous experience of team teaching where the team members had spent a considerable amount of time designing the course together and thus had

> some sort of shared commitment to the content of the subject ... to thinking about and learning about the process itself so we had to spend time together.

This had led to an experience of the process described as 'a kind of interactive dance, much more integrated and interwoven'.

Feelings of vulnerability

Whereas the lack of time for mutual planning and reflective discussion is an easily recognised barrier to deepening a team-teaching partnership in the direction of productive reflection, there are other barriers that are less tangible but equally powerful. One of these is the feeling of vulnerability that may be experienced when teaching in front of an academic colleague. Teachers in all areas of the education system are used to working in isolation from their colleagues; the classroom or lecture theatre is rarely observed by others apart from the students. Team teaching, where colleagues work alongside each other in the teaching situation, invades this privacy and requires the development of a particular kind of relationship, a *teaching* relationship. This is the kind of relationship which can provide particularly fruitful ground for collaborative reflection because of the equality of investment in the successful teaching outcome (Knights and Sampson 1995: 58). However, it also presents challenges for teachers used to sole responsibility for their teaching spaces. Signs of this vulnerability can be seen in several responses from our interviewees, even though they had all volunteered to be part of the team-teaching project. For example a very experienced teacher said:

> When the whole proposal for the team-teaching exercise came up I thought 'Oh!' because I really had never done anything like that in my whole life so I thought 'Oh gosh, will I be able to do this? Will my team partner be able to deal with me?' because I know I'm all bloody over the place.

One aspect of the vulnerability that may arise from the sharing of the teaching space is the potential for a feeling of inequality through different levels of experience, or status. One of our interviewees indicated a strong awareness of the differences in academic status between herself and her teaching partner and spoke of her

> apprehension as to whether or not I would be a bit of a shadow where A. was concerned because she was a senior person, she had a tremendous grasp of the material.

This apprehension was clearly evident to her team-teaching partner who commented that:

> B. came in with, I think, a good deal of awe about working with me, very much the 'humble servant' and I guess that I said, 'Look this is absolutely crazy, we can't do it this way.'

A similar sense of anxiety was evident in an interview where a newly appointed staff member described her experience of a team-teaching relationship with a more experienced colleague as extremely professionally productive but her description indicated a certain amount of vulnerability.

> I think that this process has told me that I have a lot to learn. I've always been very harsh on myself, I've always told myself that I have to do the very best. I think when you're teaching with experienced people you tend to look at your shortcomings and I thought, 'Gee, I've got a lot to learn here.' Not to put myself down but to note things I've got to learn.

A comment from her senior colleague suggests that she was not unrealistic in feeling that she was to some extent 'on trial'.

> Well if ever there was an opportunity to say, 'We put this person in this job. Can she really do it?' there it was.

Whose interests are served?

The sense of vulnerability reflected in the quotations above would obviously be far worse in situations where the members of a teaching team had not chosen to teach together but had been required to do so because of the need for different content expertise or the large size of a cohort of students. Accounts of team-teaching partnerships which have been seen to lead to productive professional learning tend to stress the value of working alongside trusted and supportive colleagues where such collaboration has been freely chosen by the participants. This is seen to provide a positive environment for professional development.

However Hargreaves draws our attention to the fact that collegiality may not always be freely chosen and may be encouraged by 'management' with a specific managerial purpose in mind.

> In these cases, collegiality is either an unwanted managerial imposition from the point of view of teachers subjected to it or, more usually, a way of co-opting teachers to fulfilling administrative purposes and the implementation of external mandates.
>
> (Hargreaves 1994: 190)

An example of this kind of concern about whose interests are served by team teaching was expressed by one of the interviewees in our study. She is an experienced casual academic who had been asked to share the teaching of a large class with a newly appointed full-time lecturer. The post he had been appointed to was one she had also applied for. She commented that she did have some worries that by teaching alongside him and sharing her knowledge and understanding of the course she had previously helped to design she might be eventually doing herself out of a job. This hardly provides a fruitful context for collaborative reflection and learning.

Another aspect of the concern about whose interests are served by the encouragement of collaborative reflection is raised in Elmholdt and Brinkmann's chapter 'Discursive practices at work: Constituting the reflective learner' (Boud et al. 2006). Their discussion poses questions about the value to workers of engaging in collaborative reflection.

> Post-bureaucratic organisational forms especially work to constitute hyperreflexive subjectivities. In such organisations, which often lack visible controls and authorities, individuals are continually asked to reflexively monitor themselves and their relations to others. Gradually employees become more engaged in different kinds of emotional labour at work, where they are asked to be specific kinds of people, rather than mere professionals with skills independent of their private personalities. ... The organisational shift from hierarchies to networks and teamwork demands increasing self-reflectivity. This is not just liberating, but also threatens to stifle personal character and makes it hard to work out a coherent structure in one's life narrative.
>
> (Elmholdt and Brinkmann in Boud et al. 2006: 176)

This somewhat bleak description suggests that rather than being supported in their professional learning by participating in reflective team teaching, the academic partners could be in danger of losing track of their individual pathways.

Voluntary collaboration or 'contrived collegiality'

Apart from the kind of situation described earlier, where team teaching may be seen to have a value to the faculty through orienting a new staff member, team teaching in universities is not particularly encouraged by the way staffing hours are allocated. This means that those who team teach voluntarily may do so at the expense of a heavier teaching load. They are likely to be colleagues who already have a positive working relationship and a commitment to professional learning through team teaching. Descriptions of the experience of team teaching in these circumstances (Knights and Sampson

1995; Crow and Smith 2005) indicate that the relationship seems to have the characteristics described by Hargreaves as typical of a collaborative culture – spontaneous, voluntary, development oriented, pervasive across time and space and unpredictable (Hargreaves 1994). For those involved, the positive outcomes clearly outweigh the disadvantages of a heavier teaching load.

Paradoxically, a greater organisational commitment to supporting team teaching for professional development could have the effect of changing this spontaneous and development-oriented relationship into something more like Hargreaves' situation of 'contrived collegiality' which he describes as administratively regulated, compulsory, implementation oriented, fixed in time and space, and designed to have high predictability in its outcomes (Hargreaves 1992 p196). It seems unlikely that such relationships will result in productive professional learning. This was the conclusion reached by a research team investigating the nature of informal workplace learning in a large vocational education institute in Sydney. They were investigating aspects of informal learning in the workplace but, having identified some of the processes at work, they advised against proceeding with one of the original purposes of their project which involved the possibility of providing organisational support for some of the informal professional development processes they identified.

> Part of the original design of the research project was a stage in which some of the practices identified through the study would be developed as formal interventions to 'improve' learning at work. This idea was abandoned at an early point once it became clear that the richness of learning we identified could be compromised by attempting to move it into the system world of the organisation.
>
> (Boud et al. 2006: p167)

So the challenge here is to enable the full professional learning potential of team teaching to be realised without stifling it through organisational regulation. This is similar to the dilemmas faced by many organisations in relation to introducing formal structures to support workplace mentoring or communities of practice.

Conclusion

Having discussed some of the challenges that can arise in attempting to use team teaching as a vehicle for collaborative professional development, it seems clear that there is no easy recipe. Sometimes the members of a teaching team may actively dislike each other or have extremely divergent views about the way to help students learn. In these cases it is probably advisable that they be allowed to divide the programme between them and do not attempt to teach together, let alone reflect together. In other situations the teaching team may like each other but because of the challenges find it difficult to develop a relationship of trust where collaborative reflection is possible. Nevertheless, the individuals may achieve a *functional* level of collaboration in their teaching and learn from observing each other.

Paradoxically it is the difficulties and hiccups encountered in planning and teaching together that seem to present the most fruitful opportunities for critical reflection and thus professional learning. These are the 'disorienting dilemmas' that Mezirow describes as the precursors to perspective transformation (Mezirow 1991). These dilemmas are likely to be acknowledged and addressed when team-teaching partners have a level of trust and respect for each other and a commitment to developing their teaching relationship. Our experience is that a structured approach to collaborative reflection (Knights and Sampson 1995) provides a framework within which a mutually respectful teaching relationship can develop, enabling open self-revealing discussion, real engagement with each other, commitment to the process and a willingness to persist through discomfort and frustration.

Our enthusiasm for the process, supported by theoretical concepts about experiential learning and action research (Knights and Sampson 1995) has persisted and been further informed by research on workplace learning and communities of practice. Although there are still questions to be answered and challenges to be addressed about the process of reflective team teaching as a form of professional development, we agree wholeheartedly with the statement of one of our team-teaching colleagues.

> You don't get rich learning for yourself and possibly the students, I don't know, but you don't get that richness unless you engage in the critical reflection, in the combined critical reflection.

Chapter 8

Preparing for patient-centred practice
Developing the patient voice in health professional learning

Penny Morris, Ernest Dalton, Andrea McGoverin and Jools Symons

Introduction

The move from a paternalistic system that emphasised the autonomy and expertise of the professional, as represented by existing representations of reflective practice, towards a more flexible and empowering model of practice is central to understanding the current transformations of health care. This new paradigm incorporates many debated elements, including notions of citizenship, choice and co-production (Coulter 2002; Cottam and Leadbeater 2004) which emphasise the quality of the relationship between flexible professionals and active and empowered patients. What we are witnessing are attempts at radical shifts in the distribution of power. These arise from pressures of cost containment and changing expectations of the public and professionals, as well as increasing understanding of effective care (Wanless 2002; World Health Organisation 2005).

More recent models of practice recognise and value patients' experience and knowledge and how these can help professionals develop their understanding and their practice. They raise questions about traditional approaches to professional learning that do not adequately support the recognition and integration of this different perspective. They are sometimes called 'patient-centred' approaches.[1]

Increasingly, professional bodies have responded to changing realities by working to involve patients in meetings about developing the professional role. One conference aimed to gather momentum for patient-centred professionalism (Picker Institute 2007): the UK General Medical Council consulted with patient groups and researchers of patient experiences to develop its 'Good Medical Practice' standards, also taken up by its US counterpart. Similar efforts have been made by the Royal College of Physicians (Levenson et al. 2008) and the Postgraduate Medical Education and Training Board (2008). Service users are involved in quality assurance of wider health professional training (Department of Health 2003; Skills for Health 2006), building on explorations of user and carer involvement in nursing education (O'Neill 2002).

'Patients as teachers' in medical education are recommended for helping doctors to work in partnership (Hasman et al. 2006). The authors of this chapter are part of national and international initiatives to promote and explore the growing role of the 'patient voice' in health professional learning.[2] (Patient's Voice Conferences 2005, 2006, 2007; see also PEPIN network at www.pepin.uk). In the UK, patient and public involvement has a concerted rhetoric and practice because of state policies (Department of Health 2001) and supported initiatives (www.invo.org.uk; www.involve.org. uk), and because of the influence of service-user movements in mental-health care and disability (Mental Health in Higher Education 2004). Involvement is now mandated in the National Health Service (Department of Health 2001) and in social care education (Department of Health 2002). In all these efforts, it is becoming increasingly important to identify the nature of the participation of the public (Arnstein 1969) and to be clear about when their engagement is token, and when powerful (Trent Strategic Health Authority 2005).

Social care is leading the way in attempts to reform practice, towards true partnership working with service users. 'Person-centred' support services make the claim to offer 'choice and control' to individuals, rather than merely slotting them in to existing provision. Practitioners and users have emphasised that this will mean 'thinking in a different way' (Glynn et al. 2008), rather than merely 'ticking boxes'. It also means shifting the focus of resources to include supporting patients' learning and development of their own capacities for self-care and decision making, as in health policy around 'expert patients' (Department of Health 2001) and personal care planning (Department of Health 2008a).

This chapter explores our experiences and understanding of the implications of this shifting terrain for professional lifelong learning and the notion of reflective practice. In particular, we focus on the changing nature of the relationships between professionals and patients. We look at theories and models of learning that help us to understand more about how professionals and patients can be encouraged to enter into fresh ways of relating. The authors write as developers of ethical, effective ways of bringing patient voices into professional learning. These efforts are based in a consistent learning approach that supports participation and collaboration. We examine examples from this work in the light of different models, including community development and service planning. We focus on one example of a method of supporting professional learning and another of building the learning of patients, and make links between the two. We examine how reflective processes, informed and supported in conversation with others, work in the personal development of both patients and professionals.

First, we outline how some of the roles and relationships in health care have evolved, in order to illustrate the complex nature of the challenge for professional learning.

Towards co-production: changes in the patient role and patients' encounters with professionals

> Co-production is a term used to redefine the relationship between service professionals and the beneficiaries of services as one of mutuality and reciprocity rather than one of dependency.
>
> (Value for People 2007)

Co-production is a useful formulation of the roles of professionals and service users that encompasses the notions of participation and collaboration. It has been embraced by practice developers from wide-ranging backgrounds and perspectives (Hart 1988; Chapman 2004; Boyle 2005). In this idea of their encounters with professionals, patients have responsibility and power.

In the early decades of the NHS, the understanding of the relationship between health professionals and patients was still based on a straightforwardly paternalistic model. Patients were cast in a passive role, the grateful, uncomplaining recipients of the benign and benevolent 'gift' of state-funded health care, in a system characterised by the almost unbridled power of the professions (Salter 2004). The subordinate nature of the patient was captured at the time by Talcott Parsons' concept of the sick role, where the role of the patient is to try to get well by complying with the medical regime and to bear no responsibility (Parsons 1985).

In this formulation, the consultation between patient and doctor (particularly GPs as gatekeepers to other services) assumed a very privileged place in the health-care system. It became the focal point for the development of a new area of research and medical education, involving many disciplines analysing and aiming to improve the doctor–patient encounter (Balint 1956; Stoekle 1987). This has included juxtaposing 'doctor-centred' and 'patient-centred' styles of consulting (Byrne and Long 1976) and widening the medical focus in the consultation on 'bio-psycho-social' matters (Engel 1977) from the patient's experience. Armstrong (1984: 738) surveyed the role of the patient's view from the 1930s to the 1980s and described how attention to what the patient has to say altered: 'the changes in perception that enable some things to be heard, and not others'.

Broadening the 'medical gaze' (Foucault 1973) in GP medical training to include wider aspects of patients' lives in a doctor-directed framework (Pendleton et al. 1984; Neighbour 1987; Silverman et al. 1998) seems to have had variable impacts on preparing doctors to be more 'patient centred'. Newly trained GPs were required to demonstrate that they elicited and responded to patients' concerns and involved them in their care management, but despite the emphasis on this in their training, many were unable to do so (Campion et al. 2002). More patients now report in NHS surveys that their GP listens to them, but almost half would have liked more say in decisions about medicines and a third were not involved in other decisions about their care (Richards and Coulter 2007).

While the approach of working with the patient as expert, paying attention to patients' ideas and frameworks of meaning (Mishler 1984; Tuckett et al. 1985), has been successfully developed in medical education (Morris 1992; Morris et al. 1998), doctors in practice have still felt unprepared for what appears to be additional to their core clinical task (Morris et al. 2001; Morris 2006a). They felt burdened by what they perceived, during their GP training in 'patient-centred' care, as extra responsibilities and demands.

Further models, encompassing the need to share decisions and acknowledging more the role of the patient (Elwyn et al. 1999; Towle and Godolphin 1999) have also proved to be very challenging in practice for many professionals who appear to be unable to trust in patient participation (Pollock 2006). The concept of 'relationship-centred' care (Beach and Inui 2006) broadens the focus to include reciprocity in all relationships in health-care, self-awareness and the emotional domains. It has built on 'person-centred' approaches (Nolan et al. 2006), to which we shall return in this chapter.

Cayton (2005) also suggests that a new professionalism in health care could be defined, not in terms of autonomy, but in terms of relationships. He defines professionalism as found in 'how people behave towards each other and towards me' and that includes having the skills to support him to engage in his own care and in making informed choices. The extent of patients' participation in everyday practice does not match the aspirational rhetoric, however (Collins et al. 2007). Studies show many doctors and nurses hold deep-seated beliefs that patients do not want to get involved and would rather professionals make decisions on their behalf (Ford et al. 2002). Power remains largely with the doctors in consultations (Thistlethwaite and Morris 2006).

Part of this difficulty with reforming professional–patient encounters is recognised to be due to factors outside practitioners' (and patients') control and more to do with aspects of care systems, e.g. time pressures and the focus on general targets (Richards and Coulter 2007).

Another problem has been the contradictions in teaching 'patient-centred consultations', with delineated structures and detailed lists of core and unchanging skills, that imply that there is a right way for doctors or nurses to conduct encounters with patients. There has been a parallel tendency to reify patients' 'stories', as if these narratives and peoples' related feelings and ideas are set, waiting to be exposed, whereas, more often, they develop afresh during conversation.

Rather, clinical encounters are dynamic, emphasising the need to support the capacity of diverse professionals in response to the diversity of patients, and a changing world. In other words, it is all, in effect, out of professional control. This means that authority in the relationship has to be negotiated, at every step (General Medical Council 2008).

Collaborative models of professional–patient dialogues have been recognised: Clark and Mishler (1992) called for a reframing of the clinical task to include acknowledging 'the reciprocal responsibilities and efforts' of both patients and doctors. Acknowledging the part that patients play means not ignoring their 'lifeworld' (Mishler 1984) and recognising the patient's autonomy in this. At the same time, the clinician also has to accept his/her own authority as the coordinator of their joint activity. Sharing this authority allows the fuller contribution of the patient and thus an appropriate, ethical sharing of the burden of care.

More recent models also argue for a greater role for the patient in directing the path of the encounter, for example, in the notion of 'joint enquiry' (Steinberg 2005) where patient and professional would 'undertake joint learning and teaching as equals'. He argues for a different style of conversation between professionals and patients, alongside the traditional clinical consultation. Launer's approach (2002) encourages patients to develop their own 'story' during the consultation. He describes this as curious questioning, to explore the problem in the context of the wider world of the patient, in which the professional has no special expertise.

This changing understanding of the role of the patient offers a similar challenge for other professionals. Those charged with introducing 'person-centred' support in social care have recognised that this is a different way of doing their work, not an addition to their workload: 'It's not another job. It is *the* job. Person-centred support is not another thing that you have got to do. It is what you have got to do' (Glynn et al. 2008).

Patients as experts

A further challenge for professional learning is the changing pattern of morbidity. The predominant disease pattern in England, and most other developed countries, is one of complex and continuing illness, rather than acute disease. In Britain alone, 17.5 million people live with a long-term condition. Professional and popular cultures tend to prioritise acute care, portraying professionals in heroic roles which give us all hope of effective medical intervention. Chronic problems, however, require continuity and emphasise the importance of beneficial, active relationships and working with patients' expertise from experience.

The Experts Patient programme has become mainstream policy in the NHS (Department of Health 2001). This educational programme for patients, delivered by volunteers who themselves have a long-term condition, is based on evidence about the positive impact of peer-support and education in supporting self-management. Some groups are more professionally led than in the self-help movement which inspired the programme, and evaluation has shown mixed results (National Primary Care Research and Development Centre 2007). Findings of a randomised trial of participants identified moderate gains in self-efficacy (belief in one's capability to produce an effect), some reductions in costs of hospital use and no impacts on routine health service use. However, the study also revealed high levels of satisfaction with the course, and social support from attending a group was highly valued, sparking debates about whether formal evaluations have elevated professionally defined outcome measures and not taken sufficient account of outcomes that are valued by patients.

Self-help groups have been described as developing self-esteem, confidence, perceived control over long-term conditions and a renewed sense of identity (Kelleher 1994). Supportive discussion of their situations and feelings helps people to reframe their experience. This not only serves to 'let off steam' (approved of by professionals who cannot allow space for this in their encounters with patients), but also to enable patients to rethink their behaviours around treatment and to develop a sense of independent expertise and legitimacy about their decisions. Their focus on reflecting together on experience enables a range of concerns to be kept alive, rather than being distorted by expert systems and the discourse of the market.

Professionals are not always supportive of the idea of the expert patient. Resistance to patient expertise is widespread in professional literature and is seen as a significant barrier to patient-centred practice (Kennedy et al. 2007). Many professional views are based on untested assumptions that not only will patients make poor decisions about treatment or care routines, but also that the floodgates of relentless demand will open. A poll in 2003 found that 76 per cent of pharmacists, 63 per cent of doctors and 48 per cent of nurses thought better-informed patients would take up more of their time, be more demanding and be harder to deal with (Hart 2006). In reality, the evidence is that more informed patients may reduce, rather than increase, demand (Pollock 2006).

The moves by governments and health-service leaders to renegotiate professional and patient roles threaten professional status and values. The resulting need to maintain professional identities can limit professionals' capacity to share understanding and power with patients (Flynn and Britten 2006). Learning opportunities for professionals with expert patients have been found to help professionals discover and appreciate how patients can contribute to improved health outcomes, while the professional's effectiveness is also increased (Morris and Trafford 2004). At the same time, patients who get involved in professional learning develop new insights into the world of the health professional.

Learning to live with complexity, uncertainty and difficult feelings

Patients continually hope for different kinds of relationship with health professionals. In general though, they are still held in high regard, with most patients very appreciative of the care they receive. The evidence is also that many patients want more involvement in decision making, more information and the opportunity to express preferences and influence decisions about their care (Richards and Coulter 2007). However, Lupton (1997) argued that consumerist notions of autonomous patients do not take into account how people feel at different times in their lives and 'the often unconscious, unarticulated dependence that patients may have on doctors'. Salter (2004) holds that, despite the many social factors that may be leading to a reordering of the doctor–patient relationship, including the decline in deference and the advent of the knowledge society, there are more continuities than changes. Instead of relying on simple dichotomies around paternalism and empowerment, he emphasises the complexity and constantly shifting nature of the relationship between professionals and patients. Above all, he argues, like the proponents of 'relationship-centred' care, that more account should be taken of the emotional domain for both sides of the relationship. He quotes one advocate: 'The reality for most patients is not that we want to be in sole control of decision making. Maybe we just don't want to feel like everything is out of our control.'

A similar need to feel in control of the disorder of disease is perhaps what keeps some professionals stuck in paternalistic mode. Patients bring much that is not within a purely medical remit – the everyday miseries and illness-causing factors of people's lives, particularly in deprived areas. Medical training has not prepared today's doctors to get to grips with these potentially overwhelming factors, as Cecil Helman (2006) describes in his latest anthropological work about his experiences as a GP. Because a broader psychosocial model for exploring patients' problems may yet be learned and applied in an essentially doctor-controlled framework, GPs approaching such aspects of patients' problems often baulk at the task (Morris et al. 2001). Some doctors and nurses seem to feel that they should always know more than their patients, even about what to do about the daily realities of their (the patients') lives. This is the 'Pandora's box' that is kept closed: pain is uncomfortable to hear, but pain that you feel unable to help, when you think perhaps you should, may be impossible to hear. Of course, the effort to keep this box closed is painful in itself. This is why learning opportunities where professionals and patients can reflect and work together to understand how to address illness are so important.

Learning to work together: building new relationships

The 'resourceful' patient

For a new relationship to work, the patient has to be regarded differently. Muir Gray (2002) describes the 'resourceful patient' as competent and responsible. The priority is to ensure resources are made available to help patients develop their capacities for self-care and independence, rather than simply investing further in educating professionals.

One criticism levelled at this idea is that it is appropriate for only some, less vulnerable, patients. An influential set of ideas has been the community development 'asset-building' approach, particularly as applied on the Westside of Chicago and elsewhere (Arnstein 1969; Morris 1992; Kretzmann and McKnight 1993). In this, people are seen as having resources in themselves, with capacities, even gifts, and the challenge for change and development is to identify, build and share these. In this way, deficits and problems and the 'discarded, discounted person' can be addressed through the untapped potential of individual and community resources (www.healthauthority.org). Similarly, illness can be viewed as a blessing which helps personal growth, not merely as a pathology – as in mental-health users' discussions of their experience of a diagnosed mental illness (Collins and Wells 2006).

These approaches argue for a redistribution of focus, resources and power from professional to patient. Some professionals have found this realignment to be helpful (Goldsmith 1999) in terms of sharing the burden of care. We have evidence that what is needed for this shift to be possible is a vital, parallel and complementary process of personal capacity building for professionals, which we unpick below.

Collaborative and person-centred learning

Such new attitudes towards active and equal consultations between patients and professionals challenge education providers to rethink traditional learning approaches. The provision of opportunities for health professionals to experience a joint enquiry approach in a safe learning environment should help to build the confidence required to develop new approaches in clinical practice.

Previous work with groups of GPs concentrated on learning from their everyday practice in difficult consultations. In a study of action learning groups (Morris et al. 2001) a process of guided reflection on videos of their own consultations was found to be instrumental in helping doctors begin to change their practice. They felt more able to support patients to deal with anxiety and to share care and decisions. This process has also worked for individuals (Thistlethwaite and Morris 2006). A common factor is safe 'scaffolding' for such experiential learning (Bruner 1973) that allows for truthful exploration of feelings and ideas and the development of new insight. Learners are helped to reflect on experience and build on their own capacities.

Learning to do their own work of facing their anxieties about difficult consultations enabled these doctors to see how to help patients to do *their* own necessary work in a mirroring process. They were clearer about where their authority lay, which was, partly, in supporting patients to discover their own strengths to solve problems. This is not training with a set model, structure and skill list for managing patients according to professional needs; rather, it is modelling collaborative communication, in common with those educators who have recognised the overriding need to help professionals to listen, remain aware, learn and respond with openness (Epstein 1999; Launer 2002; Skelton 2005; Bub 2006; Bleakley and Bligh 2008).

One participant in a later programme asked 'Can I be myself then [in consultations]?' Integrating our sense of self within our professional identity is a necessary part of taking on professional responsibilities, and requires support to the personal in professional development. This means being learner centred, not catechism centred.

Bringing patient voices to professional learning supports this movement away from some traditional models. The role of the patient in medical learning has been developing over many years (Wykurz and Kelly 2002; Thistlethwaite and Morris 2006). However, many traditional approaches to learning that have involved patients have mirrored the same kinds of relationship found in practice. Where patients were brought into the classroom or involved in bedside teaching, this was often as raw material, as an audio-visual aid, rather than as an acknowledged contributor, that is, a co-teacher. In social work, where the user and carer role in education has been most developed, con-temporary theory and practice of more collaborative ways of working with users has been promoted by their meaningful involvement in learning toge-ther with professionals (Waterson and Morris 2005).

Given the changing roles in health care, an emphasis on mutuality, and on ethical behaviour in relation to others, is the starting point for fresh approaches to professional learning. What kinds of model will most help professionals change their practice?

Models of reflective practice, emphasising the value of engaging in learning from experience (and in dialogue with others through mechanisms like all-round feedback) are clearly relevant. We have found, like others (West 2001; Burton 2006), that refining and supplementing the reflective model helps further understanding of the processes needed to ensure learning for trans-formation. Like others who have involved patients in service design and research (Gillespie et al. 2002), we have learned what this new voice brings to our progress. We shall now focus on an example of a learning method with a patient voice to bring in other helpful concepts.

Example 1: Reassembly: the 'Spanner' model for learning with simulated patients

Learning skills with simulated patients (SPs) is now ubiquitous in clinical education. Learners practise talking with SPs, usually in small groups with feedback, sometimes including feedback from the person role playing the patient.

Our approach with this learning method includes a significant focus on reflection and review. Students have the opportunity to experiment with different approaches, both in response to their own reflection on how an interaction went and also to feedback from the SP, peers and facilitators in the room. When this practice was brought into medical-student learning (Whitehouse et al. 1984) and analysed, it was most closely linked to learning and psychoanalytical theories applied in community and family development and medicine (Freire 1972; Balint 1956; Bowlby 1969). Together, they emphasise a focus on capacity, rather than on deficit, self-awareness, and safe structures for learning and creative change.

Rather than an information-giving, 'banking' approach to education that treats learners as empty vessels into which professional educators deposit knowledge, Freire argues that transformative learning occurs only through a process of dialogue with teachers and other learners, based on mutual respect. In this way, learners and teachers are involved in an active and equal relationship in which both sides learn from each other. We see a parallel with this process and that of the different form of discussion in encounters between patients and professionals, raised in the previous section. In both processes, ways forward are constantly negotiated; there is no single, right answer and the final learning and decision rest with the learner or patient.

During the SP method, learners need to be encouraged to venture into new territory. It is risky interviewing in public, often about sensitive matters. Where the role-played encounter will go is unknown to all present. Bowlby pointed out that clear structures and encouragement must be in place for a 'safe space from which exploration is possible'. Learners are enabled to identify their abilities, then use and build on these to respond to difficulties discovered by themselves or others. SPs who are trained to bring a patient voice understand how this works (because of their own group preparation, described later); theirs is often the most powerful voice in the room.

Too often though, the 'rules of feedback' by which similar such sessions are run and the comments made by others when a learner steps forward to rehearse an interview with an SP, can be applied in a rote, perfunctory fashion that does not encourage real dialogue and honest reflection. Participants in this case, often because of the lack of a feeling of safety, are hidebound by ideas of what they are supposed to say and do, rather than doing the careful 'work of attention' (Scott Peck 1987) to what is actually happening in front of them or within themselves, as Balint encouraged. Similar distractions can occur when learners fill in reflection sheets or draft personal development plans without real engagement (Harris et al. 2008).

This is the core challenge for the learner when talking with the patient, of course. The patient, as in Freire's model of learning and development, has to be part of defining the problem in order to take an active role in finding a solution. Professionals at all stages of learning need confidence to apply their own clinical expertise while facilitating the patient's involvement. Confidence building by the facilitator entails engaging with the person in the professional, respecting their perspective and offering, transparently, others' perspectives.

Professional educators have to learn how to be open to the yet unknown, in order to model this demanding task for learners (Burton and Morris

2001). In the 'Spanner' SP method, this would mean not writing a 'script' for the SP (which risks stereotyping patients, leaving out the perspective of the person playing the role who, in turn, must be open and able to give voice to the person within a patient role), but, rather, creating or refining a role in collaboration with the SP. It would also mean, wherever possible, that the patient voice is engaged in the development of SP roles and the whole learning process. SPs need to have the insight and confidence to bring forth the patient voice so that their role play and feedback are authentic and bring the 'other' perspective, rather than reinforcing professional ideas and stereotypes. Further, the scenario to be explored should be based on the learner's experience, which will mean negotiating this with the learner, often creating or adjusting it on the spot in collaboration with the group and SP.

In this way, simulated practice is a rehearsal of unpredictable life rather than the performance of a set learning agenda with little core engagement of learners or patients. Learners are free to express anything, rather than being manipulated or exhorted to perform for their seniors – or, indeed, for patients – with a rigid idea of what students need to know, rather than an approach which facilitates learning for change. Here, students can access their own voice and the patient is a co-facilitator.

At the University of Leeds School of Medicine, people from patient and carer groups have joined clinical teachers and professional educators in devising roles for medical-student clinical teaching and assessments, as well as scenarios for inter-professional student learning. Significant adjustments to the original clinician-authored briefs have arisen from these discussions. Patients and carers have also trained as SPs and facilitators and become co-teachers, particularly working with students in difficulty (Dalton and Morris 2005) and assessing final year medical-students' clinical skills (Kilminster et al. 2007). These patient teachers are core to a fledgling 'patient council', helping to envision and implement a new medical curriculum (www.mbchb2010.leeds.ac.uk).

An increasing focus of the developing pedagogic understanding of these programmes is on how to ensure an effective learning 'crucible', where personal change in understanding and behaviour can occur. An important emphasis has also been on testing educational development in the context of daily practice: learning processes for students have been tried out with clinical teachers, as a model of self-review. A key finding is that doubting patients' capacity and expertise is behind doctors' lack of listening. Connecting to their common experience with the patient – realising that learning and healing are mutual processes – enables doctors' to shift to listening and collaborative practice. Once doctors and students realise the potential of working with the patient, they are able to change their behaviour.

Our aim in SP sessions is to provide opportunities for patients and professionals to learn to engage in different kinds of encounter. In these, we do not concentrate on the technical matters that are often the focus of consultation and communication-skills teaching, but go deeper, explore attitudes and reach new understandings. We have found that, once the intention in the learner's communication has changed towards collaboration, their skills grow.

There is growing evidence of the positive contribution the patient voice can make in service improvement (Fisher and Gilbert 2002), but, despite the exhortations of government, these efforts have often been token, minimising their effect. We know that effective learning with SPs as co-teachers helps students demonstrate involving patients in consultations (Morris 1992). Whether this new patient voice in learning will make a real difference to clinical consultations in practice is still an open question; what is clear is that it can make a substantial difference to patients, professionals and students involved in learning together.

Example 2: Learning from the patient experience – patients as learners

The Patient Learning Journey programme prepares patients and carers to become involved in professional learning. It follows the core principles of engagement that are used with health practitioners: a group examination of difficulties through the expression of ideas and feelings, in order to move forward. The group explores each person's account of illness in turn. They identify their learning from voicing their own experience and reactions and from listening to each other, discussing common threads. Only then do they consider how this might be applied in professional learning. Their understanding of how they have learned helps them to be more effective teachers with both students and practitioners, as well as to be more authentic collaborators with the faculty of clinicians and academics or with service leaders.

A group of local people, mainly with arthritis and connected to the Expert Patient programme, helped to develop our approach for enabling and supporting people to become involved. The group discovered that many patient-training approaches failed to recognise the importance of listening to, and building on, the experiences of patients. By starting with the personal experiences of patients and only then moving on to consider how these insights and knowledge could become part of professional learning, barriers to an authentic expression of patient expertise could be overcome. These patients have applied their growing self-awareness to understanding the needs of learners, and ways that providers and patients could work together differently. They do this in a participative, action-research process. Their present focus is on defining what professionals need to learn to be able to support patients and their carers play a greater part in care and decision making.

The programme is now led by a carer advocate who works with the university to support patient and community voices, and who has herself been engaged through a parallel, iterative process of reflection within the University of Leeds School of Medicine. It has been taken forward in collaboration with the University of Leeds School of Healthcare and the universities of Bradford, Huddersfield and Leeds Metropolitan. Funded by the local strategic health authority and now made available across the Yorkshire and Humberside region, the programme is preparing patients and the public to play their part in health professional education.

Throughout this process, people have reflected on the experience in pairs and groups, and these reflections have been recorded and analysed. Diverse participants benefit greatly from the programme, describing, as in self-help groups, increased confidence and self-esteem. Many talk of an improved patient experience and enhanced relationships with clinicians. Some report changing their concept of living with the condition and feel better. Like the patients in Jackson's study (2006) of learning from long-term illness, some feel they have learned about themselves and undergone self-development. They enjoy varied opportunities to feel valued by contributing to professional learning. These often provide earnings, as well as expenses. Some have moved straight into full employment, citing the programme as an important contributing factor in their rehabilitation. Through this innovative programme, the university is able to offer tried and tested educational approaches that directly benefit its wider community.

Patient Learning Journey groups: preparing for dialogue

Throughout the group sessions is a sense of mutual learning, rather than training. As in self-help groups, supportive listening is key. This is not easily found elsewhere.

> In the end it was a secure, confidential environment for people to share their experiences. Not one was the same, but there are threads. ... Where else can I talk like this? I don't want to bore my family and professionals haven't the time.
>
> (Carer and lead group facilitator)

Too much of what needs to be said feels too painful for people who are close.

> It's too emotive, too naked, to say some things to people around you at home. You're all too vulnerable – you see their suffering, they see yours.
>
> (Patient Learning Journey group member)

Participants are encouraged to uncover the meaning of their experience.

> We've kept it hidden, not realising its value.
>
> (Patient Learning Journey group member)

A particular theme is the sense of moving on, through sharing difficulties.

> It was a revelation. I discovered all these things in common with other people. I'd felt anxious, depressed, but had put on a brave face. I could say – yes, I'm suffering, ... [It was] a privilege to have a chance to get all that

emotion out, share with other people, learn something about myself. ...
People get to see themselves differently and others see them differently.
(Expert patient, member of original Patient Learning Journey group and
co-facilitator of further groups)

Others also talk of the 'revelation' of being part of a group.

> It seemed like a revelation to me: hearing your own thoughts, spoken
> out loud – it hits you ... whatever condition we have, it's the same for
> him too. It's taken me out of a small group and put me in a wider group
> in society. I've more in common with a wider group of people and don't
> feel so different any more.
> (Patient advocate, co-facilitator of original Patient Learning Journey
> group and patient teacher)

Then, an empowered position from which to contribute is created.

> I've been wheeled out as a token user. ... [Then] I'm pushed back out
> the door and the meeting goes on – the message there is how tragic, sad,
> poor old thing – there's no learning from it. ... In this work, you feel you
> have a priority and a place, rather than being wheeled out as a token. You
> can share what you understand, translate it for them, fill a gap.
> (Patient Learning Journey group member and wheelchair user)

These examples – learning with patients and learning by patients – show
how to ensure the place in professional learning for the patient voice. They
also illustrate shared assumptions with the Council of Elders model (Katz *et
al.* 2000) where elders attending a day-care centre receive junior doctors,
who present their challenging clinical and moral dilemmas in caring for the
elderly. Here, the elders have acted as a 'senior faculty' to listen and advise in
a 'special kind of "open dialog" in which moral dilemmas could be presented,
discussed, and reflected upon'. Katz et al. also stress the careful preparation
that these new conversations require and the learning that arises for both
parties through their dialogue.

Conclusion

In discussing the examples of learning to work together given above, we
consider afresh how we learn. One insight is offered by Sfard (1988) who
describes a fundamental difference between the 'participation metaphor'
(PM) rather than the 'acquisition metaphor' (AM), which is illustrative of
our approach: 'While the AM stresses the individual mind and what goes
into it, the PM shifts the focus to the evolving bonds between the individual
and others.'

We argue for more attention to be paid to effective group processes and support for realistic personal review. Too often, 'reflection' in education is attempted in groups where it is difficult to discover and express individual views, let alone work together to create a new vision (which is a requirement in modern health care).

Such 'free group discussion' with medical students was pioneered by Jane Abercrombie (1960). She helped to make conscious and explicit the effect past experience and personal beliefs have on perception and judgement – and applied this insight to the inherent complexity of interpretation and decision making in medical science.

When patients bring out their 'hidden, not realising its value' experience; when students find connections between their own and patients' experience and begin to have a dialogue, they are similarly examining evidence from experience. In effective groups it is possible to check out assumptions and to question one's own assertions, supporting reflection.

When patients have explored painful feelings with each other, they feel stronger and are in a better position to meet professionals in a learning group. They can then help those health professionals to tolerate patients' pain. Patients as teachers in early student experience are particularly helpful to model such coping skills (Morris et al. 1998).

When discussion is focused on experience in groups where a wider context has to be considered because of the diversity of participants, unvoiced or unheard concerns can be kept 'alive'. The concept of deliberative practice is useful here (Forester 1999): originally applied to involving people in town planning, it has been widened to include people in decision making in government and business (National Consumer Council 2008). There is an emphasis on listening and not pushing for solutions too soon, before all parties have had the chance to listen to each other. It also includes 'safe rituals of small group meetings' that 'enable participants to develop more familiar relationships or to learn about one another before solving problems they face'.

This allowance of time and space for voicing is crucial to successful joint working: social-work educators talk about the time needed to ensure effective participation by 'vulnerable citizens' and how universities and funding bodies must take this into account (Brown and Young 2008). We too have found the need to take the time to develop relationships, working towards the 'patients' council'. This has to be planned into the medical school's curriculum development and assessment cycle by the faculty leadership, if a useful community input is to be ensured.

Clinicians under time pressure, used to multitasking and being in control, find it hard to engage. This has always made reflection and listening difficult and is not healthy for them, nor effective (Bub 2006). Deciding to work jointly, with clarity, on a task within a set time frame is one way to ease this frustration for professionals and patients – in the clinical encounter or in evaluating practice.

Notes

1 We acknowledge 'patient centred' to be a contested term (albeit in everyday use in our institutions) as it can describe approaches that involve little patient participation and is rather more about the focus of professional attention. In medical education research particularly this notion has given way to 'relationship-centred' care. The patient contribution to learning is perhaps best captured in the existing concepts of person-centred and collaborative practice, applied to both patients and professionals.

2 By 'patient voices' we mean the active contribution to professional learning of patients, carers and the community. The term 'patient' is used here as shorthand also for other terms used in different settings: client, consumer, service user, survivor and lay person. The meaning is debated about these and more independent and equitable terms such as citizen, community, stakeholder and public.

Chapter 9

Informal learning by professionals in the United Kingdom

Geoffrey Chivers

Introduction

A previous publication co-authored by Graham Cheetham and myself (Cheetham and Chivers 2001), provided an opportunity to review the literature to the beginning of this millennium on how professionals learn. While this literature is now extensive, it is rather fragmented, reflecting particular schools of thought about adult learning, vocational learning, formal versus informal learning, learning on and off the job, etc.

In terms of this chapter, the seminal work of Marsick and Watkins (1990) on formal, informal and incidental learning in the workplace is significant. More recent research by Eraut et al. (1997) into the development of knowledge and skills in the workplace should also be acknowledged. This latter study included some professional occupations, although it was not specifically focused on professions; but rather on higher-level workers in three occupational fields: engineering, health care and business.

Eraut's team conducted semi-structured interviews with managers, technicians and a number of professionals from each sector. The interviewers established the nature of the interviewee's job, then sought to identify 'learning episodes' which had helped them acquire necessary knowledge and skills.

This research identified nine broad types of learning episode as follows: working for qualifications; short courses; special events; access to learning materials; organised learning support; consultation and collaboration within the work group; the challenge of work itself; consultation outside the working group; and life outside work (Eraut et al. 1997: 9–10).

This study did not include any quantitative element, therefore the researchers were unable to consider the relative importance of different types of learning episode or confirm their general applicability. Nevertheless, this research revealed once more that higher-level workers, including professionals, learn a great deal by informal (and incidental) methods at work (and even outside work), and do so in a wide variety of ways. This study also pointed up the benefits of asking workers themselves about their vocational learning, rather than relying on others, such as their managers, and training and development staff to explain the how, what and why of their learning.

In considering the Eraut et al. list of learning episodes, it is also notable that learning by reflection on practice does not explicitly appear. Given that the study included professionals in the sample of interviewees, and given the generally very strong emphasis on Donald Schön's work on reflective practice when considering professional learning and development, this result may seem anomalous.

There is no doubt that Schön's research and publications have had a major impact on thinking and practice concerning the development of professionals in the USA, the UK and many other countries around the world (Schön 1983). Indeed, for certain professions in England, such as teaching, nursing and social work, initial professional-development programmes include much formal teaching and learning about reflective practice. It has seemed to me for many years that learning largely arises from reflection upon experience (including the experience of being formally taught), and that the workplace provides a huge variety of experiences from which to learn. However, to sum up these 'learning episodes' or 'learning experiences' as just an arbitrary aspect of the overriding importance of 'reflecting on practice' seems unjustified, whether for professionals or for other workers. Having supported the learning and development of many professionals, younger and older, across a wide range of professions, I am certainly aware that many of them were quite unfamiliar with the concept of learning by reflection on practice, and were learning well at work without any overt attempt to follow any 'recipes' for learning from reflection on practice.

This is not to state that professionals do not learn from reflection on their practice. Indeed, again with Graham Cheetham, I have argued that this process is the key driver of improvements in individual professional competence (Cheetham and Chivers 1996, 1998). The Cheetham and Chivers model of professional competence acquisition and professional learning, with reflection on performance its essential motor, has gained widespread credence in the UK.

This chapter reports briefly on empirical research conducted to investigate the validity of this model, and to determine in detail how experienced professionals in England have in fact developed their professional competence through learning (especially their informal learning) since qualifying.

Literature review

The literature on informal learning at work generally is now extensive, and a full review would be beyond the scope of this chapter. Marsick and Watkins (1990) have made a distinction between formalised learning in the workplace and what they call 'incidental learning'. Reber (1993) also recognised the existence of an implicit process that leads to the acquisition of knowledge without conscious effort or any explicit awareness of what has been learned. Indeed, this learning generates the tacit knowledge, understanding and skills on which workers draw, for example, to make decisions, apparently intuitively.

Marsick and Watkins (1990) went further to argue that while the workplace provides opportunities for learning, there are personal characteristics which, if present, make work-based learning more likely to take place, or take place more extensively. These are:

1 Proactivity – a readiness to take the initiative in situations.
2 Critical reflection – a tendency to reflect, not just on events, but on underlying assumptions.
3 Creativity – to enable a person to think beyond their normal point of view.

Mumford (1995) has identified four broad approaches to learning used either tacitly or deliberately:

1 Intuitive approach – learning is unconscious and a consequence of experience.
2 Incidental approach – involves learning by chance from activities that cause a person to reflect on them at the time or soon after.
3 Retrospective approach – looking back over time at what has happened and reaching conclusions.
4 Prospective approach – involves retrospective elements, but focuses on planning to learn from events *before* they happen. Future events are seen as important, not just in their own right, but as opportunities to learn.

Mumford suggests that different people may be inclined to one or other of these approaches in much the same way as they lean towards a particular learning style.

While informal learning at work is seen as worthy of encouragement by these authors, and by those concerned with or promoting organisational learning and the learning organisation (for example, Argyris and Schön 1974; Fiol and Lyles 1985; Jones and Hendry 1992), Zuboff (1988) cautions that much work-based learning is likely to be context-specific. This means it will not transfer readily to other work environments.

Research concerned with professional development has until recent years largely focused on specific professions. Research into continuing professional development (CPD) has tended to focus on formal learning, and particularly on the requirements of particular professional bodies (Becher 1999).

Gear et al. (1994) reported that up to the 1990s there seemed to have been a dearth of research which was cross-professional rather than profession specific, and which had a significant focus on informal learning. Gear et al. (1994) themselves carried out an investigation across seven professions in regard to 'informal learning projects'. Informal learning methods involved included: reading, visits, meetings, practice, audit and conversations.

More recently Eraut et al. (1997) have looked at the development of knowledge and skills in the workplace. This study included some professional occupations, but was not specifically focused on professions. The study involved semi-structured interviews with managers, technicians and a number of professionals drawn from the engineering, health care and business sectors.

These researchers identified nine broad types of learning episode. Studying for qualifications featured significantly, as did learning from short courses, and events such as conferences and workshops. Other forms of organised learning support were referred to, as was self-learning from a wide variety of learning materials.

However, the work carried out by these professionals itself was seen as providing important learning opportunities, as it was ever changing and continually challenging. Consultation and collaboration within the working group was seen as a key form of informal learning, as was consultation outside the working group. Importantly, life outside work was also frequently cited as providing rich learning opportunities by these professionals.

Eraut et al. (1997: 13–14) also sought to identify various factors that affected the extent of learning at work. They found that confidence and motivation to learn, together with capability and prior knowledge of relevance were key to professional learning, as with other learning. However, the nature of the organisation in which a professional works also has a strong influence, as does the micro-culture in their particular workplace, and how he or she is managed.

Professional bodies were also found to have an influence on the extent and nature of professional learning.

Poell et al. (2000) have gone further into how the nature of the work of different types of work organisation influences the ways in which workers, including professionals, seek to gain knowledge. These researchers have studied in considerable depth how some groups of professionals organise themselves to learn from so called 'learning projects'.

However, the focus of the empirical research reported here has been on how professionals learn through their careers from an individual perspective.

Empirical research methods and results

The research conducted by Cheetham and Chivers (2000, 2001), which forms the substantial basis of this chapter, took the form of interviews with eighty practitioners from twenty professions, and a questionnaire survey of practitioners from six professions, which yielded 372 usable responses. The six professions selected for the survey were dentistry, accountancy, the Civil Service, surveying (chartered), the Anglican Church and training.

Both interview and survey respondents (N = 452) were invited to rate the importance of each of ten types of informal learning or experience (drawn from the literature) in helping them to become fully competent (on a 1–5 scale).

The ranking of the contributions of the various forms of informal learning showed:

1 On the job learning;
2 Working alongside more experienced colleagues;
3 Working as part of a team;
4 Self-analysis or reflection;
5 Learning from clients, customers, patients, etc.;
6 Networking with others doing a similar job;
7 Learning through teaching/training others;
8 Support from a mentor of some kind;
9 Use of a role model;
10 Pre-entry experience.

Significant differences were noted between professions when the results from the six surveyed professions were looked at separately. For example, pre-entry experience scored reasonably well amongst clergy, whereas amongst dentists the score was much lower. The church scored highest on both the use of role models and mentors, while trainers (as might be expected) rated most highly learning through teaching others.

The empirical research methods, especially the in-depth interviews, were able to draw out a great deal of qualitative data. In each case, respondents were asked to describe experiences that had proved particularly formative for them. In the case of the interviewees, the probing went considerably further, for example, by asking them about particular difficulties they had faced in their earlier practice and how these had been overcome.

The experiences reported could be grouped into a number of general themes. The most obvious of these was learning by repetition of tasks, through rehearsal, simulation and actual professional practice; indeed there was a stress on 'over-learning', that is practising a task (such as giving a talk) so that the performance was to a higher standard than was really necessary.

There was also a stress on learning from extensive observation of professional performance. This included what not to do as well as how to perform competently. The value of role models was emphasised in this context, as was working alongside more experienced colleagues, and team working in general.

Frequent reference was made to learning from complex or multifaceted problems, and from innovative and pioneering experiences. Learning from multidisciplinary working, learning from clients, patients and customers, and from switching perspectives (for example, working in a different part of the organisation or secondment to a partner organisation) were also stressed. Networking featured strongly as a mechanism for learning, and learning through moving outside the work organisation to represent it was also seen as valuable.

Learning through explaining one's work or one's organisation's work to outsiders was seen as very effective, culminating in acting as a teacher or trainer.

Being able to learn from feedback and criticism was seen as an important issue, as was developing self-knowledge and self-image in the professional role. Building understanding by linking new learning to existing knowledge or by linking elements of new knowledge together was seen as crucial in professional learning. In doing this, developing imagery, mental models and other psychological devices were seen as very helpful.

Learning was not always seen as steadily progressing, and some of those interviewed discussed quite rapid mindset changes, and sudden, profound 'Damascus Road' experiences as key learning steps. Learning to cope with the demands of professional work at ever increasing levels of responsibility, especially the stress this could create, was seen as important in the long term. Reflection on practice overall, and on particular areas of performance, was seen as crucial to learning and improving as a professional. Such reflection could be informal and conducted in isolation, but more formal reflection techniques and processes were also seen to have value in learning. Mentoring was seen to have a significant place in learning by some interviewees, although others had never been in a position to benefit from a mentor.

Discussion of research findings

It is clear from the above findings that professionals learn informally in a wide variety of ways. By no means do all professionals learn by all these methods. It seems clear that some informal learning methods are favoured in certain professions and less so in others. The research by Eraut et al. (1997) reminds us that the circumstances of the workplace as well as the nature of the work may determine to a considerable extent which learning opportunities present themselves to particular professionals, indeed particular professions. Mumford (1995) stresses that particular workers may prefer to learn (informally or indeed formally) by particular methods.

A detailed content analysis has suggested that twelve general types of learning process can be identified from all the data collected in the Cheetham and Chivers (2001) research. These components can be arranged into a taxonomy of learning mechanisms along the lines of Bloom's Taxonomy of Educational Objectives (Bloom 1956):

1   Practice and repetition
2   Reflection
3   Observation and copying
4   Feedback
5   Extra occupational transfer
6   Stretching activities
7   Perspective changing/switching

8　Mentor/coach interaction
9　Unconscious absorption or osmosis
10　Use of psychological devices/mental tricks
11　Articulation
12　Collaboration.

A number of general comments were made by respondents about other factors they considered important to becoming a competent professional. Synthesising these suggests five general factors:

1　The opportunity to experience a wide range of developmental experiences;
2　The motivation to acquire the necessary competencies and to improve these continuously;
3　Adequate practice in carrying out the various key tasks and functions in order to master the requisite competencies;
4　Persistence in overcoming difficulties and in persevering when things are not going well;
5　The influence and support (when needed) of others.

One further point was repeatedly made in relation to more formal training. This was having the opportunity to put something into practice immediately. This finding accords with one, at least, of Knowles' 'principles of androgogy' (Knowles 1980).

The professionals researched placed little emphasis on formal learning processes in regard to their learning and development beyond initial qualification to enter the profession. However, it should be remembered that the interview and questionnaire samples included a large number of experienced professionals. These respondents may have had little opportunity, or incentive, to engage in formal learning (for example, group-based learning in a training environment) in the earlier stages of their careers.

Certainly, as the newer professions emerged in the 1970s onwards, there would have been few qualified to take forward the development and delivery of relevant training courses. For the older professions there will have been some formal CPD courses offered during the career span of relevant respondents. However, take up may well have been quite low due to lack of encouragement from employers of professionals, or any demands from professional bodies to undertake CPD.

In the light of the Cheetham and Chivers (2001) research, I have undertaken some initial research into the learning being achieved by a younger generation of professionals undertaking part-time postgraduate, post-experience qualification courses in my own university (Chivers 2008). This research has involved analysis of email and postal correspondence with professionals undertaking postgraduate study in the field of occupational risk management. The results indicate that the learning challenge for many of these professionals is to achieve or develop further the meta-competencies of the Cheetham and Chivers professional competence model (1998). These include creativity, problem definition and problem solving, analysis and synthesis, communication, understanding how best to achieve self-development, etc.

In brief, this research in progress suggests that for many professionals there is still not sufficient challenge in their day-to-day work to require them to step up their learning levels so that learning at the meta-competence level is constantly taking place. Equally this research suggests that for most professionals informal learning at work is not sufficient to enable them to become competent at the highest levels to which a professional may aspire.

Conclusions and practical implications

The results of the Cheetham and Chivers (2001) research attest to the wide variety of ways in which professionals acquire their competence. They suggest that much of the learning required to attain full professional competence actually takes place after the completion of formal training to enter the profession. Until recent years, opportunities and incentives to undertake formal training once a professional is established on the career track have been limited. This conclusion highlights the critical importance of informal learning.

However, the results also suggest that different individuals find different kinds of experience formative, and this should caution against being too prescriptive in respect of 'best-practice' learning methods. Indeed, these results show up the limitations of any single theoretical perspective in fully explaining the complexities of learning. They counter against too rigid an adherence to any particular theoretical approaches and the development of practices these may have generated.

Those in the professional development field should start by explicitly recognising the key contribution of informal learning to the acquisition of full professional competence. Conversely, they should accept the limitations of formal programmes and acknowledge that much of the necessary learning will be beyond their control.

At the very least they should concentrate within formal programmes of study on imparting core knowledge (including widening and updating knowledge) and basic professional skills, and, very importantly, on developing a range of learning skills, especially those linked to informal learning.

In planning development methods beyond formal courses, developers should avoid too much reliance on a single approach. Mentoring, for example, may well strongly benefit one professional but not another. Developers should encourage trainees to recognise, seek out and fully explore as wide a range of potential learning opportunities as possible. Indeed, they should encourage trainees to view all experiences as potential learning experiences. Developers should encourage and help professionals to become self-directed learners who are skilled at getting the best out of learning opportunities.

The research in progress on professional learning from higher-education qualification courses suggests that formal learning, and feedback on this learning, may play an important role in the achievement of the powerful meta-competences necessary to perform at the highest professional levels (in any profession). However, this assumes that the core competences upon which any effective professional performance are based have already been imbued by earlier formal and informal learning. It does seem that developers should be looking to help professionals learn via a well thought out mix of formal and informal learning methods. The 'practicum' or practical work placement period which features in many undergraduate, postgraduate and other professional development courses is, of course, a recognition of this need.

Whether in initial professional development programmes, or in subsequent post-qualifying progression or CPD courses, any such placement period should preferably involve real-work situations and specific projects. As wide a range of such placements as possible should be organised. Within these, the learning sought should be clearly identified (possibly through a learning contract), and a strong emphasis should be placed on the development of workplace competence, and its assessment.

Work placements require effective supervision to ensure time is not wasted through trainees not being offered suitable development opportunities. During placements regular feedback should be offered to trainees. Practice-orientated development should also be sought through the use of project-based learning methods, which include substantial elements of team working. Programmes should seek to achieve a smooth integration of theory and practice, both in terms of coordinating the timing (so that trainees get a chance to practice something they have just learned about in theory) and in making suitable links before and after placements.

Trainees should be encouraged to give presentations and to articulate and defend their work. The effort to explain and justify professional thinking, decisions and practice is a major driver of professional competence development, especially at the meta-competence level.

When mentors are used within programmes, they should be carefully selected to ensure they have the necessary qualities and should be adequately trained. Where practicable, mentors should be matched to trainees or, better still, selected by the trainees themselves to ensure compatibility. Too often people are asked or encouraged to take on a mentoring role without adequate explanation of what is expected of them, let alone any mentor training.

There is much merit in organising 'reflective-practice interviews' on a periodic basis where one professional can talk at length with another experienced professional (or human-resource developer or learning facilitator) about their learning achievements and challenges (Chivers 2003). The potential power of peer mentoring and collaborative learning should not be overlooked. Trainees can learn a lot from each other and this should be encouraged.

In assessing practical competence, a variety of assessment methods should be used. These should be as close as possible to real professional practice. A number of real-life examples are given by Cheetham and Chivers in their book *Professions, Competence and Informal Learning* (2005: 223).

Most professional-development providers will already be doing some of these things. However, our experience suggests that few will be doing all of them. This is often because certain approaches have grown up by trial and error in particular professional-development fields, but not in others.

There is a great need for the sharing of good practice in regard to both informal and less formal professional learning practices across the professions. Inter-professional conferences, seminars and meetings are important in this respect. However, there is a need for cross-professional trainer training courses or seminars, in which professional-development providers can be exposed to development methods used in other professions with which they may be unfamiliar.

Newly trained professionals should embark on their careers recognising that the greater part of their professional learning is still to come. They should not shy away from daunting or stretching tasks, in the knowledge that some of the best learning can come from these. Where possible, trainee professionals should collaborate with others in their learning, sharing what has been learned and comparing experiences. They should reflect regularly and systematically on recent experiences and what these have taught, seeking where possible to codify and articulate the lessons learned.

Individuals should also endeavour to find out from their more experienced colleagues as well as their peers the sorts of things that are particularly important for them to learn. They should learn from their more experienced colleagues about their tacit skills leading to mastery of the profession, and their personal tips for effective performance.

Beginning professionals should strive to make mental links between their informal learning experiences and any relevant theory or principles they have been taught through their formal learning or follow-up reading. From this stage they need to formulate their own concepts of excellent professional performance, discussing these with peers and more experienced colleagues and testing them against future experience.

As learning progresses it is important for newer professionals to discuss their learning processes, learning achievements and learning needs with relevant work colleagues. Professionals at all stages of development should regularly and systematically take stock of what they have learned and how it can be used to improve performance, drawing from all known reflective-practice techniques to support their learning from performance.

All professionals should also accept that they have a professional obligation to facilitate the learning of other professionals (not just new professionals). They should be aware that their own practice and behaviour may, possibly unknown to them, be proving particularly formative to others. Indeed, other professionals and potential professionals may be observing them closely, even seeing them as a role model.

Chapter 10

Judgement, narrative and discourse

A critique of reflective practice

David Saltiel

Introduction

Reflection and reflective practice are ideas that have been so enthusiastically adopted within social work and other caring professions in the UK and elsewhere as to constitute a new orthodoxy.

While the stresses and strains of practice in managerial environments have inhibited the growth of reflective practice in the workplace, the reflective practitioner is seen as an ideal. Much work has gone into developing reflective peer groups and, in health care, clinical supervision, which are seen as vehicles for promoting reflective practice. Students on qualifying and post-qualifying courses spend a great deal of time compiling learning journals, case studies, critical-incident analyses and reflective learning statements: all seen as educational tools for producing reflective practitioners.

Yet at the same time it has proved difficult to define precisely what we mean by reflection and how it might be assessed (Ixer 1999). Key terms have been criticised for their imprecision (Eraut 1994; Moon 1999), there has been a lack of clarity about how to write reflectively (Rai 2006) and a review of the literature suggests a lack of rigorous research and debate about the nature and process of reflection (Fook, White and Gardner 2006).

The purpose of this chapter is to consider some perspectives that may unsettle some of the increasingly taken-for-granted assumptions about reflection, and yield insights into the professional contexts within which reflection takes place. One perspective is that more emphasis should be placed on thinking of practitioners' accounts of practice as narrative constructions rather than as unproblematic accounts of their work. Another is to think of the reflective learning model as a discourse, 'a rule-governed socio-historically situated language' (Cotton 2001: 514) that lays claim to knowledge as truth, that constitutes those doing reflection in particular ways and is therefore not politically neutral. This chapter also draws on debates within the nursing profession which perhaps deserve to be better known in the social-work literature. Reflection in nursing is closely linked in the UK to clinical supervision which was introduced into the profession in the UK following the murder of some children by a paediatric nurse, Beverley Allitt, and has an explicit dual purpose of encouraging reflection and monitoring (Clouder and Sellers 2004); although some branches of nursing already had well-established cultures of clinical supervision. This has led to a focus within nursing on the way professional cultures and discourses shape reflective practice; a focus that has not been so clear within social work (see Janet Hargreaves' discussion in this volume of how cultures of caring in nursing have developed). It may be that an exploration of reflective practices within different professions will help develop models of reflection that are useful in multi-professional contexts. Finally it is suggested that seeing reflection within the context of debates around what constitutes critical thinking may give us a more holistic model of professional learning and development.

Reflective practice is often seen as a counterpoint to the technical rationality of evidence-based practice, the other approach that dominates current thinking, and has been generally much more warmly received by practitioners and educators (Taylor 2003). It is perhaps easy to see what the appeal is: where evidence-based practice seeks order and certainty – what *ought* to happen (Taylor 2003) – reflective practice engages with the messiness, the unpredictability, the uncertainty of practice, focusing not on abstract theory but on the real experiences of practitioners and the skills they develop as they try to make sense of those experiences. It emphasises the expertise – the skill and artistry – of professionals in a world where procedural and managerial approaches predominate.

What Gould refers to as the 'reflective learning paradigm' (Gould 1996a: 1) has redefined our understanding of the skills and knowledge of practitioners. The epistemological basis of this paradigm is that practical expertise derives not from the application of deductive rules and procedures but through an inductive process of analysing and theorising experience and practical activity: what Schön (1983) calls reflection in- and on-action. Theories become 'frames or metaphors ... from which practice can be reviewed and deconstructed' (Gould 1996a: 4). What Moon (1999: 11) refers to as the 'backbone philosophies' of reflection derive from the work of Dewey, Habermas, Schön and Kolb, all of whose work focuses on how knowledge is developed through the processing of experience.

Some writers have distinguished between reflection and what has been variously described as critical reflection (Fook and Askeland 2007) and reflexiveness (Taylor and White 2000). The distinction rests on the degree to which deep lying assumptions are left unexamined, and those assumptions are centrally about the workings of power (Fook and Askeland 2007).

The work of John Dewey is often taken as a starting point. Dewey (1991) differentiates between routine action and reflective action, arguing that knowledge is created when we are faced with difficulties that must be carefully defined so that possible solutions can be hypothesised and then tested. Through 'imaginative thinking ... [the practitioner] moves from the known to the unknown, creating a sort of cognitive disruption' (Ixer 1999: 515) in which new knowledge and solutions are found. Knowledge, then, is primarily derived from experience and problem solving rather than the application of deductive theory. But this does not mean we enter the realms of untheorised 'common sense': Dewey argued that through reflecting on problems and possible solutions we synthesise and integrate theoretical concepts into our practice. Dewey sets out some of the key underpinnings of reflective practice: that expertise is a mix of different kinds of knowledge – formal and informal, that we learn by thinking on our feet and then reflecting on this, that abstract theories do not provide ready-made answers but need to undergo a transformation to make them useful for practice.

Building on this work, Donald Schön's (1983) concepts of reflection-in-action (thinking creatively while acting) and reflection-on-action (thinking about what we did afterwards) have been widely influential, particularly in professional education and training where a wide range of teaching methods have been developed to encourage students to reflect on their practice and integrate theory with action.

Schön has been criticised for his imprecision and his failure to argue his points rigorously (Greenwood 1993; Eraut 1994; Ixer 1999). Eraut argues that reflection-*in*-action is best seen as a theory of metacognition, concerned with the ability to make rapid judgements in problematic situations.

In both health and social care there has been a movement away from defining expertise purely in terms of factual, technical knowledge to a wider definition that includes both practice-based knowledge and skill, and service user perspectives (Horwath and Thurlow 2004). Some of this is said to defy technical definition: 'people do not simply think, they intuit, they have the feeling of what happens' (Taylor and White 2001: 52). Benner's (1984) study of nursing suggests that expertise comes not from the ownership of technical knowledge but from the ability to understand situations swiftly and holistically in all their layers of meaning. This 'situation-based interpretive approach' (p. 46) comes from long experience once the nurse has learned to move beyond a reliance on formal rules and use his or her rich store of experiential learning to be constantly flexible and creative. Benner argues that this is not a process entirely open to rational analysis: much expert knowledge is tacit and highly contextualised and grows without the nurse being fully aware of it.

Benner's (1984) study of nursing has its counterpart in social work in Fook et al.'s (2000) research into how expertise is developed in practice. They found that social workers were defined (by their peers) as expert not by their ability to articulate theory but based on their capacity to be adaptive to complex and uncertain situations, being alive to the vast numbers of variables and competing interests in such situations and swiftly arrive at creative interventions. Skills of 'process' (thinking on your feet to manage situations: Eraut 1994: 81) were more important than outcome skills.

There are other examples from health and social care that emphasise this view of expertise as based on reflective, practitioner knowledge rather than technical, rational theory. For example, Taylor (2003) cites evidence that doctors need to render biological and medical knowledge into anecdotal narratives, based on experience of similar cases to enable them to make judgements in individual cases. Alderson (1998) argues that pain is a personal, subjective experience, providing medical staff with no directly observable evidence and so providing pain relief is a matter of fine judgement based on experience and the patient's subjective view rather than any technical theory.

Schön (1983) saw the risk that reflection-in-action could become stale and routinised and argued that reflection-on-action prevents this by revisiting previous judgements in a more analytical way designed to make tacit knowledge explicit. Judgement making is not just intuitive and context based but also requires a more reasoned approach after the event. Quick judgements are necessary to resolve practice situations but may be 'good enough' rather than optimal, based on untested assumptions and prone to error. More deliberative judgement after the event allows decisions that were made quickly, in the heat of the moment, to be revisited, and a wider range of options and theories considered (Munro 2002). In the rush to embrace reflection, the more formal and theoretical aspect of judgement making can be ignored as can the fallibility of practice knowledge (Usher and Bryant 1989; Eraut 1994; Gould 1996b).

Both Benner's and Fook's studies are heavily influenced by the work of Dreyfus and Dreyfus (1986), who argue for the importance of experiential learning and map out a schema in which the practitioner moves from a novice stage characterised by a reliance on universalistic rules, to a level of competence where more context-specific procedures are followed, to a condition of expertise where rules and procedures become irrelevant, even counterproductive, because the worker's deep tacit knowledge allows them to comprehend and respond to situations with the intuitive artistry suggested by Schön (1983). Both studies emphasised the degree to which tacit knowledge and intuition are critical to expertise in unpredictable situations. Eraut describes the strength of this model as '[depicting] not so much the simple skill of riding a bicycle but the more complex process of riding ... through heavy traffic' (1994: 128). But he also criticises it for its rejection of the more deliberative, rational, technical element of judgement making, and in particular its failure to discuss how professionals control and evaluate their own behaviour. Usher and Bryant (1989) suggest some serious limitations to this kind of informal knowledge: it is likely to be primarily concerned with immediate problem solving, coping and surviving, and is lacking in multi-causal analysis and suggestions for longer-term improvements in practice. Indeed, they question the degree to which reflection-in-action really takes place, as the practitioner is likely to play safe and opt for routinised solutions: the problem that Schön (1983) argued made reflection-on-action necessary.

And Schön's apparent privileging of practice over theory has itself been criticised (Barnett 1997).

Sheppard (1995) suggests that practice knowledge can be made more rigorous by treating it as inductive theory, and following a process of developing hypotheses and searching for disconfirming evidence, but the range of hypotheses available to workers (and supervisors) may be limited by preferred professional formulations (White 1997) and in the multiplicity of competing hypotheses it may not be possible to objectively determine which is best. In a complex and uncertain world, judgements may then be made on moral grounds (Taylor and White 2001).

It is clear that reflective learning models privilege practitioner accounts. A great deal of work has been done to develop typologies and models of the reflective process to enable practitioners to analyse their practice within coherent frameworks (see, as examples across professions, Johns 2005; Moon 2006; Rai 2006). Moon (2006) is careful to distinguish between common-sense notions of reflection, and reflection in contexts where it has a clear purpose and defined learning outcomes. Problems remain, however, and it has been argued that reflection is too vague and imprecise a term to be reliably measured (Ixer 1999).

A key issue is how practitioner accounts are treated. It is argued in the post-positivist world of the reflective paradigm, that language, and the subjective meanings our language embodies, construct our view of the world so that we never see an objective truth, only constructions of reality mediated by our language and culture (Henkel 1995; Gould 1996b) and so language is not merely a reflection of objective reality but is constitutive and is a complex, imaginative and metaphorical phenomenon (Gould 1996b). As a consequence, when we construct accounts of the world, rather than following the rules of scientific objectivity we use forms of knowledge and mental processes that are highly subjective and interpretive.

Bolton (2001) argues that storytelling is the way we make sense of a chaotic world, and the many roles we have within it. Taylor (2006) argues that practitioner accounts should be seen as narratives, constructions made by a storyteller to an audience, rather than unproblematic accounts of what really happened. A key element of narrative theories is that people order their experiences into causally coherent stories and that this ordering into stories varies according to the audience (Wilks 2005). Narratives, then, may be defined as versions of reality designed to be plausible and convincing to the recipient (Taylor and White 2000). It is central to their construction that 'they include an implicit proposition that they are true and moral' (Parton and O'Byrne 2000: 49). They are not 'the truth' but actively created, rhetorical performances which may be full of inconsistencies and contradictions. Their meaning will change according to the social context and the relative power of the storyteller and the recipient. If the storyteller is seeking to tell a liberatory, subjective 'truth' but the listener (or reader) wants to assign to the narrative a politically convenient status then there will be a struggle over the narrative's meaning in which one voice, invariably the least powerful, will be silenced (Parton and O'Byrne 2000).

When practitioners give reflective accounts they do so using vehicles of expression which they themselves have not chosen (Taylor 2006). Such vehicles include learning journals, case studies and critical-incident analyses – all widely used to assess reflection in academic contexts and work-based supervision. It is important in these contexts, Taylor argues, for the practitioner to give an account of themselves as both a competent practitioner and a competent reflector, creating and sustaining an identity that is firmly located within social work's professional ethics and practices. It is also inherent in such contexts that there is a power imbalance between student and academic assessor, between practitioner and supervisor. Even where there does not appear to be such an imbalance, narrative processes are at work. Reviewing the literature on qualitative research methods, Murphy et al. (1998) argue, following Goffman (1971), that interviews do not give unproblematic access to respondents' perspectives but are an opportunity for 'impression management' (Murphy et al. 1998: 120), ensuring that the interviewee presents themselves as morally competent.

Practitioner accounts, then, can be seen in terms of how narrators are constructing morally and ethically acceptable stories about their professional identities in situations marked by imbalances of power between narrator and assessor/supervisor. They form only a part of what is happening in care settings on a day-to-day basis and they tell us as much about how professionals construct their identities, and the contexts within which this happens, as what is 'really' happening: as Taylor puts it, they allow the narrators to 'pass as social workers' (2006: 203).

An example from current practice is the use of 'atrocity stories' (White and Featherstone 2005) designed to demonstrate the narrator's (and the narrator's profession's) competence and moral worth by highlighting the lack of those qualities in others (from different professions). White and Featherstone, in their study into practice at the interface of health and social care, found that many of the accounts elicited by their research were dominated by such atrocity stories which in the current practice climate could be said to have a particular purchase. In current policy and practice in the UK there has for some time been a considerable emphasis on working across agency and professional boundaries to provide integrated delivery of services (Weinstein et al. 2003), and partnership working was identified as one of the core areas of teaching and learning for the new degree in social work in the UK (Department of Health 2002). Social workers and students are increasingly working in partnership with practitioners with very different professional identities, starkly differing levels of status and pay, and different codes of accountability and discretion, all of which can cause considerable difficulties in communication (Frost 2005): difficulties which have been identified as contributing to tragedies such as the death of Victoria Climbié (Reder and Duncan 2004). Partnerships between health and social-care practitioners have a particularly long history of friction (Lymbery 2006). Moreover, the increasing specialisation within social work means that social workers often work across radically different teams and cultures, creating potential difficulties in communication (Horwath and Shardlow 2003) and fruitful ground for atrocity stories to be told about each other. Similarly, the increase in managerialism and tight budget control within social work can foster tensions between practitioners and managers.

Some years ago I conducted some research into processes of judgement and decision making in a local authority children's team, based on the theories and methods of Fook et al.'s (2000) work. I was struck by the consistent ways in which the practitioners I interviewed constructed their stories about their practice. Almost all my research interviews involved atrocity stories about management, giving the workers the opportunity to assert their sensitivity, 'client'-centredness and adherence to social-work values in the face of management's proceduralism and resource-led instrumentalism. Lymbery (2000) argues that the very essence of social work lies in the worker–service-user relationship, and while managers can determine *what* will happen, it is the worker who determines the *how*. The respondents were able to assert their status as bearers of social work's core values by telling stories that emphasised this and demonstrated their person-centred process skills rather than outcomes. They were also able to assert their moral autonomy by showing that they could work for large bureaucratic organisations, which are widely seen as unfeeling and incompetent, without agreeing with their every action or condoning the behaviour of less morally and professionally competent colleagues.

My research was small in scale and unpublished. However, I was interested to then encounter two recent linked studies that attempt to apply Fook et al.'s theories of professional expertise in a study of mental-health workers in Australia and the USA (Merighi et al. 2005; Ryan et al. 2005). Both are based on interviews with practitioners and contain powerful accounts of the stresses and strains of practice, the particular nature of which might be gauged by the categories Ryan et al. used to structure their work around the themes identified by the workers, including 'we are here for the clients', 'a lot of hard grind' and 'going ten rounds with the system'. Analysing these themes by applying narrative theories, by a consideration of the limits and fallibilities of practice knowledge, by using the concept of the atrocity story or the Foucauldian analyses discussed below, which link reflective practice to Foucault's writings on the function of the confession, might have significantly affected the status given to the practitioner accounts.

It has been suggested that reflective practice has been widely accepted within a number of the caring professions in the UK. It may be useful to look at some of the literature and debates within nursing, specifically the debates generated by the introduction of clinical supervision which discuss ideas that have been relatively neglected in the social-work literature on reflective practice. Practice, including reflective practice, takes place within professional organisations and cultures that are sometimes taken for granted but have a profound influence on how that practice is shaped (Fook, White and Gardner 2006). The introduction of clinical supervision into nursing as a vehicle for reflection has led to some useful debates on this issue which could be very relevant within social work.

Ideas of reflective practice are well established in the nursing profession in the UK and derive from the same theoretical sources as in social work (for example, Benner 1984). Clinical supervision can be defined as a regular and protected time for practitioners to reflect on their practice, develop their skills and increase their accountability (Bond and Holland 1998). It is seen as essential to lifelong learning and therefore part of clinical governance, the process whereby the NHS in the UK is meant to continually improve its standards and services (Department of Health 2008a). It was introduced in Scandinavia as long ago as the 1950s (Hyrkas 2006) but it was not adopted in the UK until after the publication of the Clothier Report into the case of Beverley Allitt, a paediatric nurse convicted in 1993 of murdering hospitalised children in her care. The report recommended that a process of reflective supervision be introduced into nursing to help nurses develop their self-awareness and learning and to uncover potential health problems (Clouder and Sellers 2004).

Many nursing professionals and educators have welcomed the introduction of clinical supervision and the opportunities it provides for reflection on practice. It has been seen as instrumental in changing the perception that nurses are less well educated assistants to doctors and emphasising the great range of responsibilities and emotionally complex tasks which nurses carry (Bond and Holland 1998). It is accepted by many within nursing that surveillance and self-regulation are legitimate aspects of clinical supervision that are intended to ensure accountability and patient safety (Heath and Freshwater 2000).

However, from the earliest days there have been suspicions amongst nursing staff that clinical supervision would be used as a form of surveillance and control and indeed it has always had a dual purpose of reflection and monitoring (Heath and Freshwater 2000). The different ways it has been introduced locally, with a much greater emphasis on managerial surveillance in some areas than in others, has added to these suspicions (Freshwater 2005). While there has been no equivalent scandal to the Allitt murders in UK social work, parallels may be made with the development of increased managerialist controls following a succession of child-abuse inquiries. Since the introduction of clinical supervision there has been a lively and at times polarised debate within the nursing literature which has not been reflected in the social-work literature on reflection.

However, Cotton (2001) has taken a Foucauldian perspective, arguing that reflection, rather than making professionals empowered learners and developing workplace learning, has constituted them as docile bodies, conforming to professional and educational imperatives. Reflective supervision, learning journals and other vehicles for reflection require private thoughts to be made public where they can be subjected to surveillance: practitioners are assessed for what they think as well as for what they do. Practitioner reflections could thus be seen as confessional practices that subject them to the panoptical surveillance that Foucault refers to as 'the gaze' (Rabinow 1984: 191) whereby bodies are observed and made docile.

Foucault has argued that the confession is 'one of the main rituals we rely on for the production of truth' (1981: 58). Originally gaining its cultural purchase in Europe because of its connection to religious penance, it has, since the decline of religious practice, spread to a whole series of relationships: to parents, educators, doctors and to the self. Confessionals, and confessional rituals, have now come to be seen as scientific, medicalised and turned into 'therapeutic operations' (p. 67).

Cotton (2001) defines confessions as statements made to a more powerful other, consisting of revelations about one's shortcomings and deviations from the norm, linked to a willingness to engage in self-improvement. Cotton argues that reflection should be seen as discourse – indeed, given its popularity, as a dominant discourse, with reflective practice and reflective practitioners constituted by that discourse. Gilbert (2001) links the confession with Foucault's notion of governmentality, the regulation of the population by a range of normalising and moral practices rather than physical force. Codes of ethics are important ways in which people regulate themselves, and through reflection they become 'ethically self-managing individuals' (Gilbert 2001: 202), incited to tell the truth about themselves and admit their shortcomings. This, it is argued, is an essential component of the modern surveillance and regulation of health and social-care professionals whose organisations are now so diverse and complex that regulation must depend significantly on self-regulation. Foucault (1981) argues that confessions are ultimately linked to sexuality and the pursuit of pleasure, and Gilbert suggests that reflection is used to resolve the tension between selfish pleasure and public duty – a commitment to the latter being an essential qualification for membership of the professional community. Professionals in health and social care have, it has been argued, been 'colonised ... into selfless obligation' (Clouder and Sellers 2004: 264). In return for being surveilled and managed, they are given rewards in the form of status, autonomy and power. Clinical supervision is seen as only an aspect of the surveillance of professionals which is ubiquitous. The media, colleagues, managers and service users all contribute to a truly panoptical 'gaze' (Clouder and Sellers 2004) (also see Janet Hargreaves' discussion in this volume on discourses of caring and devotion within nursing).

While debates about reflective practice in nursing are in many ways similar to those in social work, the introduction of clinical supervision as a vehicle for reflection, with the dual purpose of both developing reflective practice and monitoring practitioners, has encouraged critical discussions about the professional context of reflection which highlight how it may function as a technique of surveillance and control. This dual purpose is mirrored in social work, where reflection takes place in particular contexts where students and practitioners are being monitored and assessed according to a variety of ethical and policy criteria.

It might be argued then that there is a strong tendency for reflection to become something superficial, conformist and confessional, a technical exercise undertaken to fulfil certain study or employment requirements, taking wider contexts of knowledge and power for granted. The view of reflection as a vehicle for creating a compliant, self-monitoring workforce is echoed by Barnett (1997), who argues that it has come to replace transformational critical thinking. While more 'critical' forms of reflection (Fook and Askeland 2007) seek to question the taken-for-granted, the emphasis within reflective practices on intuitive, tacit knowledge may limit its effectiveness as a vehicle for transformative thinking because insufficient account is taken of more deliberative judgement making, so that reflection, however 'deep' or 'critical' is always exploratory (Moon 2008). Seeing reflection as a constituent part of a critical-thinking schema that also encompasses more analytical critical reasoning may be helpful. Ford et. al. (2005) use Barnett's work to suggest that reflection is not enough: that a critical understanding of traditions of thought and practice is required to bring about a transformation of the self and the contexts of knowledge, power and action within which the self is situated.

Critical thinking might be briefly defined as a pedagogical approach that begins by emphasising the nature of all knowledge as problematic and bound within wider contexts. Thus, making discriminating judgements and decisions based on what we understand as knowledge will always be complex and involve a consideration of many perspectives including a critical examination of the self. Both inductive and deductive forms of thinking will be needed to do justice to this complexity (Moon 2008; Phillips and Bond 2004). Barnett's work widens critical thinking to 'critical being' (Phillips and Bond 2004: 280) by arguing that criticality covers the three domains of knowledge (critical reason), the self (critical reflection) and the world (critical action). This schema places reflection within a wider context of how we think about and act in the world and, by making the link with action, has been of particular interest within social work (Ford et al. 2005).

Within social work the idea of critical practice is associated with taking a questioning approach that seeks to interrogate assumptions, explore wider contexts, consider competing perspectives and analyse inequalities (Adams et al. 2002). It is also seen as a way of resisting the conforming power of agency procedures, managerial control and budgetary restrictions, and keeping alive social work's progressive possibilities (Stepney 2006).

There is of course as much debate and uncertainty about the nature of critical thinking as there is about reflection, but it may be that locating reflection within models of critical thinking may help us move towards a new balancing of deliberative and analytical reasoning alongside more personal experiential knowledge. Analysing practitioner accounts as narratives taking place within particular discourses about professionality and the 'reflective practitioner' could be a fruitful way of bringing reflection and critical thinking together.

Conclusions

The notion of the reflective practitioner is an enticing one. To assert the importance of experiential knowledge and creative practice, to start from – to embrace, in fact – the messiness and unpredictability of practice and then to unpick what is going on by generating inductive hypotheses which are dispassionately analysed to reveal the nature of expertise and judgement; these are ideals to strive towards. And there is much about the reflective paradigm to hold on to. Indeed it seems an essential counterbalance to the school of evidence-based practice which sees certainty and technical rationality as its highest ideals.

Reflective practice takes account of the mix of rationalities that underpin judgement, so that we do not take scientific evidence for granted but weigh it in the balance along with other competing versions of events (Taylor and White 2001). It raises practitioners above the status of mere technicians, emphasises the richness and creativity of their practice and leads to persuasive new formulations of professionalism based on diversity and flexibility. By unsettling dominant, modernist conceptions of knowledge and expertise, it enables many new perspectives to develop. An example of this is the development of clinical supervision in nursing which by seeking to 'de-medicalise' nursing and emphasise its expressive role has contributed to studies of the gendered nature of health care which have rethought traditional working practices and hierarchies (Parton 2003).

But while the reflective paradigm has led to important developments in teaching and learning, it has also created some problems. Reflection is notoriously difficult to define, and loose definitions and uncertainty about how to assess it can lead to oppressive practice (Ixer 1999). Educators should be much more aware of the issues in requiring less powerful people to perform confessional reflective tasks and not be so quick to assume that reflective learning is always about positive development.

Practitioners' reflective accounts are often extolled as giving access to the raw material of practice but this is a naive approach that fails to take account of the imagistic and metaphorical nature of language which constitutes rather than reflects reality. Reflective accounts are as artfully constructed, as storied, as any other uses of language. They give access to how professionals construct their identities (and those of service users) and their practices but they are not, by themselves, enough. Service-user perspectives are essential, and so is the kind of ethnographic research which seeks to analyse day-to-day practice realities and professionals' verbal and written accounts (Taylor and White 2000; White and Featherstone 2005).

Considering reflection as just part of a wider range of critical practices may help to maintain a critical rigour and prevent the tendency for reflection to become a set of conforming and instrumental activities designed to produce docile and self-monitoring students and practitioners.

If reflective practice has become the new orthodoxy, the dominant discourse within professional education, it is essential that we keep a critical perspective so that we are as alive to its problems and limitations as to its strengths.

Part III

New practices

Nick Frost, Helen Bradbury, Sue Kilminster and Miriam Zukas

Having examined conceptual challenges and professional perspectives in the previous parts we now move on to explore how new developments are put into practice. In the ever-changing worlds of work and education it is important that reflective practice itself is changing, dynamic and innovative. Here we examine new practices that might take us beyond reflective practice to consider how change can be implemented in relation to the workplace, qualifying professional education, continuing education and inter-professional training.

As we saw in the Introduction to this volume, the four chapters are connected by a key theme – putting change into practice and connecting individuals so that reflective practice can move beyond the individual towards collective change. This Part III is therefore crucial to moving beyond critical reflection.

The initial chapter has been written by Kate Collier and focuses on the issues of creativity and the arts and how to build a relationship with reflection. She utilises the concept of 'self-spectatorship' to enable her to demonstrate how putting action 'on stage' changes the relationship between the professional and the act of reflection. This is a practical chapter that demonstrates how the author has worked with adult educators to enable them to reflect on their practice in new and exciting ways. Collier is keen to makes links between reflective practice and issues of creativity, imagination and the creative arts.

Cheryl Hunt's chapter addresses the issue of spirituality. Her chapter draws on her practice in initiating a module about reflective practice as part of a Masters degree, and explores issues arising from a seminar series she organised. The chapter argues that issues relating to spirituality can be a key element of reflective practice. Hunt suggests methods for taking practice forward and argues that the relevance of spirituality can easily be lost in the world of 'rationality' and targets.

The chapter written by Kate Karban and Sue Smith makes links between inter-professional working and reflective practice. They demonstrate how inter-professional working is becoming increasing dominant in the worlds of health and social care that they explore. The authors argue that barriers and obstacles to effective reflective practice can be addressed by creating space for reflection across the traditional professional boundaries. They demonstrate how this can been encouraged through a professional qualifying module that brings together nurses, social workers, dieticians, speech and language therapists, physiotherapists and occupational therapists. The students meet together and their learning is facilitated by reflective practice as a thread connecting their learning. The authors argue that this approach enables emergent professionals to reflect on the challenges of their practice and the issues of power and status that will confront them in their professional practice.

In the closing chapter, John Sweet demonstrates the emergence of new practices with a group of dental students. In common with other chapters in this section he also suggests that there are methods for building space for collective reflection – so that reflection moves beyond the personal and private. Sweet provides a critique by exploring what he calls RPIIA (reflective practice as individual incident analysis). He provides an analysis of a group form of reflective practice with undergraduate dental students and how this contributes to wider organisational change.

All the chapters in this Part III make realistic and achievable suggestions for a way forward, drawing on theory and empirical research. In the conclusion to this volume we take forward some of the suggestions, and reflect on a creative future for a truly creative reflective practice.

Chapter 11

Re-imagining reflection

Creating a theatrical space for the imagination in productive reflection

Kate Collier

Introduction

This chapter focuses on the creative and imaginative aspects of the reflection process within the framework of productive reflection. I propose that a creative approach to reflection can offer an extra dimension to 'productive reflection': an arts dimension. I will argue that reflection can potentially be seen as a creative arts process and will present a theatrical model of reflective practice that is designed to stimulate creative reflection in professionals at both the individual and the collective level.

Boud, Keogh and Walker (1985: 19) describe reflection as being 'an important human activity in which people recapture their experience, think about it, mull it over and evaluate it'. They argue that it is through this deliberate process of returning to an experience, and the consequential conscious reconsidering of it, that people are encouraged to make 'active and aware decisions in their learning'.

Reflection has been presented as an essential tool for continuing professional development (Argyris and Schön 1974; Brookfield 1995, 2005; Schön 1983, 1987) because it encourages professionals to be more conscious of their practice. Brookfield argues that this increased consciousness helps professionals change and continue their learning in the workplace.

Recently, Boud, Cressey and Docherty (2006) reconceptualised the process of reflection at work and renamed it 'productive reflection'. They extend ideas of reflection as an individualised examining of experience, to a collective process integrated into workplace practice. Productive reflection is seen as providing 'a key to unlocking vital creative forces in employees' (Boud et al. 2006: 5) and this helps workers deal with the changing demands of the modern workplace. Sternberg reinforces the connection between creativity and work effectiveness.

> The economic importance of creativity is clear because new products or services create jobs. Furthermore, individuals, organizations, and societies must adapt existing resources to changing task demands to remain competitive.
>
> (Sternberg 2003: 89)

Productive reflection can therefore provide a valuable framework for thinking how it is possible to move beyond conventional ideas of reflection and make reflection relevant to professional development and lifelong learning.

Even though creativity is seen as something that productive reflection promotes, the place of the imagination and creativity in the reflection process is rarely discussed. This appears to be an oversight because reflection can be seen as a creative process closely linked to imaginative thinking as it involves participants 're-experiencing something that happened earlier, projecting into the future or transforming someone or something through action learning' (Taylor, Marienau and Fiddler 2000). Professionals involved in reflective processes are recreating their experience and therefore need to learn how to use their imagination to re-envision their past and to create new futures.

Once the elements of imagination and creativity are recognised as integral to the reflective process, it is possible to draw on theatre arts literature and ideas of the aesthetic to develop new reflective practices that can enhance workplace learning. Reflection can be seen as the process of creating imaginary pictures or scenarios of experience and as such have a theatrical quality. The reflective process, like theatre, re-imagines and fictionalises certain workplace experiences and 'brackets them off' for further noticing and contemplation. For example, if I want to reflect on a training session I facilitated yesterday I have to be able to recreate a picture in my mind of myself and my students in that class so that I can discover what was professionally significant for me in that learning event.

Creativity, the imagination and reflection

One of the qualities of productive reflection that is identified by Boud et al. (2006: 22) is that reflection is a dynamic 'open, unpredictable process' that changes over time. This refers to the creative nature of reflection. It is the creative quality of reflection that is crucial to the learning that can emerge from reflective practice because it encourages learners to deal with ambiguity and with change. When reflection is considered in these creative terms it can be viewed as a space for professionals to re-imagine their practice and re-vision it. This can be seen as a particularly important quality for professionals to develop in the uncertain conditions of the globalised workplace (Tovey and Lawler 2008; Burns 2002).

If the imaginative aspect of reflection is neglected then there is a danger that it becomes an instrumental tool, little more than a task-focused, 'ticking the box' exercise (Boud et al 2006). Heron (1992: 139–40) also stresses the importance of the imagination and warns that if this dimension of thought is absent there is a danger that an 'intellectual approach to problem solving, with its fixed assumptions and head-on strategies' will be adopted.

It is easy to see, however, why the creative aspect of reflection may not be at the forefront of discussions on reflection and professional development.

Creativity is an extremely difficult concept to describe and is often viewed as a quality that is impossible to measure (Athanasou 1999) or as having 'ineffable properties that are impervious to scientific investigation' (Sternburg 2003: 105).

Heron (1992: 139) has attempted to capture the essence of creativity focusing on the 'imaginal nature of the creative process'. He attempts to describe what imaginative thinking might be and links it to reflection in his 'up-hierarchy of the four modes' which is a dimension of his psychological theory of the person (Heron 1992: 20). By looking at Heron's ideas of the imagination it is possible to gain a better understanding of imaginative thought and its place in the reflection process.

For Heron (1992) the imagination is a 'presentiment' that is felt by the person doing the imagining. Feeling is at the heart of the imagination. It is packed with latent meaning but this meaning is apprehended through metaphor or analogy and is therefore not fully comprehensible. 'There is a play of imagery in the marginal mind which is felt to be inherently mean-ingful and this felt meaning has to be brought to a certain point before it can be expressed in linguistic and logical terms' (Heron 1992: 21).

The ability to create mental images is seen as a key component of imaginative thought. Heron (1992: 139) suggests that this imaging is 'pre-conceptual' and should firstly be sensed, 'divined and received' rather than logically dissected, as this kills creativity. He stresses the value of promoting imaginative thought: 'The imagination has the capacity to sense what you do not know, to intuit what you cannot understand, to be more than you know.'

The valuing of creativity and the imagination in the reflective process allows the experience of the professional to be 'mulled over' and apprehended first, before it is analysed in detail. The ability to apprehend images, to be present in the imagined moment, links reflection to aesthetic understanding. Once the ability to imagine becomes a key component of reflection, then it is possible to align reflection to the arts because the capacity 'to think in images and then transform them into other dimensions of reference is vital to art' (Thompson in Heron 1992: 138).

I will examine ideas of the aesthetic and the arts in more detail and show how they can be connected to the imaginative process of reflection. Then I will look at the concept of 'self-spectatorship' created by the drama-in-education specialist Gavin Bolton and explore whether this theatre arts perspective could add a new perspective to reflection. Finally I will show how I tried to put theory into practice and describe a reflection exercise I developed from researching these areas. I used this exercise with a small group of professional adult educators and evaluated their responses.

The aesthetic experience and reflective imagining

The term 'aesthetic' derives from the Greek word *aisthetika* which refers to 'things perceptible through the senses'. For Abbs it denotes 'a kind of bodily knowledge, an apprehension of patterns through the power of sensibility, especially as it is formally expressed and developed through the arts' (1989: 172). Nicholson highlights that 'aesthetics is more than an arid branch of philosophical discourse. It is an attempt to explain how and why art matters, to find words to describe the special powers with which the arts can illuminate, move and excite' (Nicholson 1999: 81). Therefore aesthetics is not just concerned with the study of what constitutes art, but also the way art engages both feeling and reason to help people 'make sense of the sensuous' (Abbs 1987: 61).

Art can be defined as 'the creation of forms symbolic of human feeling' (Langer 1979: 40). Abbs believes that art 'embodies the invisible logic of the life of feeling and sentience and, in so doing, brings it to conception and consciousness' (1994: 224). In other words, art makes the intangible (feelings, sensibility) knowable (conscious) through its creation of 'significant form'.

Both Abbs and Langer identify feeling as being at the centre of the arts experience and this links the arts and the aesthetic to Heron's ideas of imaginative thought. The symbolic form of art is also relevant to Heron's description of the imagination as is the proposition that the arts and aesthetics are pre-lingual and reside in the senses. However, in addition, art frames the imagination and gives it form. It is this form that highlights or 'brackets off' images and makes what is imagined significant. Dewey (in Jackson 1998) suggests that this highlighting of 'the significant' is the ultimate purpose of art as it is designed to reawaken our senses, causing us to see once again what we overlooked. Once imagined ideas become significant they demand to be looked at and contemplated and that is where the aesthetic dimension comes into play. Langer (1979 5) argues that art allows us to 'objectify feeling so we can contemplate and understand it'. While the 'audience' responds emotionally and engages with the work of art, they nevertheless see it as separate from reality, hence they are able to feel with conscious detachment. This process of aesthetic contemplation could be seen as a form of reflection.

If reflection is conceived as a creative process where the person reflecting creates an image of a past event, it is possible to view this imagining as a form of art. Once pictures are conjured up in the mind and given form, they take on a special quality because they are filtered into particular 'scenes' which are 'bracketed off' from the chaotic mess of our everyday experience. This allows a situation to become like a scene from a play and as such it can be viewed differently and contemplated in a way that eliminates distractions. At this point there is the opportunity to engage in aesthetic responding. Through this response, the imagined experience is felt but at the same time comprehended in an involved or detached manner. It is this process of aesthetic responding that has the potential to add an extra dimension to reflective practice.

There is one aspect of art and the aesthetic that has not been discussed so far that has an impact on whether the arts are really relevant to reflection. This is the place of the audience in the aesthetic experience. Abbs (1987) makes it clear that if there is no audience then there can be no aesthetic, and Newman (2006: 145) notes that, for the artist, the reaction of the audience to a piece of art 'is the objective, and in a sense the only, reality'.

If this is the case, then it is important to question whether it is possible for a person to be both the creator of an imaginative image or scenario and audience to it during reflection. I will argue that this is possible, and explain how Bolton's (2000) concept of 'self-spectatorship' is relevant to ideas of audience and reflective practice.

Bolton's concept of 'self-spectatorship'

The problem of theatre only existing if it has an audience is solved through Bolton's (2000: 24) concept of 'self-spectactorship'. The idea behind this concept is that 'whenever we make anything we are spectators to it'. He gives an example of a child drawing a picture of their mother and at the same time being the audience to what has been created. A self-spectator is looking at what they are creating or have created, rather than being absorbed in what someone else presents to them. According to Bolton, self-spectatorship promotes a special kind of attention and noticing. This has already been identified as a crucial factor in aesthetic responding.

One of the ways that self-spectatorship is encouraged is through the placing of action in a significant space, for example, in a painting or a theatre space. Even if this space is allocated to the mind, it will still have a special focus and this will affect the concentration of the person who enters this space and the way they view the actions in the images created within it (Collier 2005). Once an action is 'put on stage' it gains a particularity that it would not have in everyday life. States (1985) calls this area 'intentional space', because everything that is put in it has a special importance and becomes the focus of attention.

In terms of reflection, once an image has been created in the mind's space and developed into a scene like that from a play, this brings about a perceptual change and encourages the reflector to pay attention to it and look at it as an audience might do. Consciousness then 'shifts into another gear' and the displayed object or person becomes 'a signifying, exemplary image' (Carlson 1996: 40). An example of this is Andy Warhol's famous screen print of a Campbell's Soup can. This ordinary object becomes extraordinary because it has been taken out of its everyday context and re-presented as a framed print.

The same thing could be said to happen in reflective practice when a person begins to re-imagine their professional practice. When they look back and recreate a training session they have just conducted or a team meeting that took place the previous week, it is similar to the process involved in creating a play or scenario. It is the recreation of an imagined reality.

Like a play in the theatre, this imaginative recreation can give the event a special focus and meaning. By recreating the scenario, the person reflecting will begin to consider how and why this event is important. Although a person reflecting on their practice is not an audience in the conventional sense, they are still observing the scenario, concentrating on it and reading significant meaning into it.

I have suggested that reflection can be likened to the creation of scenes from a play, which we stage in our minds and then watch with the special concentration that theatre demands of its audience. Having put forward this proposition, I decided to test it and developed a reflection exercise that capitalised on the imaginative and theatrical possibilities in reflection. I also considered how this kind of reflection could be given a broader collective and organisational focus so that it could meet the demands of productive reflection as set out by Boud et al. (2006).

Putting theory into practice

I am a lecturer in adult education working on a graduate diploma program in vocational and workplace learning. The participants on this program are all experienced, mature students who are working as professionals in areas of adult education as diverse as nursing, information technology, events management and horticulture.

One of the subjects that I facilitate is titled 'The Practice of Workplace Learning'. As the title suggests, this subject is designed to help students reflect on their practice and by doing so enhance their professional development. The students are encouraged to use a range of different reflection strategies such as keeping learning journals and being part of a learning partnership. Throughout the program I set aside time for reflection and use a variety of exercises to help stimulate the imagination as I find some students find the process difficult to engage with.

The exercise I developed from this research had three stages. The first stage involved a visualisation exercise and the second the development of a case study from the visualisation. The third stage was a peer-learning exercise where the case study was discussed and then interrogated through the use of 'strategic questioning' (Peavey 1994). This stage was added to give the reflection the wider collective focus demanded of productive reflection. The three stages also indicated a move from imaginative thinking to a more analytical mode of reflective thought.

The visualisation was designed to create a theatrical space for imaginative reflection. This space was designed to prompt students to notice aspects of their professional practice in more detail and contemplate it as an audience might a play. I was hoping that this approach to reflection might stimulate an aesthetic response from students, and concentrate their focus and attention on the event so that it became more significant to them.

As the facilitator, first I told the students that they were about to participate in a visualisation exercise that would encourage them to reflect on a recent teaching or training experience. I then asked them to close their eyes and imagine that they could see the curtains of a traditional theatre before them – red plush with gold trim! They were told that the curtains before them were closed and that when they opened in a few seconds there would appear on the stage a scene from their professional practice. Once the curtains were open, the students were asked to imagine what the scenery was like in this scene: the furniture and props that adorned the stage and the actors who were part of it. Then they were asked to look at the dramatic focus of the scene and consider what made it significant. Gradually students were encouraged to flesh out a dramatic scenario in their imaginations.

After the visualisation, students were asked to share their image with their learning partner. This part of the exercise was designed to help students clarify the image they had created and also shift the learning from an individual to a more collective focus. Students were then required to go away and write a short case study, based on what they had seen in the visualisation. The following week students worked with their learning partners and read and discussed each others' case studies.

Learning partnerships have frequently been employed as a strategy to encourage critical reflection. They provide students with the opportunity to share their experiences and learn from the different perspectives offered by their partners from their work experience (Collier and McManus 2005, Sampson and Cohen 2001). After a general discussion of the case study, students took turns in using strategic questioning to further interrogate their partner's professional practice.

The strategic questioning approach is designed to help people think more deeply about an event by moving them from 'what was' to 'what might have been and what could be'. This focus on 'what may be possible' involves imaginative speculation and is another reason why I added this approach to the reflection exercise. After the strategic questioning exercise was completed, I asked students to fill in an evaluation sheet that asked them to comment on the reflection exercise as a whole.

The evaluation form was designed to find out if the visualisation exercise had stimulated imaginative reflection in the participants. It also explored whether the visualisation helped students to concentrate on the imagined event so that it became significant for them. The form also looked at whether the visualisation exercise acted as a creative force in developing the case study, and it explored the impact of the strategic questioning exercise and what was learnt from it. Finally students were asked to comment on the strengths and limitation of the exercise in terms of their professional development.

Four questions eliciting a 'Yes', 'No', or 'Neutral' response were provided for each stage of the reflection (twelve questions in all), which allowed for some quantitative evaluation of the data. For example, in the section dealing with what happened after the visualisation exercise, students were asked if visualising the scene from their professional practice helped make the incident more significant. The rest of the form asked for qualitative responses on the strengths and limitations of the exercise and on what was learnt.

Student response to the reflection exercise

Ten students participated in and evaluated the reflection exercise. Their responses give an indication of the potential of a creative, theatrical approach to reflection.

All the participants felt that the visualisation exercise helped make the incident more significant for them. Nine out of ten of the students could see the picture vividly in their mind and found that the visualisation exercise made it easier to write up the case study. Interestingly, only six out of the ten respondents said that the teacher's prompts helped with the development of the picture in their mind. Given that most students were able to strongly visualise their scenarios, this suggests that the facilitator's detailed intervention in the visualisation process may not have been the most important factor. Perhaps the instruction to open the theatre curtains and then observe the scene they had created would have been sufficient, though the cues given were designed to highlight the theatrical form of the reflective image and, by doing so, strengthen its significance. All participants found the strategic questioning helped them gain new insights into what they could learn from the case study.

I will now focus on the qualitative data received in the responses, in particular on what were the perceived strengths and limitations of the imaginative aspects of the exercise and what was learnt from it.

Overall students felt the exercise helped them reflect more deeply on their professional practice. For example, one student commentated on how the exercise had allowed 'deepening insight [in]to specifics in my practice'. Another student noted that the strength of the exercise lay in 'the concept that each event in our life can be reflected upon for development and growth'.

Some students commented on 'the quality of the picture' they created in their minds and how the exercise helped them remember the 'strong links' to the event being recalled and the emotions attached to it. They could clearly recall 'things such as faces' and 'could see the impact I was having on people at the time'. The clarity of the image and the participants' emotional connection to this image are characteristic of imaginative thought and of aesthetic responding.

The visualisation not only highlighted participants' emotional response to the scenario, but also enabled them to 'step back and look "objectively"' at their case studies. This suggests that the aesthetic quality of being able to objectify feeling for the purposes of contemplation was present in the exercise.

There were many different responses to what were considered to be the limitations of the reflective exercise. One person found the image of pulling back the curtains 'very prescriptive' as 'it doesn't allow for other images to occur'. A couple of students found it hard to do the visualisation in the class and wanted to reflect in private, but used the prompts to successfully reflect later. There was one student who commented on the need for preparing the students 'psychologically, emotionally and physically' for the exercise, though another saw it as a 'challenging yet safe process'. The need for more time to be given for the exercise was an issue for one student.

What participants learnt or discovered through the reflection exercise

It is in some of the comments on learning that the connections between reflection and imaginative thought and the arts become clearer. The idea behind the exercise was to create a theatrical space that would make what was placed in it significant and worthy of contemplation. That did seem to happen for some students.

> It surprised me how much information I was able to recall, in significant detail from the reflection ... to be focused on detail initially, thicken the story, give it detail and strength.

Another student appears to reinforce Bolton's ideas that the creation of a theatre space can stimulate us into becoming a self-spectator: an audience to our imagined experience. The language used suggests the student was watching him/herself feeling. He/she was able to feel but with detachment, which has been identified as an important aspect of aesthetic responding.

> Seeing how I felt, what would I change to avoid the negative feelings?

The development of the case study and the strategic-questioning exercise did appear to help some participants link their personal reflection to a wider context. One of the students was able to 'think about strategies I could have used [if I'd stayed at the workplace] or could use in the future if needed'. The students also noted that the reflection had allowed them to 'think about self-change as well as strategies for bringing about external changes'. This focus on using the imagination to think creatively about change relates to ideas of productive reflection. Another student noted that the strategic questioning exercise

> revealed some interesting new facts/ideas for my learning partner's case study which I could relate to my own experiences. Provided greater depth of understanding.

There is an indication here that the reflection that occurred during the strategic questioning stimulated reflection that led to some collective learning which once again is seen as a feature of productive reflection.

Conclusion

I have explored the imaginative dimension of reflection and stressed its importance in the reflection process. By doing so I have suggested that it could be usefully connected to aesthetic understanding and the arts. Aesthetic consciousness requires a person, through focused contemplation, to be acutely present in the moment, a quality that is also relevant to reflective thought.

I have argued that an arts perspective can offer a framework that gives imaginative thought form and significance. One of the forms presented as being a useful aid to reflection was theatre form. Reflection if viewed from a theatre arts perspective can be seen as a process that uses the imagination to develop scenarios from a person's past experience and at the same time observe these scenarios as an audience might watch a play. Theatre, even in the mind, can provide a special space that makes everything that is placed within it worthy of notice and contemplation.

I developed and trialled an exercise that used visualisation as a strategy to promote the imaginative, arts dimension of reflection. This visualisation exercise was then used as a platform to extend personal reflection into productive reflection. The sample of students who participated in and evaluated the reflection exercise I developed from my research was small, and could provide only an indication of how an arts approach to reflection may contribute to productive reflection and professional learning. I hope, however, that this will stimulate further investigation into the imaginative nature of reflection and consider whether it really has dramatic potential.

> Imagination is indispensable to understanding the unknown. We imagine alternative ways of seeing and interpreting. The more reflective and open to the perspectives of others we are, the richer our imagination of alternative contexts for understanding will be.
>
> (Mezirow 1991: 83)

Chapter 12

A step too far?

From professional reflective practice to spirituality

Cheryl Hunt

The real magic of discovery lies not in seeking new landscapes but in having new eyes.
(Marcel Proust *c.*1899)

A human face with a third eye. This eye sees what the other two do but in addition it sees beyond normal perception – not just 'I see' but 'I see why'.
(An image of reflective practice, Masters degree student 1998)

Introduction – scene setting

Outline

This chapter is based on a personal journey. It begins with reflections on the development of a module on reflective practice within a Masters degree over a decade ago and ends with a discussion of the issues arising from more recent work on researching spirituality as a dimension of lifelong learning. It suggests that, especially for people who have a 'transpersonal orientation' to their life and profession, questions about spirituality are integral to reflective practice – and that the implications of such questions now need to be addressed more widely and openly in the context of professional learning.

Approach

I first became knowingly involved in reflective practice in 1994. I have included the word 'knowingly' because I had engaged in reflection, of a sort, much earlier than that – primarily in terms of thinking and worrying about my professional practice and how best to go about it, especially when things went wrong. As Janet Hargreaves indicates in her chapter, a worry about being 'not good enough' is often a driver of reflective practice; I suspect that gendered assumptions may make this particularly so for many women. In 1994, I designed a new module on reflective practice as part of a Masters degree (MEd) in Continuing Education (I will say more about it in the next section). Since then, I have worked alongside many different professionals who have been formally required to engage in reflective practice as part of a qualification and/or as a statutory requirement of their job. In consequence, I now firmly believe that reflective practice can and should involve much more than a basic 'functional' examination and enhancement of what we do *professionally* (Susan Knights, Janet Sampson and Lois Meyer refer in their chapter to Head's (2003) notion of functional and effective processes).

Besides helping to identify how one might become ever more 'effective' in the exercise of one's profession, reflective practice can also be a means of exploring our own *personal processes of meaning making,* enabling us to state clearly, for ourselves and others that 'this is where I am and what I do now; this is how I got here; and these are some of the reasons why I think/feel/act as I do'.

I will attempt to make this chapter congruent with that statement by grounding it in my own experience. Adopting an autoethnographic approach,[1] therefore, I will describe something of my own reflective journey – which is currently taking me towards an understanding of what it means to engage, personally and in professional practice settings, with spirituality. I will leave open the question of whether, in the current outcomes-driven, technical rationality of much professional education, engagement with spirituality goes a step too far beyond established conventions of reflective practice to be widely acceptable.

Background

In the early 1990s, I was working in the adult education department of an old civic university in the UK. I was director of the MEd in Continuing Education which had been in existence in a 'face-to-face' format for fifteen years. Designed to enhance the professional development of mid-career educators from a range of settings, a key espoused value of the course had always been to encourage students to link theory and practice. Much of this had hitherto been done in weekly seminars which drew extensively on students' experiences as educators and learners.

Keeping pace with trends in many other universities at that time, a decision was taken in 1994 to restructure the MEd in order to make it available for distance learning as well as on campus. As part of this process, I introduced a new module entitled 'Becoming a Reflective Practitioner'. It was designed to underpin and accredit a process whereby all students, including those working in remote locations, would be encouraged to bring their own experiences to the foreground, reflect on them in the light of academic and policy literature, and critique 'practice' in the light of 'theory' – and vice versa. To some extent, evidence of this process was required in assignments for all modules, but it was not 'rewarded' separately and could easily become occluded within the final grade by other marking criteria, especially when a student's writing style and/or grasp of theoretical issues was particularly good. The reflective-practice module was therefore to carry one eighth of the total number of credits for coursework.

I collaborated in the development of the module with two colleagues from the local college of nursing and midwifery which was about to become a department in the medical faculty of the university. They were setting up a new Masters course (M.Med.Sci) in Clinical Nursing and Midwifery and wanted to incorporate the module. It was later also included in three other courses, including an MEd in Medical Education.

I now shudder both at the naivety with which I approached this development and at my failure to recognise that I had stepped onto something of a bandwagon. At that time I had a passing acquaintance with Schön's (1983) work on 'the reflective practitioner'. I knew about reflection as a stage in the learning cycle (Kolb 1984; Boud et al. 1985) and I recognised the usefulness of reflection as something which, to use an old adage, might enable practitioners 'to have twenty years' experience instead of one year's experience twenty times over'. Primarily, however, I saw the reflective practice module as a practical solution to the issues outlined above and was largely unaware of either the literature about, or the developing critique of, reflective practice.

In the next section I will refer to some of this in order to contextualise within its own time the framework for reflection we recommended to students; and to indicate how it relates to my own subsequent thinking about the nature of reflection in professional contexts, including links with spirituality.

Literature and practice

Bandwagon?

By 1996, as Bright demonstrated, reflective practice had been:

> adopted by the teaching, nursing, police, counselling, social service and clinical pharmacy professions, and appears in virtually every professional training mission statement or policy document as an espoused objective of professional training.
>
> (Bright 1996: 163)

He argued that this 'suggests a superficial and token acceptance of "reflective practice", rather than a genuine and committed awareness of what it involves and a serious attempt to implement its principles fully' (ibid.). In the same year, Ecclestone (1996) similarly questioned whether reflective practice had become a mere 'mantra' in professional training and development programmes. As she pointed out, Eraut (1995) had already developed an extended critique of Schön's work while Furlong (1995) had argued that it legitimised the removal of theory from teacher education and its replacement with personal reflection. Ecclestone (1996: 154) was particularly concerned about the inculcation by reflective practice of 'unintended apolitical introversion', endorsing Clark's view that:

> *by urging teachers to focus mainly on their inner lives, we draw their attention away* from the larger, collective, external forces and entities that may be manipulating and controlling them and the entire system of education.
>
> (Clark 1986: 8, my emphasis)

Brookfield, too, was concerned about the lack of 'a certain critical "edge"' in reflective practice, noting:

> The terms *reflection* and *reflective practice* are now so overused that they are in danger of becoming buzzwords denuded of any real meaning – of taking on the status of premature ultimates, like *motherhood* and *democracy*. A premature ultimate is a concept that, once it is invoked, stops any critical debate dead in its tracks.
>
> (Brookfield 1995: 216, original emphasis)

Arguing the case for *critical* reflective practice in teaching and teacher education, Brookfield (1995: 217–18) claimed that 'reflection in and of itself is not enough; it must always be linked to how the world can be changed'. He cited Gitlin and Smyth, who argued that:

> Because most teachers do not have the opportunity to reflect critically on practice *with others*, the inadequacy [of] those practices often remains hidden, and analysis remains fixated at the level of attending to technical problems. Moral, ethical and political issues that may be the cause for alarm often remain invisible or impenetrable to the teacher.
>
> (Gitlin and Smyth 1989: 6, my emphasis)

There are two particular notions highlighted in the texts I have just cited that I will take up again later in the context of spirituality: first, that a focus on 'inner lives' may be problematic; second, that reflection 'with others' is significant.

Guidelines

As will be evident, most of the texts cited above post-date the development of our 'Becoming a Reflective Practitioner' module. Back in 1994, those of us working on it were in fairly blissful ignorance of the thundering of the bandwagon we had inadvertently stepped onto, and of the gathering critique that was about to be aimed at it. Having begun our discussions in May, our greatest concern was simply to get the module up and running by September – which included being clear about how it was to be assessed.

For my nursing colleagues, reflective practice was already a required element of their clinical work. They stressed the importance of having a common framework and clear guidelines for reflection on 'critical incidents'. However, wanting to get away from the idea that a crisis was a necessary preliminary to reflection, we agreed on a four-stage process, adapted from Flanagan (1954) and Benner (1984), to enable students to select, record and reflect upon what we called 'practitioner incidents'. Students would be required to submit 'rough' written accounts of three of these for formative comment before preparing a final 'polished' piece for assessment, together with an overview of learning points extracted from reflection on all three incidents.

The guidelines devised to frame this writing remained largely unchanged throughout the subsequent life of the module (a further ten years). In a slightly amended and more alliterative form, they currently appear in a popular textbook on human-resource development where four headings are recommended: Process (describe what happened; make judgements; analyse); Personalise (use personal rather than general statements, e.g. instead of 'It was good/bad' write 'What I understood/felt irritable about/enjoyed etc. was … '); Probe (instead of settling for a statement of how things seemed to be, ask questions like 'Why did that annoy me so much?'); and Plan (from the previous statements, begin to identify favoured learning techniques, 'hang ups', responses etc. and, focusing on one feature at a time, make plans for the future, including appropriate adjustments to practice) (see Hunt 2005: 248–49). This step-by-step structure represents a fairly standard approach to written forms of reflection in professional learning settings, where the desired outcome is usually some form of change that will enhance practice and/or learning. However, I now recognise that, because of my own orientation to reflective practice (to which I will return in the next section), these particular guidelines are heavily biased towards understanding personal meaning making and action rather than effecting change in organisational or political structures.

The original version of the guidelines contained an additional step which I continue to regard as vital in the context of a Masters degree programme: 'Illuminating the incident through appropriate academic literature'. However, we debated at length the appropriateness of this step. For one colleague, who was also a practising counsellor, the implication that the meaning and interpretation of a personal experience would be more 'valid' if it could be 'illuminated' by concepts embodied in academic literature sat very uncomfortably with a firmly held belief that people should be encouraged to value their own experiences and interpretations of them, and not made to feel that these are better or worse by virtue of their similarity to those of someone else. For another, whose background was in the natural sciences, the notion of 'validating' the interpretation of a personal experience against those of other people was crucial to his world view and self-concept. The debate was never fully resolved, but it made us very sensitive to the differences in our own backgrounds and world views and to the impact these were likely to have on our interactions with students (Hunt 2001a: 279).

It was nearly a year after the first pilot run of the module before I encountered Brookfield's (1995: 29) model of four different lenses through which to view practice: '(1) our autobiographies as teachers and learners, (2) our students' eyes, (3) our colleagues' experiences, and (4) theoretical literature'. It helped to illuminate the debate we had had about this very concept. Thus, in a subsequent review of Brookfield's book, I wrote:

> Is it in the nature of reflective practice that one goes through what seems to be an enormous struggle in uncharted territory in order to identify and name assumptions and patterns that shape one's work – only to find that someone else has already been there, done that *and* prepared a map? ... To come across Brookfield's beautifully signposted map of this whole territory after we had crossed it was somewhat galling! It was, nevertheless, wonderfully affirming that, albeit by a different route, we had reached the same viewpoint: 'Theory can help us "name" our practice by illuminating the general elements of what we think are idiosyncratic experiences' (p. 36).
>
> (Hunt 1996: 300–301)

As I have indicated, I first got involved *in* reflective practice for pragmatic reasons and encountered literature *about* it sometime later. Accessing theory – whether relating to reflective practice or anything else – in order to shed new light on, and to help me to 'name', what I know has now become a significant feature of my own learning. However, in terms of what it means to be a 'reflective practitioner', it is the practical rather than theoretical aspects of the question that have continued to hold the greater significance and interest for me. I sensed in the early discussions of the MEd tutors that the personal 'struggle in uncharted territory' that is often involved in getting to grips with one's own thoughts and feelings, whether about professional practice or life in general, represents a different kind of engagement with knowledge from that involved in much intellectual debate.

As Bernstein (1977: 7) put it, 'It is very rare to have an intellectual dialogue which is not at some point transformed into symbolic cannibalism; my formulation can eat up yours.' That is, in a sense, the academic game. By contrast, the 'embodied'[2] knowledge generated through personal struggle can result in what Willis (2004: 324) calls 'unitary transformation' whereby 'a person works to define and enrich her or his authentic "inner self"'. In this situation, the boundaries between what might be defined as 'reflective practice', 'professional learning' or 'lifelong learning' become somewhat fuzzy.

Ultimately, of course, whether we know something because of a structured process of reflection or because we discussed or worked with an issue in a professional or a personal context does not really affect the knowledge itself. Nevertheless, the context in which we give voice to that knowledge and, especially, how the context influences what it is possible to say and do, is highly significant.

I want to suggest that, while guidelines for reflection – through writing or other means – may help professionals to focus upon aspects of their everyday practice and whether changes might be desirable, there seems to be a growing need not for more such frameworks but for 'unfettered spaces' – spaces in which professionals feel it is safe to explore, with others, their 'inner self' as well as their professional role.

In her chapter, Hargreaves argues that nurses 'need to have a much clearer vision of what they want nursing to be and to have realistic expectations of the extent to which this threatens the central discourses that control them'. I sense that the exploration and articulation of a shared vision, and its connection with personal, professional and political values and related discourses, can best be facilitated in the kinds of 'unfettered spaces' to which I have referred – and which I saw in operation within a recent series of seminars. In my view, such exploration is associated with spirituality.

I am aware that, for many people, 'spirituality' is an uncomfortable concept but, in the next section, I hope both to locate and 'legitimise' its place within reflective practice as well as to illustrate how and why spirituality has featured in my own learning journey. After that I will return to the seminar series and the notion of unfettered spaces.

Orientations

Theory

Building on the work of Habermas (1974), Van Manen (1977) and Grimmett et al. (1990), as well as on their own extensive analysis of the literature on reflective practice and 'hundreds of journal entries written by practising teachers', Wellington and Austin (1996: 307) propose that, within the field of education, there are five different orientations to reflective practice: immediate, technical, deliberative, dialectic and transpersonal. These can be represented as end points on a three-stage decision pathway on which the key questions are: (1) Does the practitioner engage in reflective practice or not? (2) Does the practitioner believe that education ought to be domesticating or liberating? and (3) Is the practitioner systems-oriented or people-oriented?

The first question determines whether the practitioner is conscious of using reflection in their practice. If they are not, the pathway leads directly to the 'immediate' orientation which 'places emphasis on pleasant survival' (op.cit.: 309). For those who do engage in reflective practice, the second question determines how they conceive of education and the relationship between individuals and society. Practitioners holding a 'domesticating' view believe it is appropriate for a dominant culture to replicate itself through education: depending on their answer to the third question, the end point of the pathway will suggest they have a 'technical' or 'deliberative' orientation. Practitioners holding a 'liberating' view regard education as a tool for personal and/or social transformation: answers to question three will suggest either a 'dialectic' or 'transpersonal' orientation. The purpose of question three is to determine whether the practitioner's values and interests are associated more with organisational structures or with personal meaning making.

Wellington and Austin (1996: 314) argue that these orientations do not represent a 'simple classification scheme designed to pigeonhole people and practices', nor are they hierarchical. Rather, they are intended to facilitate understanding of different points of view, thereby enabling practitioners to identify their own predominant mode of reflection and practice; to respect the modes in which others prefer to work; and to re-view personal values and beliefs and professional practices in the light of others. Figure 1 draws on Wellington and Austin's text to represent key elements of each orientation in diagrammatic form.

Practice

I first came across Wellington and Austin's work when I was in the final stages of writing a PhD thesis that had been many years in gestation. Although the thesis was rooted in the practicalities of a large action-research project in community education that I had facilitated, it had long since strayed into a more theoretical exploration of 'community'. This is one of relatively few English words that does not seem to have an opposing term: I felt this might be because, deep within the human psyche, it is associated with a sense of 'oneness'. From that perspective, I had tentatively begun to engage with the notion of spirituality – but met with enormous resistance from my then supervisor. His implicit message seemed to be that 'spirituality', especially a personal exploration of it, was not an appropriate topic for study within an academic thesis on community education (Hunt 2001b).

For some considerable time, I had accepted the message and virtually abandoned both exploration and thesis. Finding Wellington and Austin's account of what it means to have a 'transpersonal orientation' was part of a sequence of events which encouraged me to re-engage with the thesis. They note that practitioners with this orientation:

> Tend to be inner-directed and to focus on self-development and on the relationship of internal to external. They question educational ends, content and means from a personal, inner perspective. Their pedagogy is typically individualised and holistic. ... Artefacts [reflective journals, stories of experience etc.] reflecting the transpersonal orientation are introspective and often highly personal. They contemplate questions such as: 'how can I integrate my personal/spiritual growth with my vocation?' ... In this perspective, knowledge is subjective and internal. The validity of research findings relies on resonance with experience.
>
> (Wellington and Austin 1996: 311)

Figure 1 Orientations to reflective practice (quotations all drawn from Wellington and Austin 1996).

View of education	Domesticating	Domesticating	Liberating	Liberating
Systems/people orientation	Systems	People	Systems	People
Orientation to reflective practice	'Technical'	'Deliberative'	'Dialectic'	'Transpersonal'
Manifestation in educational practice	'Build educational structures and employ instructional methodologies designed to efficiently and effectively achieve predetermined ends'	'Create environments and employ methodologies that help individuals find meaning and success within existing educational establishments'	'Build coalitions which promote political empowerment and social equity'	'Promote the personal and holistic development of individuals in a context that extends beyond the existing educational establishment'
Characteristics	Likely to 'accept institutionally determined educational content and ends'. *Asks questions like*: How can I achieve my goals for students most efficiently? What are the most efficient and effective teaching techniques I can use to transmit information to my students?	Likely to 'accept given educational ends but may negotiate with authorities for changes in academic content'. *Asks questions like*: How can I make learning meaningful and relevant to my students? What meanings are embedded in student behaviours? How can deeper communication with students enhance meaningful learning?	Likely to 'question educational ends, content and means {...} to be outer-directed and to focus on political and social issues'. *Asks questions like*: In what ways do institutions replicate the status quo? How can we redesign institutions on more democratic principles? How can I help students to liberate themselves from cultural oppression?	Likely to 'question educational ends, content and means from a personal, inner perspective.' *Asks questions like*: How can I integrate my personal and spiritual growth with my vocation? What is my personal responsibility to myself and others?
Key words Focus (applicable to most professions)	Efficiency/ effectiveness *of the* work context	Self-development of the individual *within* the work context	Empowerment of the individual leading to *change* in the work context	Integration of individual's subjective/ objective (inner/ outer) experiences *beyond* the work context

I read this account with great glee! Not only did it give a name to the way in which I had worked on the thesis but I felt it 'legitimised' my interests. In Brookfield's (1995: 36) terms it illuminated for me 'the general elements of what we think are idiosyncratic experiences' and signified that, despite the view of one academic gatekeeper, other people shared, and were likely to be accepting of, my approach and topic.

Additionally, I found the notion of different orientations enormously helpful in understanding where my students were 'coming from' in their selection of, and reflections on, their 'practitioner incidents'. It also helped me to make sense of differences of approach within the MEd tutor group and within the wider body of literature on reflective practice. Although Wellington and Austin's model is rooted in teacher-education and social-science research, I sense from working on reflective practice with doctors, nurses and other health and social-care professionals that it also has resonances within these professions. In the bottom line of Figure 1, I have incorporated the key words and foci that seem to be applicable in a range of work contexts.

Interestingly, however, while efficiency, self-development and empowerment are familiar and usually legitimate aims within many work contexts, the notion of integration – whereby the links between an individual's 'inner life', including their spirituality, and the enactment of their working life are made explicit – is much less common. Indeed, simply within the literature on reflective practice cited in this chapter, there is a strong implication that a focus on an inner life might occur *at the expense of* more 'important' activities in the workplace rather than alongside them. I think this is why holding and, perhaps more significantly, giving voice in professional contexts to a transpersonal orientation often feels like taking a defensive position. Nevertheless, the time may now be right to redress the balance so that the notion of 'integration' becomes a more familiar and acceptable element of reflective practice and professional development. It is arguable that already:

> [A] Grassroots Spirituality Movement is attempting to integrate consciousness, soul and spirit into our societal dialogues. Slowly it is weaving these into our understandings of the nature and purpose of life and reality, into our workday and family lives, into our global politics, and into our future.
>
> (Forman 2004: 4)

Time for integration?

Seminar series

If the so-called 'Grassroots Spirituality Movement' is no more than another bandwagon, then at least this time I am aware of climbing onto it. In 2003,

I received funding from the Economic and Social Research Council (ESRC) to convene a seminar series entitled 'Researching Spirituality as a Dimension of Lifelong Learning'. The following is an abbreviated version of the introductory paragraph of the proposal (in the interests of space, supporting references have been removed unless they are linked to direct quotations).[3]

> Spirituality is a highly contested concept but we start from the view that: 'Human beings are essentially spiritual creatures because we are driven by a need to ask "fundamental" or "ultimate" questions ... to find meaning and value in what we do and experience' (Zohar and Marshall, 2000: 4). We also associate spirituality with the capacity to be fully alive and connected to every aspect of existence, including interpersonal relationships, psychological processes and the global environment. Some people seek guidance and resolution in such matters using religious teachings and traditions; others within a humanistic framework that is often shaped by principles of social justice (e.g. Van Ness [1996] refers to 'secular', and Berry [1988] to 'public' [action-oriented] spirituality). Some may reject the language of spirituality altogether but espouse what might nevertheless be called 'spiritual values' in their lives and work through their commitment to others (e.g. English, 2000: 30 refers to 'care, concern and outreach to others [as] integral aspects of authentic spirituality').

The series spanned two years and incorporated six open meetings in which, overall, there were more than 200 participants; and five closed meetings of the core group of seven members in which we took a cooperative-inquiry approach to the exploration of our own understandings of spirituality and the issues arising from the seminars. Throughout the series, we sought to ground discussion in participants' own experiences and not to get immersed in a purely intellectual debate about definitions of spirituality (Hunt and West 2006).

I have selected the following comments because they are not only fairly typical of the discussions and subsequent feedback but they touch on a key issue raised by the seminars: the relationship between academic/professional knowledge and something 'deeper'.

> I often interact with robots and, frequently, I am a robot myself. And until now, I hadn't even noticed. For most of today, though, I was real. It felt good, and I liked myself. I felt as if I was floating. Most days I feel as if I am walking uphill, but today I was floating. I was simply being and simply seeing, rather than trying, doing, thinking and judging.
>
> (Feedback: PhD student, February 2005)

> I left feeling very excited that I'd found a way to unite all parts of myself and my work. I discovered that the connection was 'me'! I also left

feeling inspired to draw explicitly upon my spirituality in my teaching and my research, rather than to hide it as something not 'valid' in academic/ professional space. Hearing from other people who are doing similar has definitely increased my knowledge and confidence.

(Feedback: University teaching fellow, February 2005)

Suddenly all the bits of my life are together in one meeting.

(Comment in plenary session, February 2006)

We need more spaces like this where people can be open and honest, touch deeper levels.

(Comment in plenary session, April, 2005)

How do we re-establish contact with deeper levels of what it means to be a professional – express a 'calling' and connection with what it means to be human?

(Feedback: College lecturer, July 2004).

Such comments give a clear sense of the fragmentation that many people feel in their lives, and of a yearning to bring 'all the bits' together and to access some deeper meaning: in other words, to seek integration. Because the seminars were explicitly about 'researching spirituality', it is likely that many participants already had an 'orientation' towards doing this. Nevertheless, as several pointed out, acknowledgement of 'deep' issues is rarely present or encouraged in most professional contexts, though they felt it would be welcomed. Participants used words like 'nourishing', 'inspiring' and 'energising' to describe the seminars, often remarking upon how refreshingly different the meetings had been from those at work. For example:

I left feeling amazed and inspired by the way people treated one another – the respect and valuing of one another which is a contrast to daily organisational life. I welcomed the opportunity to be in that environment.

(Feedback: University lecturer, June 2005)

It has been very energising – most research and professional development is not about that deeper sense-making process.

(Comment in plenary session, November, 2005)

The question arises, therefore, of where and how such nourishment, inspiration, energy or refreshment – and a sense of integration – might be found within professional environments. I think this takes us beyond the boundaries of conventional frameworks for reflective practice and professional learning – and, as I noted earlier, I will leave open the question of whether or not this may be desirable, though I will make my own position clear in my conclusion.

Reflections

In the final core-group meeting of the series, we explored what we felt had been particular about the nature of the Researching Spirituality seminars. We acknowledged that the content had been rich, raising numerous issues about political and personal understandings of spirituality. However, the *process* had been even more significant. We had consciously tried to make the process of each seminar congruent with our own understanding of spirituality as something to do with 'interconnectedness and community', 'a search for meaning' and 'situated experience'; and, in our facilitation of discussions, we had deliberately drawn on knowledge within the core group of transpersonal psychology, auto/biographical research and the processes of storytelling.

We saw the seminars as 'unfettered spaces' in which participants had been free to re-view and, if they wished, share their own embodied knowledge; and, with others, to co-create new meanings. The only boundaries had been those of mutual respect, which included attentive listening. In essence, the seminars seemed not just to have been about 'researching spiritu*ality*' but 'researching spiritu*ally*' (Hunt and West 2007: 301–6).

In terms of academic theory, Heron's (1996) concepts of cooperative inquiry and 'levels of knowing' had been especially important in shaping this process. The former because 'It sees inquiry as an intersubjective space, a common culture, in which the use of language is grounded in a deep context of non-linguistic meanings, the lifeworld of shared experience' (Heron 1996: 11); the latter because it actually gave us a language with which to refer to 'non-linguistic' understandings. It enabled us to admit into discussion, and to explore, what Heron calls 'experiential' and 'presentational' knowledge – knowledge embedded (or embodied) in sensory perception and in imagery.

Also significant in shaping, and subsequently in trying to understand what had taken place within the seminars, was the notion of *mythopoesis* (Macdonald 1981). This refers to a process of sense making by which individuals come to know their world and their relationship with it through myths and images. As Bradbeer argues in the context of teacher education, we feel it was important for participants to be regarded:

> as a consciousness rather than an informed intellect – ... as a person consciously and deeply within the myths and narratives of his or her own world both as a person and a worker ... [who] attends to, or listens to, the intangible fabric of his or her own experience of life.
>
> (Bradbeer, 1998: 47–48)

Evidence from the seminars suggests that the approach suggested above would also be welcomed in workplace contexts. There would seem to be a real need for opportunities in professional settings where practitioners can feel free to share and reflect with others not only on the how and why of practice situations, but on the myths, narratives, life experiences and ultimate questions that are integral to the 'intangible fabric' of being human as well as a professional. Indeed, there is a strong argument in the emerging field of consciousness studies that the mutual examination of the metaphysical premises that sustain our life-worlds is integral to the creation of a more peaceful and sustainable world (see Laszlo 2003, especially 46–48)

Conclusion

In keeping with my understanding of what it means to be a reflective practitioner, I have drawn heavily throughout this chapter on aspects of my own learning journey. I have highlighted events and readings that led me from the relatively calm waters of curriculum development in Masters degree programmes, onto the 'bandwagon' of reflective practice, through personal struggles with meaning making, and into the realm of spirituality. Because this journey is now part of my embodied experience, it is almost impossible for me to see its elements as separate, so, in my eyes, questions about reflective practice lead seamlessly into those about spirituality – and, especially, about what it means to research/work spirit*ually*.

In the current climate of much professional education where written action plans, audit trails and ticked boxes are common requirements, I am aware that to speak of spirit and/or to advocate an appreciation of *mythopoesis* and intersubjective inquiry as an element of reflective practice may well seem a step too far. Nevertheless, I believe, as the opening quotations to this chapter suggest, that it is not really necessary to 'step' anywhere – but simply to look at the landscape, and the potential, of reflective practice with new eyes.

Acknowledgements

My thanks to the colleagues and students who worked on the Becoming a Reflective Practitioner module, and to the core group and all the participants in the ESRC seminar series Researching Spirituality as a Dimension of Lifelong Learning (ESRC grant no. RES-451-26-0008), for helping me to explore the landscape of reflective practice and to see it differently.

Notes

1 In Burdell and Swadener's (1999: 22) terms, autoethnography is 'a form of self-narrative that places the self within a social context. It is both a method and a text.' I am only too well aware of arguments which suggest that both autoethnography and reflective practice, especially of the type I am advocating here, are nothing more than an indulgent form of navel gazing. Nevertheless, I continue to be attracted to Stenhouse's (1980) vision of 'systematic inquiry made public' (be it through case study, autoethnography, reflective practice or other means) as a vital means of acquiring deeper understanding, individually

and collectively. Knights et al. advocate a similar view in their chapter, citing work by Crow and Smith (2005: 493) which demonstrates how 'opening up one's reflections to public scrutiny' can create 'an ideal forum for collaborative learning'.

2 Davies (2004: 4) notes that feminist post-structuralist theory now 'enables a different sense of what is knowable, and what can be done with that knowledge'; writing in this context can 'reveal a certain clarity that comes with specificity, with the insistence on an embodied (rather than abstract) knowledge of that which is written about, and with the refusal to run away from ambivalence and ambiguity'. Todres (2007) explores the theory and practice of embodied enquiry, particularly in the contexts of phenomenological research, psychotherapy and spirituality.

3 The full text is available at www.education.ex.ac.uk/research/documents/ESRCSeminarSeries_info.doc. [Accessed 21 March 2008.]

Chapter 13

Developing critical reflection within an inter-professional learning programme

Kate Karban and Sue Smith

Introduction

The imperative for 'joined-up working' in health and social care is fundamental to the 'modernisation' agenda for health and social-care policy in the UK (Department of Health 2000a) and has led to the need to promote skills and knowledge for inter-professional practice at all stages of professional education and training (Barr 1998). A wide range of approaches to developing inter-professional practice can be identified involving practice based and 'formal' education opportunities at all stages of the professional development continuum. Within preregistration education the majority of these incorporate inter-professional learning as one component of the overall curriculum alongside a primarily uniprofessional approach.

Reflective practice, traditionally viewed as underpinning the core uniprofessional curriculum has tended to remain a uniprofessional activity. However, this chapter will analyse the relevance of models of reflective practice as they relate to inter-professional learning, recognising the need to facilitate and integrate reflection on the process of learning with the practice of inter-professional working by exploring some of the wider issues concerning identity, communities of practice and managing boundaries. In particular, attention will be drawn to the nature of learning as a social and participatory activity founded on dialogue, thereby endorsing the nature of education as negotiated meaning rather than information transmission.

The central importance of the service-user perspective and experience in the approach of the inter-professional team will be emphasised, linked to the need for a holistic and multifaceted model for understanding issues of health and welfare. This in turn will be placed in the wider context of issues of power and inequality, diversity and inclusion, manifest in the public-health agenda that increasingly influences the planning, organisation and delivery of health and social-care services in Britain.

The changing landscape of health and social care

Health and social care is characterised by rapid policy and organisational change, some of which reflect deeper-seated and longer-running themes. Within the past twenty-five years there has been a move from institutional to community care and, more recently, an increasing role for primary care in the commissioning of services with a mixed economy of care including the growing influence of the private sector. The public-involvement agenda, recognising the need to involve the service users and carers, and the role in shaping services and in determining the type of care and treatment available, as well as the recognition of the service user as the 'expert' in their own care has also emerged (HM Government 2007b). A key strand within this changing landscape is also the recognition that the role and contribution of traditional professional groups is undergoing a significant transformation. Whilst elements of this can be seen as a response to feedback from users and carers, based on their experiences, and public concern regarding the lack of coordination of services, often in response to high profile events, these changes can also be seen to reflect other changes including economic constraints, the need for a more flexible workforce and a challenge to the traditional power associated with the professions.

Firstly, a challenge to what was traditionally seen as the expertise, authority and role of traditional professional groups, leading to the curtailment of the traditional expectations can be found in the public scrutiny of the medical profession leading to a less unquestioning approach to the power of doctors and concerns regarding the behaviour of individual practitioners, following the Shipman Inquiry and the report of the Royal Liverpool Children's Inquiry (Redfern 2001; Smith 2002).

Secondly, the roles and tasks associated with various professional groups can also be seen to be changing, with increasing numbers of nurse practitioners and consultants as well as other senior practitioners such as physiotherapists taking on tasks such as referral for specialist services and being trained to undertake non-medical prescribing, with corresponding changes in the traditional role of doctors. Changes to the mental-health legislation as set out in the Mental Health Act 2007 (HM Government 2007a) and the creation of the new role of the Approved Mental Health Professional, including other mental-health professionals alongside social workers (previously the sole incumbents of the role of the approved social worker in making applications for hospital admissions) also highlight changing roles and expectations. The increase in the number of support workers, assistant practitioners and others in many areas of health and social care has also been interpreted as a move towards 'deprofessionalisation' with a consequent eye on cheaper services and a training agenda focused on competences rather than years of professional training.

Thirdly, the increasing recognition of the contribution of service users and carers in many and various aspects of care and treatment delivery can be seen as a challenge to a definition of professionalism that was premised on a form of benign paternalism summed up as 'doctor knows best'. As Hugman has suggested:

> The very existence of occupations which make claims to expertise in areas of health and welfare may be said to have been founded on the exclusion of users from the definition of need or appropriate responses to its remedy.
>
> (1998: 137)

A final point concerning what it means to be a professional at the beginning of the twenty-first century can be found in the continuing imperative to 'work together', manifest in a number of different ways and contexts with 'joined-up working' in health and social care viewed as one of the cornerstones of the 'modernisation' agenda in health and social-care policy (Department of Health 2000a). The need for closer working and greater collaboration, coordination and communication between different professional groups has also been highlighted by a number of major inquiries into varying aspects of health and social care, especially child protection and mental health. This is summed up by Margaret Hodge, Minister for Children, in the wake of the inquiry into the death of Victoria Climbié.

> That sort of lack of mutual trust and respect for the different professional backgrounds ... not sharing the same vocabulary and language, certainly not sharing the same sort of understanding of child development and child protection – is an enormous problem. Changing that culture so that people value each other's professional competence and recognise each other's work is a hugely difficult and complex thing to achieve.
>
> (Hodge 2004)

These wider trends influencing the role of the various professional groups involved in health and social care have raised concerns relating to the future of the professions. The nature of training and education for the professions, whether at the preregistration stage or in terms of continuing professional development, is also affected, recognising that students and practitioners will need to tolerate and work with change and uncertainty. At the same time, there is a need to promote skills and knowledge for inter-professional practice at all stages of professional education and training (Barr 1998). This can be seen as requiring the challenging of traditional barriers, compartmentalised thinking and professional 'tribalism' (Carlisle et al. 2004; Smith and Roberts 2005).

Furthermore, in order to work together and to develop interpersonal and team working skills, students will require opportunities to recognise and value the diversity of others' beliefs and prior life and learning experiences.

The recognition of service users as the central focus of this collaborative enterprise is paramount, as is the identification of multiple perspectives, personal and professional, within and outside disciplines. In addition, as the public-health, rather than illness, agenda gathers momentum, it has been suggested that models of health and well-being that acknowledge the impact of inequalities, poverty and oppression will be necessary to provide the raw material for a critical analysis of theory and practice requiring reflexion as well as reflection (Fook 2002).

These changes to the traditional expectations of distinct professions have not been unfolding without, at times vociferous, opposition and an underlying anxiety. The concept of 'role overlap' has been seen as offering a challenge to role security (Booth and Hewison 2002) which, at its extreme, leading to the notion of generic workers, has been met by an increased emphasis on professional uniqueness through role delineation.

Reflective practice

A working definition of reflective practice, for the purpose of this discussion will be based on Clouder's view that:

> In its broadest sense reflective practice involves the critical analysis of everyday working practices to improve competence and promote professional development.
>
> (2000: 211)

Within this general meaning, reflective practice is accepted as being a key component of professional education and practice in health and social care, adopted by traditional models of professional education as a fundamental foundation of professional development, essential for the integration of theory and practice. However such approaches have tended to be located within uniprofessional frameworks, albeit drawing on some key theoretical underpinnings. Additionally, whilst the notion of reflective practice is almost universally agreed to be a 'good thing', it has been suggested that reflective practice has taken on a 'common-sense' meaning, 'used in common-sense terms rather than with reference to the literature' (Dyke 2006: 115). In reality, variations in meaning and practice within and between professions have the potential to obfuscate rather than promote effective communication and sharing of thinking and practice.

Within the uniprofessional context, the main reference points appear to be educational models of reflection, originating with Dewey (1933) and further developments highlighting the importance of experiential learning, for example, Kolb's (1984) experiential learning cycle. Schön's (1983) model of reflective practice, frequently cited within professional education, highlighted the need to negotiate the theory–practice gap in dealing with 'messy' problems and the distinction between 'reflection-in-action' and 'reflection-on-action'. The application of Schön's model has, however, been seen as limited, particularly in terms of the context for learning within which he was located (Kember 2001). Other models are viewed as more profession specific, including, for example, Johns (1988) and Gibbs (1988) for nursing and allied health professions and parallel developments found in social work (Yelloly and Henkel 1995; Gould and Taylor 1996). The extent to which the emotional or affective component of reflection is acknowledged within these models is variable, despite this being originally acknowledged as important by Dewey (1933) and more recently by Boud et al. (1993).

There are a number of limitations and critiques that have been offered concerning many of these models of reflective practice. In particular three concerns will be examined here. The first is that reflective practice does not necessarily result in reflexive practice, that is, in putting oneself into the picture. The second is that reflective practice may fail to take account of wider social relations, including dimensions of power and also inequalities that may be significant influences in the overall picture. A third issue concerns the extent to which reflection itself is an individual activity.

Reflexivity is frequently confused with reflection although some would argue that the two are inextricably linked. Payne explains this by referring to the process of circularity whereby the process of reflection itself influences future action in an ongoing feedback mechanism.

> Reflexivity means that we constantly get evidence about how effective or worthwhile our actions are, and we can change what we are doing according to the evidence of its value. To do so, of course, requires being reflective.
>
> (Payne 2002: 127)

In comparing this to Clouder's definition of reflective practice above, it can be seen that the purpose of reflection in order to 'improve competence' would suggest that the two are inseparable. This point is also made by Fook (2002), who comments that although the notions of reflection and reflexion may have different origins, they are not mutually exclusive and that the process of the former may assist the latter.

A further dimension, however, concerns the extent to which the presence and action of the practitioner in the practice is also included in the reflection, including not only the emotional component but also wider issues of power which may be present in any communication, whether that be related to the role and professional status of the practitioner vis-à-vis the service user or to the personal components of this relating to issues such as gender, ethnicity and age. Ghaye (2005) suggests that a review of models of reflection suggests that an emphasis on self-reflection may frequently be limited and fails to broaden the lens to take into account wider issues of power and inequality, to move beyond technical rationalism and remains at the individual level rather than being embedded within relational notions of dialogue both within teams and across professions. For example, Donaghy and Moss (2000) propose a framework based on systematic critical inquiry, deliberately eschewing reflection on beliefs and attitudes and focusing on the examination of the patient and the clinical reasoning process through the use of personal reflective accounts.

The work of Ghaye (2005) moves the discussion further into the realm of critical reflection which has been seen by Fook (2002) as linking a reflective approach with a critical analysis. Fook (2004) also proposes that critical reflection can be of value in the analysis and making sense of power relationships within organisational structures, a dimension seen as lacking in the work of Kolb and Schön (Fook and Napier 2000) Such an understanding of power and power structures offers the potential for a transformational approach, allied to the concept of perspective transformation (Mezirow 1991) and the development of *critical consciousness* (Freire 1972). Linked to this is the contribution of critical theory in recognising and making visible systems and structures of power. In particular, Barnett (1997) draws on critical theory in bringing together three domains of critical practice comprising critical analysis, critical reflexivity and critical action, whilst Fook refers to the potential of critical reflection for 'emancipatory practices' (2002: 41).

The need to reflect on issues of power and inequality encountered within professional practice may also require students to develop their own self-awareness, drawing on critical theory and post-structuralism. From such a position, Foucault's (1980) analysis of power as a dynamic force operating from the grass roots rather than top down draws attention to multi-directional power relations within groups. Such a perspective, informed by notions of discourse and deconstruction can be seen to contribute to conceptual frameworks for critical reflection on practice in relation to the complex power relationships between practitioners and service users and between practitioners within the multi-professional team. Ghaye (2005) links this to critical action, referring to 'a team's capacity to see themselves in new ways and to do different things' (2005: 24), inherently requiring a political dimension involving influencing empowerment and change at both the individual and team level.

Drawing on such an approach, Heron (2005) highlights the distinction between social location and subject position in discussing how wider socio-economic structures produce personal troubles, a premise clearly in line with today's public-health agenda in which issues of inequality and social exclusion are seen to represent strong influences on health and access to health care. She argues that 'admitting one's privilege does not necessarily unsettle its operation' (2005: 344) and that for those on the other side of the privilege coin, the citing of privilege by those in dominance amounts, however inadvertently, to a re-inscription of marginalisation.

Finally, the notion of inter-professional working itself needs to be opened up to the reflective process. Whilst models of reflection continue to be taught only as part of the uniprofessional curriculum, it is possible that professional boundaries and traditionally delineated roles may be re-enforced rather than reduced. In particular, they may encourage the 'othering' of other professions within stereotyped expectations, as individuals reflect on their experiences of colleagues from different backgrounds. Such a process is unlikely to promote questioning and critique of dominant discourses of uni-professionalism. Heron's reference to 'claims of innocence' (2005: 350), whilst made with reference to anti-oppressive, social-work practice, may also apply to inter-professional working and the inter-professional team, requiring that the power relations of inter-professional working are themselves open to question. The conditions for this require that, rather than being understood as an individual activity, reflection should instead be understood, as suggested by Dyke, that 'experiential learning benefits from constructive engagement with the experience and knowledge claims of others' (2006: 112).

It is important to acknowledge, as emphasised by Ruch (2007), however, that the development of reflective practice can meet with both organisational and individual obstacles. Responding to the complexities of inter-professional working in child-care practice, Ruch suggests that the level of anxiety and uncertainty present in this area of work requires the availability of safe spaces for individuals and teams to address the challenges of practice together, and that it is the interdependence of both the individual and the collective conditions that is crucial in promoting holistic reflective practice. A similar point is made by Askeland (2006), who refers to 'risk taking' by tutors in order to promote learning and the development of critical reflection.

Key themes

Having briefly considered some of the issues concerning the relationship of models of reflective practice to inter-professional learning, it is possible to identify a number of key themes which might inform the development of an inter-professional approach to reflection and in turn promote reflection on inter-professional working. These include both the content and the process of reflection, recognising that there is a dynamic, complex and closely inter-woven relationship between these concepts and that each will inform the other. Firstly, the scope and content of the reflection will be discussed, and, secondly, the 'doing' of reflection will be considered with regard to the relevance of concepts of 'dialogue' and 'community', recognising the influence of professional and cultural context within which reflection takes place (Boud and Walker 1998).

As already suggested, reflection needs to move beyond the individual level to include a critical perspective on wider issues beyond that of the individual practitioner, taking into account issues of power and inequality (Ghaye

2005) and the 'impact of the social world' (Dyke 2006: 118). Germane to both are the interpersonal encounters at the heart of health and social care and also wider societal issues that may frame and influence such encounters. With respect to the former, an acknowledgement of both social position and location (Heron 2005) may shed light on the unique dynamics of any inter-action, whether that be between practitioners or with service users, recog-nising that factors such as race, age, class and gender may be influential in determining the level of ease or discomfort as well as effectiveness in such an encounter. Additionally, the requirement to promote health and well-being as well as to 'treat' illness or alleviate adversity, of necessity requires a broader lens to take into account issues such as nutrition and exercise, the impact of stress relating to, for example, social exclusion, poverty or home-lessness, and the consequences of such factors in determining access to and engagement with health and social-care services.

In addition to this increasing complexity, engendered by the 'public-health' agenda and the central importance of the user experience, practitioners are faced with yet another challenge in both working in and reflecting on the inter-professional team. This requires that practitioners are familiar and comfortable with wider issues than simply a level of technical knowledge and skill, and can locate themselves and their practice within the political, social and economic world.

The process of reflection associated with this needs to move beyond the individual and is informed by Ghaye's (2005) notion of dialogue both within teams and across professions, a concept that Mezirow (1991) also refers to as leading to perspective transformation. Tsang (2007) also refers to dialogue as being both internal and external, drawing attention to the work of Burbules (1993) to emphasise that power differences need to be acknowledged and that dialogue between individuals must be supported by mutual respect and commitment to the process.

Such communication within and between teams also needs to be premised on a shared language as a means of overcoming the cultural and language differences that Wenger et al. (2002) describes as existing between groups. Similarly, with reference to the development of critical reflection within human resources development, Corley and Eades (2006) refer to Gewirtz et al.'s (1995) notion of 'bilingualism' involving the negotiation of two or more sets of values and cultures. This would appear to be an important component of inter-professional practice in managing differences of language and dis-course within and between professionals and of service users and carers. The development of such a shared language would seem to underpin the devel-opment of an 'expert team', rather than a 'team of experts' (Engelstrom 2004), and which, for example, Bleakley et al. (2006) draw on in their investigation of team work amongst operating-theatre staff, where authentic collaboration involving considered communication, debate and feedback and reflection on practice is viewed as essential.

In considering the concept of 'communities of practice', Wenger (1998) identifies some issues that are pertinent to the concept of inter-professional working and learning. In particular he refers to the nexus of multi-membership defined as the 'living experience of boundaries and that it involves "creating bridges across the landscape of practice"' (1998: 158–59).

In this sense, professional identity entails both an experience of multi-membership and the work of reconciliation to maintain identity across boundaries, all of which would be relevant to the experience of inter-professional learning when students frequently question whether the uniprofessional or the multi-professional team is their primary allegiance. The notion of 'community' as the basis from which practitioners share experience and learn together is also highlighted by Dyke as providing 'a means whereby practitioners can share experience and learn from each other' (Dyke 2006: 113), a point echoed by Mallinson et al. (2006) with reference to public health and multidisciplinary working across organisational boundaries. Developing a professional identity and learning to work as a member of an inter-professional team is therefore a dynamic process involving 'multi-membership' and communication within an inter-professional community, fostered by learning together in which 'building social relationships' becomes the very 'enterprise of a community' (Wenger 1998: 269).

These strands need to be embedded within shared frameworks for practice and learning, influencing both the process and content of reflection. Together with notions of dialogue and community, these will inform an approach to promote the development of critically reflective practitioners, able to communicate and work together. A shared approach to facilitate reflection on and in practice will also require a rethinking of traditional and uniprofessional approaches to reflection in order that practitioners can engage in shared, critical reflective practice. In many respects, given the various histories, philosophies and theoretical frameworks of the various professions in health and social care, this may be an ambitious agenda. However, the potential for embedding news ways of thinking and working at an early stage of professional education and development will be discussed further. An important aspect of this discussion also concerns the support and development needs of tutors involved in delivering the inter-professional learning programme, and their capacity to endorse and promote the process of critical reflection, recognising the needs of both tutors and students for safe spaces in which to explore shared issues.

Embedding critical reflection in inter-professional learning

Previous practice in promoting inter-professional learning within the faculty of health in one English university brought students together in a range of workshops at various points in their preregistration training. Whilst successful in a number of areas, the programme lacked overall integration and coherence, and its 'bolt-on' approach had the potential to lessen its value from a student perspective. Reorganisation within the faculty and a re-prioritisation of inter-professional learning as an essential and intrinsic element of the student's pre-professional experience led to a revised approach, embedded more explicitly within each professional group's curriculum and assessment strategy.

A key element of the revised programme is that multi-professional workshops involving nurses, social workers, dieticians, speech and language therapists, physiotherapists and occupational therapists are supported by small multi-professional groups of students who will meet regularly during the year to provide opportunities for students to reflect on the issues associated with working together within and across boundaries. An accompanying workbook provides a focus for the analysis of practice and the process of inter-professional learning. A key aspect of the programme is that inter-professional learning is integrated and embedded throughout the students' journey before, during and following their pre-qualifying education. Whilst the evidence base for inter-professional learning is relatively undeveloped (Freeth et al. 2002), this approach is underpinned by the 'contact' theory (Allport 1954), although it is suggested that this in and of itself may be only a necessary rather than a sufficient condition of success in creating positive working relationships, and that complex social processes and dynamics require further understanding.

Working together, students can begin to develop their capacity for critical reflection, to acknowledge, explore and challenge their own values and assumptions. Challenging the theory–practice gap and promoting praxis will also facilitate critical thinking about the compartmentalisation of different professional disciplines and ways to move beyond the boundaries that both protect and defend traditional professional practices (Holmes 2005), thereby limiting the potential for integrated, creative and, above all, user-centred practice. Within the small multi-professional groups and the workshops, students will have the opportunity to engage in 'situated learning', developing uniprofessional identities as members of inter-professional communities through shared practice, communication and reflection that will mirror the reality of inter-professional practice.

This process needs to be supported and enhanced by appropriate pedagogic approaches that will enable students to develop the capacity to develop multi-memberships, to form their own 'communities of practice' and to learn together. Strategies that will promote critical reflection and dialogue will need to move beyond the notion of reflective accounts and journals, although these may be a valuable part of the process. For example, as students progress in their education, the use of 'real' case material from practice, narratives (Blickem and Priyadharshini 2007), critical-incident analysis and frameworks such as the questions posed by Tate (2004) or Fook (2002) may be introduced to promote the critical discussion of wide-ranging issues from a macro perspective. These are incorporated into the student workbooks that accompany the students at each stage of their learning.

The workbooks themselves are structured around key themes including reflection, team working, ethics and values and the assessment experience of service users, with each area being introduced with associated material and exercises at the first stage, normally corresponding to the first year of the preregistration programme. The second and third stages will revisit each theme with the increasing levels of complexity and criticality required as students increase their practice experience and gain confidence in working together. This may take the form of being joined by additional professional groups or working in various teams and roles as well as increasingly complex case scenarios (D'eon 2005). The use of the workbook, to be assessed at the end of the year, will also offer an opportunity for cooperative learning and enterprise as a record of a shared journey, reflecting the experience of a multi-professional team in practice.

An essential component is also to ensure that the perspectives of service users and carers are central to the process. This will include the involvement of simulated patients in role-play activities and feedback from users and carers at workshops, as well as the involvement of service users and carers in the development of case studies and 'checking' for authenticity. Promoting critical reflection on these encounters will move beyond the individual and their 'diagnosis' towards a wider perspective which will enable students to share and compare their perspectives, locating individuals within wider social and political processes and enhancing their understanding of their own role within these.

Promoting shared learning and adopting a model of critical reflection amongst students also must take into account the needs of those tutors involved as facilitators. The importance of preparing teachers for inter-professional education has been broadly recognised (Barr 2002), although Page and Meerabeau (2004) comment on the lack of attention paid to the experiences of course facilitators within the multi-professional literature. There is, however, a recognition that learning may be enhanced by the way in which the inter-professional team engages in role modelling (Cooper et al. 2004) or 'walking the walk' (Rees and Johnson 2007), whilst Rolls et al. (2002) describe how students may learn by a process of 'osmosis' when exposed to the philosophy and practice of inter-professional education. The notion of a parallel process in which both tutors and students engage in the complex business of working together, recognises that the teaching team itself has also undergone a process of professional 'socialisation' and has experienced, at first hand, the dynamics of team working in practice (Smith and Karban 2006).

This complex mix of educational and professional agendas suggests that tutors will need to engage in their own critical reflection (Brookfield 1995) and to develop approaches based on mutual dialogue (Brockbank and McGill 1998). The need for a high level of engagement between students in inter-professional learning also requires that tutors are supported in taking similar risks and managing the uncertainty of changing roles, drawing on their own experiences, both as practitioners and as educators to facilitate learning. Such a process also requires that tutors move beyond their own professional identities to form new identities and multi-memberships and, as highlighted by Wenger (1998), are able to form their own inter-professional communities of practice where the process and meaning of teaching is valued rather than simply the transmission of information.

Conclusion

Developing a critically reflective approach for inter-professional working offers a significant challenge. An important element of this goal concerns the need to embed learning and the application of learning within the seemingly constantly changing environment of health and social-care services within which the experience of practitioners is that the only certainty is uncertainty, and the consequent anxiety that this can engender. For students engaged in the process of developing their skills and knowledge within a paradigm of uniprofessional practice and discourse, this is particularly complex.

The concept of critical reflection is also potentially problematic within the educational as well as the practice domain. A general acceptance and agreement amongst many different professional groups that reflection is a fundamental and shared element of preregistration programmes will, in all likelihood, conceal more deep-seated and diverse views and opinions concerning the relationship between a technical-rational approach to education and one where the examination of power relationships and the importance of process take priority over an instrumental concern for the transmission of knowledge. Related to this is the risk that critical reflection may itself be seen as a bolt-on concept for the inter-professional curriculum alone rather than permeating all aspects of students' learning, creating tensions for students and tutors alike in both uniprofessional and inter-professional aspects of the educational process.

Despite such concerns, it is argued here that a model of critical and reflective practice offers a way forward, drawing on an approach that will enable future practitioners to develop a shared understanding of the world and ways of working together based on creating shared dialogue within communities of practice that will enhance the experience of service users. In doing so, it is anticipated that previously compartmentalised ways of thinking and practice will be transformed, enabling news ways of working to emerge.

Chapter 14

Beyond reflection dogma

John Sweet

Too much 'reflective practice' has been described as if it were a psychological, lonely affair, thinking about what the individual apprehends in the outside world. I call this extreme 'reflective practice as individual incident analysis' (RPIIA). Fortunately there are alternatives, which suggest reflective activities with an interpersonal group dynamic, whilst advocating, protecting and encouraging concepts of personal growth,and even development, of an inner-life quest. This chapter outlines later an example of such a group reflective encounter which delivered some practical and unexpected outcomes. But before we can get to this, I will describe some of the ruts that can bog down 'reflective practice', as well as some more liberating concepts, to try to explain the context for doing this work.

Reflective practice in context

There is a current dogma, especially in the health-care professions, that reflective practice is an individual activity (RPIIA) that largely comprises of incident analysis (Atkins and Murphy 1994; Johns 1994), carried out alone. For instance, a current piloted reflective 'e-portfolio' for dentistry 'e-portfolio 2004' does not stand as a student self-selected offering of materials to occasion a claim to values and objectives but acts as a means of assessment and part self-assessment, and consists mainly of a closely monitored record of activity. A check-box mentality appears self-perpetuating and cuts off reflection from its academic roots. Early exponents of reflective practice were attempting to encourage students and lecturers to move from prescriptive learning and ask students to take responsibility for their own learning. Elliot (1976) and Eisner (1979) saw reflection as the icing on the cake, as it were, to the educational process in producing a freethinking 'connoisseur'. A less prosaic idea about reflection is that it is simply 'slowing down our thinking processes to become more aware of how we form our mental models' (Senge et al. 1994). But in RPIIA, by tightening and restricting freedom of choice and action, I describe a whole range of topics, which appear to have been conveniently 'forgotten'. The rigid clockwise cycle of experience, reflection planning and action are often attributed to Kolb (1984), without giving Kolb the credit for adapting the original Lewin cycle. The dynamic across the centre of the circle is forgotten, as is the vigorous contrast that can exist between the opposites, and also the possible harmony and sense of balance that can be achieved. For instance, in a situation of 'research' learning inquiry there will be a continual grasping towards the concrete and the abstract, whereas clinical practice will make demands for reflection reaching across to active planning (Sweet 2003), not some gradual and predicable movement around a circle. In a journey marked out in RPIIA, just around the periphery of a cycle, the focus can be entirely based on external events, and if assessed, it will record the students' attempts to please those in authority, rather than the students attempting to identify their own group identity and individual life quest. Whilst a number of professions would equate a high level of ability to reflect on their practice as an admirable aim for expert leaders, there is an interesting anomaly for the professions such as dentistry and dietetics, which in particular have been influenced by Chambers (2004). They advocate the adoption of the skills-based concepts of novice, beginner, proficient and expert (from Dreyfus and Dreyfus 1986), and transfer them directly and apparently unthinkingly as a pathway for professional development as well. The outcome of using this protocol is an unintuitive situation where 'reflection' is stigmatised as a necessary process for the novice and beginner, but quite unnecessary for the expert consultant who can intuit what to do. Presumably a good number of consultants are content with not having to take the trouble to reflect and instead take a leap of faith! However, for the student who is put through a course of reflective practice that is not shared or valued by their superiors, there is a danger that unremitting reflective cycles can provide a dogma of order. Jarvis (1992) warns that 'all actions are subject to habitualisation and run the danger of degenerating in to presumption, ritualism and eventually alienation'.

The current RPIIA genre of reflective practice does not advocate the strong case for situated learning, where the new environment or situation is the main driver for reflection and subsequent change. Schön's (1963) early work on 'displacement of concepts', essentially a situational reflection hypothesis, is currently largely neglected. This early view of Schön's was a reaction to how difficult it is to get people to change their views directly. He discovered that it was easier to change people by moving them to a new situation where their old ideas could not work. They were then willing to modify or displace their old concepts and make changes to their actions and attitudes far more easily, without being directly challenged.

Schön's (1983) later concepts of reflection-in-action and reflection-on-action are well known. Reflection-on-action is the most straightforward concept, that of thinking about an event or action after it has occurred. This is what the RPnIIA (reflective practitioner of independent incident analysis) considers reflection to be and reflection-in-action is neglected. However, have we passed beyond the usefulness of reflection-in-action? Should it be removed or returned into use with greater vigour? Asking, 'How can one reflect when one is working at something?' Court (1988) says that momentary 'times out', which could perhaps be called 'reflection-in-action', might better be seen as moments of quick deliberation leading to decision taking: deliberation not reflection-in-action. Heywood (2000) suggests that, like a physician, we can often be surprised when the evidence is contradictory and/or ambiguous. This is the stage of surprises that causes us to review what has gone before to see how it differs from previous cases. He equates this with Schön's stage of reflection-in-action. But is this a situation of being, for a moment, just conscious of the learning process? Marton and Booth (1997) propose that learning occurs when something is viewed differently. There are also three conceptual candidates in the educational arena that could be seen as instances of reflection-in-action, the first at a micro level and the others at a macro level. First, are the latest 'threshold concepts' (Meyer and Land 2005) with reference to 'getting over difficulties in learning', referring to the 'lucky ones' who can reflect and the raison d'être for the 'threshold concepts' enterprise is then to get 'the others' to become reflective practitioners skilled at reflection-in-action? Second, can the cry for 'constructive alignment' (Biggs 1999) be seen as a dynamic reflection on the components of the teaching and learning process so that the whole concept draws itself together in a way that is larger than its constituent parts? The third concept is from the social constructivist school. The reflection-in-action could represent the individual's reaction to enculturation, a preliminary transitory realisation of knowledge and identity. By engaging successfully with the discipline, students can make progress through the outer skin of the discipline – or have found a pore or portal as a port of entry. They would meet with surprise as they see the world differently enough to see the outside of the discipline, to find a way in, and make the realisation that they have penetrated the discipline stockade. Bruffee (1993) talks about the importance of peer collaboration so that student groups may develop as intermediary cultures.

RPIIA does not fit well with feelings, especially where there has been little inner work to unpack emotions and feelings. This is where the poverty of a rigid concept of reflection merely as a rational introspection becomes apparent. An indoctrinated RPnIIA novice is trained to follow a fixed cycle, 'reflecting on' encounters to come up with propositional knowledge, which will, at best, result in an ethical response based on a consideration of justice. But this process is a recipe for 'meanness' as it is self-centred, whilst at the same time inculcating fear that it must fit some particular order of acceptability. A different approach altogether places reflection as central to the individual's response to others in an interpersonal interaction. Heron (1992) helps to make concepts of reflection broaden by widening his epistemological overview of what types of knowledge are possible. Apart from rational knowledge about things, and propositional knowledge and practical knowledge on how things work, he values experiential knowledge, which he defines as participation in and resonance with one or more beings. Reflection is then very much a part of the response to the being of another person. Levinas (1981), from a different tradition, says we have an immediate ethical responsibility to act for other persons as we 'see their face', on an individual basis. Reflection then becomes a genuine intuitive and immediate ethical response to an 'other' in need, based on the experience of the moment, rather than some intentional rational calculation.

In fact, if reflective practice is central to a learning relationship with others it should link with the prime educational tool of dialogue and its many more modern variants. Dialogue is vital to gain feedback from others and this is where debriefing is useful. A debriefing session is held to identify specific problems that occur and the learning needs to be pursued to overcome problems. Debriefing (Ments 1990) can be used to close the loop and the best reflection takes place at the point of action. This could be in the workplace but commonly in an informal community of practice, and on the Web, in particular, affinity spaces (Gee 2005) have been described where high levels of interaction occur but without complications of membership or fixed status. Action learning is probably the most established group practice method for enhancing the reflection by individuals on the spot in response to questioning (Weinstein 1999). Forgotten possibilities of group reflection have been brought to the fore by Cowan (1998) as he openly experimented with his students in attempts to resolve difficulties in their learning. Heywood and Biggs agree that Cowan's addition of reflection-for-action is a useful adjunct to Schön's terms reflection-in-action and reflection-on-action. For it is that thrust across the centre of the Kolb cycle diagram from reflection directly for planning that is the primary action of practitioners. Cowan (1998), however, describes a social process, how the main focus of the reflection can be to make public reflections from both teacher and student on what has impacted on their lives at a pre-judgemental level. The immediate value of this is that the activity takes on group energy as the writing is not solely for the individual student and vicarious tutor. The degree of 'confidentiality' of reflections are made more explicit – they can be set for circulation just within the group or for wider use, especially if the student contributions are anonymised. Possible group-reflection modification of the Kolb cycle is presented by Senge et al. (1994) who translate the cycle of individual reflecting, connecting, deciding and doing into the collective cycle they describe of public reflection, shared meaning, joint planning and coordinated action, but this is difficult to envisage for anything other than a tightly defined project, and, further, they do admit that, in their experience, groups often think they can skip stages in the cycle they describe.

One of the most unexploited resources for reflection looks like first sight as a contradiction – that of a group activity where the participants work alone.

Ira Progoff researched a group of biographies of creative lives and found that each one of them used some sort of reflective-journal record keeping. This led to further research on the use of reflective journals in the 1960s with the publication of the Intensive Journal method in 1975 (Progoff 1992). Participants in this journal method can initiate their journal, by following the book and working alone. Alternatively they can attend a workshop where they also work alone on their journal but have the advantage of a facilitator introducing the various sections of the journal and the positive atmosphere created by non-interfering workshop participants, working in their own journals. The sections are of a log type for entering data or an exercise type where the logged data is creatively explored and reworked. One advantage of the Intensive Journal is that it does not come with content and is one of the least intrusive journal methodologies so that data is solely that of the individual. The outcome of using the journal can be a comprehensively researched documentation of the inner life of a person as they move through their life course. It may help that person develop a more robust approach to life that Progoff calls having 'inner muscles'. Mezirow (1990) indicated that reflection in adults is an inner process and creates change within the person that could result in the transformation of the person. Whilst holding his or her identity, the person moves on with a different outlook and a response to events. The Intensive Journal can hold a wide range of reflections, which can include spontaneous elements such as reflection-in-action, reflection-on-action and Cowan's reflection-for-action; they can deal with feelings, work, people and life in general. Reflection in depth can invoke 'aha' moments, including some spiritual experiences that can stand with or without religious beliefs. There are three problems with the depth approach. First, is the perceived rather unusual nature of pursuing the inner-life quest, which has, in the West, not generally followed a secular reflective route. Second, moments of peace and stillness needed to gain access to inner experience are only too rare. Third, it can be time consuming and at times hard work. However, there are few other ways in which reflections drawn from so many quarters can produce a self-balancing approach across time as a resource for living.

What conclusions can be drawn about reflective practice?

The literature on reflective practice is very varied and derived from different philosophies. The opportunities for groups of individuals to contribute to an overall reflective issue is of great interest for future developments, which go beyond current reflective practice. The conceptual argument here is that, clearly, reflection can be carried out only by individuals, but the dogma that a RPnIIA should follow a mandatory cycle of fixed events involving that individual alone is restrictive. With additional suitably directional course materials, RPIIA can provide a resource for authority and control that inflicts conformity, rather than the original concepts to which reflective practice espouses: to give the students the impetus to take responsibility for their own learning, behaviours and attitude.

A further complication is that the original writings by Schön and Kolb have been selectively plundered in such a way that the original vibrancy and open possibilities have been changed with a stereotyped cycle of reflection; imposed – cast in stone as a truth (Moon 1999; Hull et al. 1996). RPIIA is usually bolt-on because other educational models do not fit well with it. RPIIA ignores reflection-in-action and keeps firmly to reflection-on-action. Reflection-in-action is something of a tease, summed up by Heywood (2000) as a stage of surprises. But it may be a resource for a number of current educational models, destined to improve the student learning experience. Trapped in reflection-on-practice the RPnIIA is unable to deal with acting in the uncertainly of reflection-in-action or take the risk of working with the moment – taking that ethical decision based on the immediate experience as a 'Good Samaritan'.

The Kolb cycle does not translate to group practice without some difficulty. Some of the most promising developments of moving reflective practice beyond an individual activity can be found where others can give support. Cowan's approach is particularly attractive because it proposes that mutual shared reflections horizontally across faculty and student boundaries appear to be most effective at resolving matters that involve a group collectively. Action learning provides support for each individual at a time in a small group being questioned by their peers. This appears to be most effective at unravelling personal work matters or projects, but with the additional caveat to act on the reflections. Affinity spaces, which are virtual sites where disparate characters are able to converse about an abiding passion, may again be a useful means of sharing reflections on a very narrow topic of mutual interest. The most demanding and possibly the most productive of ways to take reflective practice beyond its current horizons is journaling. I have described an established paper based system that works particularly well in workshop format. Once the decision has been made to take time out as a retreat, the participants have protected time and space for reflection and the temporary relocation may also contribute to a displacement of concepts.

The RPIIA genre of reflection works as a fixed cycle of processes that occur within a static individual carrying out his work with a focus on the exterior world, mainly the world of work. RPIIA, like the skills development concepts of novice, beginner etc. may have a place at the starting block, but should be discarded before the first hurdle! Perhaps rather than just working out from where we are now we need to work backwards to find out what it is we want to achieve and from this select an appropriate model to use to move forward. Maybe we want to resolve a specific work issue or be ready to help and respond with a group of colleagues, or maybe there sits a question of how to 'know thyself'. A final irony might be that the beyond in 'beyond reflection dogma' may be centred within.

A study in group reflective practice

An innovative group-reflections method recommended by Cowan (1998) was utilised, where 114 clinical undergraduate dental students in Years 3 and 4 (of a five-year course) in groups of twelve to sixteen shared reflections with their colleagues on what impacted on their learning during their clinical practice. They wrote down their thoughts at the end of a clinical session towards the end of term, and were asked to give their reflections on their clinical skills, what clinical work they had completed, and who and what had impacted on their clinical work positively or negatively. Attempts were made here to elicit both analytical and evaluative reflections – what and how well. These groups of students had experienced the start of a new way of group working, with a pair of students taking responsibility for running the everyday aspects of the clinic and taking occasional videos of interesting clinical cases for debriefing, and also experienced the advantages (when it worked) of a new computerised appointment-booking system for their patients. The hand-written comments were typed up by a departmental secretary and circulated to the group. In addition, one clinical facilitator who attended most clinical sessions shared reflections with all the students on what impacted on his teaching during their clinical-practice sessions so that reflections were shared. The results of the three reports were compared and contrasted.

Group-reflection study findings

The group-reflection exercise entailed asking about issues that had an overall impact on students' clinical working. Reflections from a staff facilitator circulated to students led to an overview of results and discussion.

Student-group reflections

In the group reflections the students highlighted the new clinical skills they had developed and included the following kinds of reflection.

> I think the most useful thing I've learnt since being on the clinic is how to give oral-hygiene instruction to patients. We had never been shown this before and now I can use this on the other clinics as well. Also looking at radiographs has given me more experience in identifying bone levels.

As to facilitation of the clinic, they reported some organisational satisfaction, but just a few reverted to the usual request to be spoon-fed rather than take responsibility for their own learning.

> The presentations weren't that useful I thought. I would rather have had lectures, so that I knew that we covered all the information on all the topics we need to know to pass exams and be confident.

The impact of having very little nursing support came up time and time again.

[Nursing support was] non-existent, we assisted each other. It is very difficult to find a nurse available to help.

The findings about group working seemed to indicate how well they worked together.

I like this group, everyone seems to get on quite well. ... Everyone shared their knowledge with each other.
The group gets on well. We all help each other out, and learn from each other. Certain people were more involved than others.
Our group works very well together. I feel we are bonded.

Reflections of staff facilitator circulated to class of students

The style of teaching that I am trying to develop is based on the idea that it is what the student learns that is of prime importance rather than what is taught by the teacher. This is even truer in the clinical situation where simple answers to fuzzy clinical situations cannot be taught directly.
To be honest, I have found the devolving of the facilitator role testing at times. It is when students individually or in pairs take the initiative themselves; I find that things don't work out exactly as I anticipate, of course. ... I think that having student facilitators has freed me up with more contact time with individual students assisting their treatment of patients, which was not possible before.

Nursing support:

It was the early reports back from the student facilitators that alerted me to the fact that we do not have on a regular basis dedicated allocated dental nurses to the student clinic. This has been a feature of the periodontal clinic for many years. ... I do intend to see if this matter can be resolved to everyone's benefit.

Comparing feedback forms and reflections

Shared reflections brought to light the need for an additional member of the support staff. A standard student feedback form that had been in use for many years had not delivered this problem as it concentrated on 'teaching' and not the overall impact on their clinical working. In contrast, the shared reflections were particularly valuable because through more open questions and through the group response they were able to ask 'big questions' and discover the collective view. It was something of a surprise to the staff because the situation had become the norm, in a 40-year-old institution and lived with for years. The case was made to management, and in response to this, a further staff allocation was made. Apart from positive personnel changes to the clinic, the joint reflections also helped to create an atmosphere of mutual trust and support between staff and students and an environment for positive change.

Conclusions

Some of the biggest learning points from the Cowan approach are that, to be educational, much is to be gained from dialogue and that some of the most useful reflections are ones that are shared. RPIIA is more likely to produce a compliant student, but the Cowan approach may contribute to resolving issues that are important to the whole group and can be resolved collectively and create positive institutional change. Many approaches reviewed are suitable for the short term, however some form of journaling may be the most productive way for an individual to reflect over their life course and take reflective practice beyond its current horizons.

Conclusions

Miriam Zukas, Helen Bradbury, Nick Frost and Sue Kilminster

A conclusion suggests some kind of ending, some sort of closure to this edited collection. As editors, we feel that this would imply a consensus or agreement about what lies beyond reflective practice which does not exist (nor is it likely to, given the nature of the debate so far). As we summarise below, there are certainly dominant questions and themes which arise from the collection. These are perhaps particularly influenced by the ways in which reflective practice has been 'incorporated' into pedagogic and professionalising enterprises, despite its radical potential for professionals seeking to change the social world. Our main suggestion is that the variety of perspectives and ways forward do challenge us to move beyond critique to take account of more complex conceptualisations of work and identity.

Whose reflection and reflective practice?

The contributors to this volume have drawn on a wide range of contexts for their discussions: some have focused on students at the beginning of their professional lives (Karban and Smith; Morris and O'Neill); others have chosen to look at mid-career professionals returning to study (Collier; Fook; Hunt); and others have considered professionals engaged in practice (Billett and Newton; Chivers; Knights, Meyer and Sampson; West). Whilst they have studied diverse professions, there has been a tendency to concentrate on what are often called the 'caring' professions. Nevertheless, what is striking from these examples is that very different kinds of profession (including what might be called 'para-professions'), engaged in quite different practices, have all taken up the same mantra (Ecclestone 1996) of reflection and reflective practice in the education and development of their members. This, in and of itself, should make us suspicious, suggesting, as it does, that one learning process suits all, regardless of stage of career, learning site or activity.

The need, therefore, to challenge the dogma of 'reflective practice' and to question what we mean by reflection runs throughout the book. Some authors have derived their ideas from empirical work including case studies (Fook, Knights, Meyer and Sampson), auto/biographies (West), historical analyses (Hargreaves) and surveys (Chivers); others entail conceptual critique, theoretical development (Boud) and reflection on practice (Sweet).

Their approaches might be summarised by the questions David Boud posed in his chapter: Should we 'reject earlier views of reflection, rehabilitate them to capture their previous potential or move to new ways of regarding reflection that are more in keeping with what we know about the context of practice'? His view is that we need to pursue each of these three directions together, and, as we show below, this is, in effect, what many of our authors have done in rising to the challenge of moving beyond reflection and reflective practice.

Rejecting earlier views of reflection

Like so many before them (for example, Boud and Walker 1998; Bright 1996; Ecclestone 1996; Eraut 1995), most authors in this volume have rejected the worst excesses of a technical or instrumental view of reflection in which educators adopted approaches which suggested that reflection could result from following a recipe and could be assessed through checklists or other instrumental means. Of course, such approaches do not discredit the idea of reflection itself, but instead suggest the need to refine and theorise our understandings of reflection in general and to develop the pedagogic processes associated with encouraging reflection in particular.

Furthermore, the contributors have rejected the ways in which demands for evidence of reflection have been incorporated into professionals' appraisals and reviews in the form of portfolios, diaries, logs, and so on. In some professions, these are scrutinised as part of the requirement for ongoing registration, and from our observations it seems likely that this will increase, rather than decrease as the conditions for professional practice change (Frost). Saltiel, for example, is concerned about the place of reflective practice in the surveillance and control of practitioners, and he also raises the important question about its emergence as 'confessional' for students.

Whilst these critiques have focused on the regulatory and normalising aspects of pedagogic and management practices associated with reflection, others have concentrated on the nature of reflection itself. Is reflection in and of itself an unalloyed positive aspect of professional work and life (Fooks; West)? Are there different kinds of reflection (Sweet)? Who is reflecting on what (Morris et al.)? What are the relationships between reflection, learning and practice (Billett and Newton; Fooks)? And what is the relationship between reflection and other aspects of our lives which normally are not considered in work (Hunt; West)? In other words, what is included in reflection – our whole selves (Boud; Collier; West)? These kinds of question open up the possibility of rehabilitating reflection through extension and refinement.

Rehabilitating reflection

Boud turns to practice to resituate reflection as do Billett and Newton, arguing for an understanding of learning as part of practice, rather than as a separate enterprise involving some other process. And this practice gives rise to other suggestions for the rehabilitation of reflection – what about those with whom professionals work? Do they have some place in our theorising about reflection (Morris et al.)? What about the fact that we work increasingly with others in trans-disciplinary ways (Boud; Karban and Smith; Knights, Meyer and Sampson)? Should we engage with others in reflection (Sweet)? These perspectives all suggest expanding the notion of reflection to acknowledge that it is not necessarily a process which happens individually within the heads of those who are reflecting. The turn towards a less individualistic, more social understanding which involves practice itself and others implicated in practice (clients, other professionals) is one of the stronger themes emerging in the book.

A second theme contributing to the rehabilitation of reflection might be considered to be a revival of old ideas – the insistence on critical (as opposed to any other) reflection as the goal for the development of professionals. Such a perspective might incorporate the analysis of power and power relations (Fook; Hargreaves; Karban and Smith), as well as the analysis of taken-for-granted assumptions and implications for the transformation of practice (Collier; Hunt; West).

New ways of regarding reflection

Many contributors suggested concepts to enrich the notions of reflection and/or reflective practice. In some cases (West's 'really reflexive practice', for example), these were suggested as replacements for the existing terms, not because the original ideas were necessarily faulty, but because of their subsequent association with instrumental and technical approaches, particularly in relation to assessment – a far cry from Schön's intentions. Others have suggested concepts which expand beyond reflection and/or reflective practice to take account of what was missing from the original conceptualisation – Boud's proposal for productive reflection is an excellent example. He argues that, if we acknowledge that in order to change work, reflection cannot be an individual matter, then we need a concept that deals with the context and purpose of work as well as the need to go beyond the individual independent worker/ learner – he proposes an embodied and contextualised refinement.

Such new concepts will, inevitably, raise new questions and fresh critiques, particularly in the fast-changing circumstances outlined by Frost. They also raise new possibilities for developing reflective practice, as explored by Collier, Hunt, Karbin and Smith, and Sweet. But we are urged by many authors (eg. Fook; Hargreaves; Saltiel; West) to remember that no matter what conceptual and practical refinements we develop, if we continue to pursue reflection and reflective practice as a 'good thing' without some kind of critical agenda, without some kind of attention to the historical and social analysis of power relations and knowledge/power, we will not end up with better professionals.

Implications of moving beyond reflective practice

It is ironic that the editors and contributors to this book should critique reflection and reflective practice so roundly when, at one level, we have tried to reinvigorate it through the extended discussion between these pages. But we have come to the conclusion that this is essential work. In continuing professional development, as well as initial education, the employment of reflective practice in continuing professional development frameworks, appraisal systems and revalidation processes is a travesty. In these contexts, reflective practice has become a chimera, denuded of most of its original meaning. The worst excesses of those educational courses which require (and assess) reflection on demand are now being replicated within continuing professional development frameworks, appraisal systems and revalidation processes.

Some professionals are required to submit each year their reflections as part of the appraisal process: but the performativity of the workplace (Frost) leaves little space for reflection – except when filling in appraisal forms. Many professions either require or are planning to require their members to submit written reflections as part of their evidence to demonstrate their continuing fitness to practise: these reflections are then scrutinised (presumably) and a decision taken about whether or not a professional has shown their fitness to continue practising. Apart from the obvious questions about the relationship between what one writes ('reflects') and what one does ('practises'), who is likely to be open, critical and reflexive when one's future career is at stake? And what values and interpretations do those who read our reflections bring with them?

Of course professionals need to be able to renew their practice in a changing world and to make 'sense of experience in situations that are rich and complex and which do not lend themselves to being simplified by the use of concepts and frameworks that can be taught' (Boud). But they (and we) need to challenge vigorously the incorporation of the concepts of reflection and reflective practice into processes of scrutiny and regulation, appraisal and control. Instead, we propose that a critical understanding of reflection and reflective practice – one in which reflection is no longer seen as an isolated, individual activity but one which has the potential to bring about social and organisational change – will move us beyond the caricature that reflective practice has become. We hope that this collection will contribute to that movement.

Bibliography

Abbs, P. (1987) *Living Powers: The Arts in Education*, Lewes: Falmer Press.

——(1989) *A is for Aesthetic, Essays on Creative and Aesthetic Education*, Lewes: Falmer Press.

——(1994) *The Educational Imperative: A Defence of Socratic and Aesthetic Learning*, Lewes: Falmer Press.

Abel Smith, B. (1960) *A History of the Nursing Profession*, London: Heinemann.

——(1964) *The Hospitals in England and Wales, 1800–1948*, Cambridge, MA: Harvard University Press.

Abercrombie, M.L. (1960) *The Anatomy of Judgment: An Investigation into the Processes of Perception and Reasoning*, London: Hutchinson.

Adams, R., Dominelli, L. and Payne, M. (2002) Introduction in *Critical Practice in Social Work*, Basingstoke: Palgrave.

Agger, B. (1998) *Critical Social Theories*, Boulder, CO: Westview.

Alderson, P. (1998) 'The importance of theories in health care', *British Medical Journal*, 317: 1007–10.

Alfrero, L.A. (1972) *Conscientization: New Themes in Social Work Education*, New York: International Association of Schools of Social Work.

Allport, G.W. (1954) *The Nature of Prejudice*, Reading: Addison-Wesley.

Anderson, J.R. (1982) 'Acquisition of cognitive skill', *Psychological Review*, 89(4): 369–406.

——(1993) 'Problem solving and learning', *American Psychologist*, 48(1): 35–44.

Argyris, C. and Schön, D.A. (1974) *Theory in Practice: Increasing Professional Effectiveness*, San Francisco: Jossey-Bass Inc.

——(1996) *Organisational Learning II: Theory, Method and Practice*, Reading: Addison-Wesley.

——(1976) *Theory in Practice: Increasing Professional Effectiveness*, San Francisco, CA: Jossey-Bass.

——1996) *Organisational Learning II: Theory, Method and Practice*, Reading, MA: Addison-Wesley.

Armstrong D. (1984) 'The patient's view', *Social Science and Medicine*, 18(9): 737–44.

Arnstein, S.R. (1969) 'A ladder of citizen participation', *Journal of the American Institute of Planners*, 35: 216–24.

Arntson, P. (1989) 'Improving citizens' health competencies', *Health Communication*, 1: 29–34.

Ashdown, M. (1934) *A Complete System of Nursing*, London: Temple Press.

Askeland, G.A. (2006) 'Turning a facilitator's critical incident into student learning', *Practice*, 18(2): 103–16.

Athanasou, J. (1999) *Adult Education Psychology*, Katoomba: Social Science Press.

Atkins, K. and Murphy, K. (1994) 'Reflective practice', *Nursing Standard*, 8: 49–56.

Atkinson, T. and Claxton, G. (eds) (2000) *The Intuitive Practitioner*, Buckingham: Open University Press.

Bailey, T.R., Hughes, K.L. and Moore, D.T. (2004) *Working Knowledge: Work-based Learning and Educational Reform*, New York: Routledge Falmer.

Balint, M. (1956) *The Doctor, His Patient and the Illness*, London: Pitman.

Baly, M. (1998) *Florence Nightingale and the Nursing Legacy*, 2nd edn, Philadelphia, PA: Bainbridge Books.

Barnett, R. (1997) *Higher Education: A Critical Business*, Buckingham: Open University Press.

Barr, H. (1998) 'Competent to collaborate: Towards a competency-based model for interprofessional education', *Journal of Interprofessional Care*, 12(2): 181–88.

——(2002) *Interprofessional Education Today, Yesterday and Tomorrow: A Review*, London: Learning, Teaching and Support Network, Centre for Health Sciences and Practice.

Bauman, Z. (1998) *Work, Consumerism and the New Poor*, London: Open University Press.

Beach, M.C. and Inui, T. (2006) 'Relationship-centered care: A constructive reframing', *Gen Intern Med*, 21; Suppl. 1: S3–S8.

Becher, T. (1999) *Professional Practices*, Piscataway, NJ: Transaction Publishers.

Benner, P. (1984) *From Novice to Expert: Excellence and Power in Clinical Nursing Practice*, California: Addison-Wesley.

Benner, P. and Wrubel, J. (1989) *The Primacy of Caring: Stress and Coping in Health and Illness*, Menlo Park, CA: Addison-Wesley.

Benner, P. Tanner, C.A. and Chelsa, C.A. (1996) *Expertise in Nursing Practice: Caring, Clinical Judgement, and Ethics*, New York: Springer.

Bereiter, C. (2002) *Education and the Mind in the Knowledge Age*, London: Lawrence Erlbaum Associates.

Bernstein, B. (1977) *Class, Codes and Control, Vol.3: Towards a Theory of Educational Transmissions*, London: Routledge and Kegan Paul.

Berry, T. (1988) *The Dream of the Earth*, San Francisco, CA: Sierra Club Books.

Bhaskar, R. (1998) *The Possibility of Naturalism*, London: Routledge.

Biggs, J. (1999) *Teaching for Quality Learning at University: What the Student Does*, Buckingham: Open University Press.

——(2003) *Teaching for Quality Learning at University*, 2nd edn., Maidenhead: Open University Press.

Billett, S. (2000) 'Guided learning at work', *Journal of Workplace Learning*, 12(7): 272–85.

——(2001) *Learning in the Workplace: Strategies for Effective Practice*, Sydney: Allen and Unwin.

——(2002) 'Workplace pedagogic practices: Co-participation and learning', *British Journal of Educational Studies*, 50(4): 457–81.

——(2003) 'Workplace Mentors: Demands and Benefits', *Journal of Workplace Learning*, 15(3): 105–13.

——(2006a) *Developing 'Learning Practice' within Queensland's Health Sector*, A submission to the Queensland Health Systems Review.

——(2006b) 'Constituting the workplace curriculum', *Journal of Curriculum Studies*, 38(1): 31–48.

——(2006c) 'Relational interdependence between social and individual agency in work and working life', *Mind, Culture and Activity*, 13: 1.

Billett, S. and van Woerkom, M. (2006) 'Older workers and learning through work', in T. Takkanen (ed.) *Older workers and lifelong learning*, 177–89, Thessalonica: CEDEFOP.

Billett, S., Barker, M. and Hernon-Tinning, B. (2004) 'Participatory practices at work', *Pedagogy, Culture and Society*, 12(2): 233–57.

Billett, S., Smith, R. and Barker, M. (2005) 'Understanding work, learning and the remaking of cultural practices', *Studies in Continuing Education*, 27(3): 219–37.

Bishop, J.H. (1997) 'What we know about employer provided training: A review of the literature', *Research in Labour Economics,* 16: 19–87.

Bishop, K. (2004) 'Working time patterns in the UK, France, Denmark and Sweden', *Labour Market Trends,* 113–22.

Bleakley, A. and Bligh, J. (2008) 'Students learning from patients: Let's get real in medical education', *Advances in Health Sciences Education,* 13, 89–107.

Bleakley, A., Boyden, J., Hobbs, A., Walsh, L. and Allard, J. (2006) 'Improving teamwork climate in operating theatres: The shift from multiprofessionalism to interprofessionalism', *Journal of Interprofessional Care,* 20(5): 461–70.

Blickem, C. and Priyadharshini, E. (2007) 'Patient narratives: The potential for "patient-centred" interprofessional learning?', *Journal of Interprofessional Care,* 21(6): 619–32.

Bloom, B.S. (1956) *Taxonomy of Educational Objectives, Book 1, Cognitive Domain* (18th printing, 1974), London: Longman Group.

Bolton, G. (2000) *'It's all theatre',* Drama Research, 1: 21–29.

——(2001) *Reflective Practice: Writing and Professional Development,* London: Paul Chapman.

Bond, M. and Holland, S. (1998) *Skills of Clinical Supervision for Nurses,* Buckingham: Open University Press.

Booth, J. and Hewison, A. (2002) 'Role overlap between occupational therapy and physiotherapy during in-patient stroke rehabilitation: An exploratory study', *Journal of Interprofessional Care,* 16(1): 31–40.

Boud, D. (2006) 'Creating the space for reflection', in D. Boud, P. Cressey, and P. Docherty (eds) *Productive Reflection at Work,* 158–69, London and New York: Routledge.

——(2007) *Professional Lifelong Learning: Beyond Reflective Practice,* Keynote address to the SCUTREA pre-conference, Leeds, 3 July 2007.

Boud, D. and Walker, D. (1998) 'Promoting reflection in professional courses: The challenge of context', *Studies in Higher Education,* 23(2): 191–206.

Boud, D., Cohen, R. and Walker, D. (1993) *Using Experience for Learning,* Bristol: Open University Press.

Boud, D., Cressey, P. and Docherty, P. (eds) (2006) *Productive Reflection at Work,* London and New York: Routledge.

Boud, D., Keogh, R. and Walker, D. (eds) (1985) *Reflection: Turning Experience into Learning,* London: Kogan Page.

Bovaird, T. (2007) 'Beyond engagement and participation: User and community co-production of public services', *Public Administration Review,* 67(5): 846–60.

Bowlby, J. (1969) *Attachment and Loss, Volume 1: Attachment,* London: Hogarth Press.

Boyle, D. (2005) *Time Banks UK: Grassroots Initiatives for Sustainable Development.* www.time-banks.org/documents/GrassrootsFoundation.pdf. [Accessed January 2009.]

Bradbeer, J. (1998) *Imagining Curriculum: Practical Intelligence in Teaching,* New York: Teachers College Press.

Bradshaw, A. (2001) *The Nurse Apprentice 1860–1977,* Aldershot: Ashgate.

Bright, B. (1996) 'Reflecting on reflective practice', *Studies in the Education of Adults,* 28(2): 162–84.

Brockbank, A. and McGill, I. (1998) *Facilitating Reflective Learning in Higher Education,* Buckingham: Open University Press.

Brookfield, S.D. (1987) *Developing Critical Thinkers: Challenging Adults to Explore Alternative Ways of Thinking and Acting,* Buckingham: Open University Press.

——(1995) *Becoming a Critically Reflective Teacher,* San Francisco: Jossey-Bass.

——(2000) 'Transformative learning as ideology critique', in J. Mezirow (ed.) *Learning as Transformation: Critical Perspectives on a Theory in Progress,* San Francisco: Jossey-Bass.

——(2005) *The Power of Critical Theory*, San Francisco: Jossey-Bass.

Brooks, J. (2001) 'Structured by class, bound by gender: Nursing and specialist probationer schemes 1860 -1939', *International History of Nursing Journal*, 6(2): 13–21.

Brown, K., Young, N. (2008) 'Building capacity for service user and carer involvement in social work education', *Social Work Education*, 27(1): 84–96.

Bruffee, K.A. (1993) *Collaborative Learning: Higher Education, Interdependence, and the Authority of Knowledge*, Baltimore and London: John Hopkins University Press.

Bruner, J. (1973) *Going Beyond the Information Given*, New York: Norton.

Bub, B. (2006) *Communication Skills that Heal: A Practical Approach to a New Professionalism in Medicine*, Oxford: Radcliffe.

Bunting, M. (2005) *Willing Slaves: How the Overwork Culture is Ruling our Lives*, London: Harper.

Burton, J. (2006) 'Transformative learning: The hidden curriculum of adult life', *Work Based Learning in Primary Care*, 4: 1–5.

Burton, J., Morris, P. (2001) 'Mental illness or human distress? Challenges for primary care educators', *Education for General Practice*, 12: 1–10.

Burbules, N.C. (1993) *Dialogue in Teaching, Theory and Practice, Advances in Contemporary Educational Thought*, Volume 10, New York: Teachers College, Columbia University/London: Teachers College Press.

Burdell, P. and Swadener, B. (1999) 'Critical personal narrative and autoethnography in education', *Educational Researcher*, August–September: 21–26.

Burns, R. (2002) *The Adult Learner at Work*, Sydney: Allen and Unwin.

Burns, C. and Schultz, S. (2008) *Reflective Practice in Nursing*, Oxford: Blackwell.

Burton, J. and Launer, J. (2003) *Supervision and Support in Primary Care*, Oxford: Radcliffe.

Byrne, P., Long, B. (1976) *Doctors Talking to Patients*, London: HMSO.

Carlson, M. (1996) *Performance: A Critical Introduction*, London: Routledge.

Campion, P., Foulkes, J., Neighbour, R. and Tate, P. (2002) 'Patient-centredness in the MRCGP examination: Analysis of large cohort', *British Medical Journal*, 325: 691–92.

Cayton, H. (2005) 'Some thoughts on medical professionalism and regulation', Defining and Developing Professionalism conference. Association for the Study of Medical Education, 28 April 2005.

Carlisle, C., Cooper, H. and Watkins, C. (2004) '"Do none of you talk to each other?" The challenges facing the implementation of interprofessional education', *Medical Teacher*, 26(6): 545–52.

Castells, M. (1996) *The Rise of the Network Society*, Oxford: Blackwell.

——(1997) *The Power of Identity*, Oxford: Blackwell.

——(1998) *The End of the Millenium*, Oxford: Blackwell.

Chamberlayne, P., Bornat, J. and Apitzsch, U. (2004) *Biographical Methods and Professional Practice*, Bristol: The Policy Press.

Chambers, D.W. (2004) 'Portfolios for determining initial licensure competency', *Journal of the American Dental Association*, 135: 173–84.

Chambers, D.W., Gilmore, C.J., Maillet, J.O. and Mitchell, B.E. (1996) 'Another look at competency-based education in dietetics', *Journal of the American Dietetic Association*, 96: 614–17.

Chan, A., Fisher, D. and Rubenson, K. (2007) *The Evolution of Professionalism: Educational Policy in the Provinces and Territories of Canada*, Vancouver: University of British Columbia Press.

Chapman, J. (2004) *Systems Failure: Why Governments Must Learn how to Think differently*. www.demos.co.uk/publications/systemfailure2.pdf. [Accessed 9 January 2009.]

Cheek, J. (2000) *Post-modern and Post-structural Approaches*, California: Sage.

Cheetham, G. and Chivers, G. (1996) 'Towards a holistic model of professional competence', *Journal of European Industrial Training*, 20(5): 20–30.

——(1998) 'The reflective (and competent) practitioner', *Journal of European Industrial Training*, 24(7): 374–83.

——(2000) 'A new look at competent professional practice', *Journal of European Industrial Training*, 24(7): 374–83.

——(2001) 'How professionals learn in practice! What the empirical research found', *Journal of European Industrial Training*, 25(5): 270–92.

——(2005) *Professions, Competence and Informal Learning*, Cheltenham: Edward Elgar.

Chiu, L. (2003) 'Transformational potential of focus group practice in participatory action research', *Action Research*, 1(2): 165–83.

Chivers, G. (2003) 'Utilising reflective practice interviews in professional development', *Journal of European Industrial Training*, 27(1): 5–15.

——(2008) 'Professional competence enhancement via postgraduate post-experience learning and development', *Journal of European Industrial Training*, 31(8): 2007.

Church, K., and Luciano, T. (2005) 'Stepping to the rhythm of circumstance: choreography of corporate disability: Reprise', Paper presented at the 3rd annual WALL conference, Toronto, 7 June 2005.

Clark, C.M. (1986) 'Ten years of conceptual development in research on teacher thinking', in M. Benperetz, R. Bromme and R. Halkes (eds) *Advances of Research on Teacher Thinking*, 7–22, Lisse: ISATT/Swels and Zeltlinger.

Clark, J.A., Mishler, E.G. (1992) 'Attending to patients' stories: reframing the clinical task', *Sociology of Health and Illness*, 14(3): 344–72.

Clouder, L. (2000) 'Reflective practice in physiotherapy', *Studies in Higher Education*, 25(2): 211–23.

Clouder, L. and Sellers, J. (2004) 'Reflective practice and clinical supervision', *Journal of Advanced Nursing*, 46(3): 262–69.

Cohen, L. and Manion, L. (1998) *Research Methods in Education*, 5th edn, London: Routledge.

Collier, K. (2005) 'Spotlight on Role-Play: Interrogating the Theory and Practice of Role-Play in Adult Education from a Theatre Arts Perspective', PhD thesis, University of Technology Sydney.

Collier, K. and McManus, J. (2005) 'Setting up learning partnerships in vocational education and training: Lessons learnt', *Journal of Vocational Education and Training*, 57(3): 251–73.

Collins, M., Wells, H. (2006) 'The Politics of Consciousness: Illness or Individuation?', *Psychotherapy and Politics International*, 4(2), 131–41.

Collins, S., Britten, N., Ruusuvuori, J. and Thompson, A. (2007) *Patient Participation in Health Care Consultations: Qualitative Perspectives*, Maidenhead: Open University Press.

Cooper, H., Braye, S. and Geyer, R. (2004) 'Complexity and interprofessional education', *Learning in Health and Social Care*, 3(4): 179–89.

Corley, A. and Eades, E. (2006) 'Sustaining critically reflective practitioners: Competing with the dominant discourse', *International Journal of Training and Development*, 10(1): 30–40.

Cottam, H. and Leadbeater, C. (2004) Health: *Co-creating Services*, RED paper 01, London: Design Council.

Coulter, A. (2002) *The Autonomous Patient: Ending Paternalism in Medical Care*, London: HMSO.

Cosh, J. (1998) 'Peer Observation in Higher Education – A Reflective Approach', *Innovations in Education and Training International*, 35(2): 171–76.

Cotton, A. (2001) 'Private thoughts in public spheres: Issues in reflection and reflective practices in nursing', *Journal of Advanced Nursing*, 36(4): 512–19.

Court, D. (1988) '"Reflection-in-action": Some definitional problems', in P. P. Grimmlett and G. L. Erikson (eds) *Reflection in Teacher Education*, New York: Teachers College Press.

Cowan, J. (1998) *On Becoming an Innovative University Teacher*, Buckingham: Open University Press.

Cranton, P. (1996) *Professional Development as Transformative Learning*, San Francisco, CA: Jossey-Bass.

Cressey, P. and Boud, D. (2006) 'The emergence of productive reflection', in D. Boud, P. Cressey and P. Docherty (eds) *Productive Reflection at Work: Learning for Changing Organizations*, 11–26, London: Routledge.

Crow, J. and Smith, L. (2005) 'Co-teaching in higher education: Reflective conversation on shared experience as continued professional development for lecturers and health and social care students', *Reflective Practice*, 6(4): 491–506.

Dalton, E., Morris, P. (2005) 'Good communication: The patient perspective'. *Newsletter*, Medical Education Unit, University of Leeds. www.leeds.ac.uk/medicine/meu/MEUNewsletterJan05.pdf [Accessed 9 January 2009.]

Davies, B. (2004) 'Introduction', *International Journal of Qualitative Studies in Education*, 17: 1.

Davies, C. (1995) *Gender and the Professional Predicament in Nursing*, Buckingham: Open University Press.

Dean, M. and Bolton, (1980) 'The administration of poverty and the development of nursing practice in nineteenth century England', Chapter 4 in C. Davies (ed.) *Rewriting Nursing History*, London: Croom Helm.

Deary, I. J., Watson, R. and Hogston, R., (2003) 'A longitudinal cohort study of burnout and attrition in nursing students', *Journal of Advanced Nursing*, 43(1): 71–81.

D'eon, M. (2005) 'A blueprint for interprofessional learning', *Journal of Interprofessional Care*, Suppl. 1 (May): 49–59.

Department of Health (2000) *The National Health Service Plan*, London: The Stationery Office
——(2000a) *Involving Patients and the Public in Healthcare*, London: The Stationery Office.
——(2001) *The Expert Patient: A New Approach to Chronic Disease Management for the 21st Century*, London: The Stationery Office.
——(2002) *Requirements for Social Work Training*, London: Department of Health.
——(2003) *Partnership Quality Assurance Framework for Healthcare Education*, London, Department of Health.
——(2005) *Supplementary Prescribing by Nurses, Pharmacists, Chiropodists/Podiatrists, Physiotherapists and Radiographers within the NHS in England: A Guide for Implementation*, London: Department of Health.
——(2006) *Mental Health Act (1983) Amendment Bill*, London: Department of Health.
——(2008a) *Clinical Governance*. www.dh.gov.uk/en/Publichealth/Patientsafety/Clinicalgovernance/index.htm. [Accessed July 2008.]
——(2008b) *High Quality Care for All*, London: The Stationery Office.
——(2008c) *The NHS Knowledge and Skills Framework and the Development Review Process*. www.dh.gov.uk/en/Publicationsandstatistics/Publications/PublicationsPolicyAndGuidance/DH_4090843. [Accessed December 2008.]

Dewey, J. (1933) *How We Think: A Restatement of the Relation of Reflective Thinking to the Educative Process*, Lexington: Heath and Company.
——(1991) *How We Think*, New York: Prometheus Books.

Dingwall, R., Raffertey, A.M. and Webster, C. (1988) *An Introduction to the Social History of Nursing*, London: Routledge.

Dominelli, L.Payne, M. and Adams, R. (eds) (2001) *Social Work: Themes, Issues and Critical Debates*, Basingstoke: Palgrave/Open University.

Dominicé, P. (2000) *Learning from our lives*, San Francisco, CA: Jossey-Bass.

Donaghy, M. and Moss, K. (2000) 'Guided reflection: A framework to facilitate and assess reflective practice within the discipline of physiotherapy', *Physiotherapy Theory and Practice*, 16: 3–14.

Dreyfus, H. and Dreyfus, S. (1986) *Mind Over Machine: The Power of Human Intuition and Expertise in the Era of the Computer*, Oxford: Blackwell.

——(2005) 'Expertise in real world contexts', *Organization Studies*, 26(5): 779–92.

Dunston, R., Lee, A., Boud, D., Brodie, P., and Chiarella, M. (2009) 'Co-production and health system reform: From reimagining to remaking', *Australian Journal of Public Administration*, 68(1): 1–14.

Dyke, M. (2006) 'The role of the "Other" in reflection, knowledge formation and action in a late modernity', *International Journal of Lifelong Education*, 25(2) 105–23.

Ecclestone, K. (1996) 'The reflective practitioner: Mantra or a model for emancipation?' *Studies in the Education of Adults*, 28(2): 146–61.

Edwards, A., Reid H., Law, B. and West L. (2003) *Challenging Biographies: Relocating the Theory and Practice of Careers Work*, Department of Career and Personal Development occasional paper, Canterbury: Canterbury Christ Church University College.

Eisner, E.W. (1979) *The Educational Imagination: On the Design and Evaluation of School Programs*, New York: Macmillan.

Elliott, J. (1976) 'Preparing teachers for classroom accountability', *College Teaching*, 100: 49–71.

Elwyn, G., Edwards, A. and Kinnersley, P. (1999) 'Shared decision-making in primary care: The neglected second half of the consultation', *British Journal of General Practice*, 50: 892–97.

Elmholdt, C. and Brinkman, S. (2006) 'Discursive practices at work: Constituting the reflective learner', in D. Boud, P. Cressey, and P. Docherty (eds) *Productive Reflection at Work*, 170–80, London and New York: Routledge.

Engel, G. (1977) 'The need for a new medical model: A challenge for biomedicine', *Science*, 196: 129–36.

Engelstrom, Y. (2004) 'Object-oriented interagency' www.edu.helsinki.fi/activity/people.

English, L. (2000) 'Spiritual dimensions of adult learning', in L. English and M. Gillen (eds) *Addressing the Spiritual Dimensions of Adult Learning: What Adult Educators Can Do*, 85, 29–38, San Francisco, CA: Jossey-Bass.

ePortfolio (2004) www.eportfolios.ac.uk/demo, 31 October 2004.

Epstein, R. (1999) 'Mindful practice', *Journal of the American Medical Association*, 282: 833–39.

Eraut, M. (1994) *Developing Professional Knowledge and Competence*, London: Falmer Press.

——(1995) 'Schön shock: A case for reframing reflection in action?' *Teachers and Teaching: Theory and Practice*, 1: 9–23.

Eraut, M., Alderton, J., Cole, G. and Sanker, P. (1997) 'Development of knowledge and skills in employment', Unpublished research paper, Swindon: Economic and Social Research Council.

Fabbri, L., Melacarne, C. and Striano, M. (2008) 'Emotional dimensions in transformative learning processes of novice teachers. A qualitative study', Paper to the ESREA conference Emotionality in Learning and Research, Canterbury, March.

Fay, B. (1977) 'How people change themselves: The relationship between critical theory and its audience', in T. Ball (ed.) *Political Theory and Praxis*, Minneapolis, MN: University of Minnesota Press.

Fineman, S. (2003) *Understanding Emotions at Work*, London: Sage.

Fiol, C.M. and Lyles, M. (1985) 'Organizational learning', *Academy of Management Review*, 10 (4): 803–13.

Fisher, B., Gilbert and D. (2002) 'Patient involvement in clinical effectiveness', in S. Gillam and F. Brooks (eds) *New Beginnings: Towards Patient and Public Involvement in Primary Care*, King's Fund, London.

Flynn, N. and Britten, N. (2006) 'Does the achievement of medical identity limit the ability of primary care practitioners to be patient-centred? A qualitative study', *Patient Education and Counseling*, 60: 49–56.

Ford, S., Schofield, T. and Hope T. (2002) 'Barriers to the evidence-based patient choice (EBPC) consultation', *Patient Education and Counseling*, 47(2): 179–85.

Flanagan, J.C. (1954) 'The critical incident technique', *Psychological Bulletin*, 51: 327–58.

Fook, J. (2000) 'Constructing Enemies and Allies in the Workplace', in L. Napier and J. Fook (eds) *Breakthroughs in Practice: Theoriesing Ccritical Moments in Social Work*, London: Whiting & Birch.

——(2002) *Social Work: Critical Theory and Practice*, London: Sage.

——(2004a) 'Critical reflection and organisational learning and change: A case study', in N. Gould, and M. Baldwin (eds) *Social Work, Critical Reflection and the Learning Organisation*, 57–74, Aldershot: Ashgate.

——(2004b) 'Critical reflection and transformative possibilities', in L. Davies and P. Leonard, (eds) *Scepticism/Emancipation: Social Work in a Corporate Era*, 57–74, Avebury: Ashgate.

Fook, J. and Askeland, G.A. (2006) 'The "critical" in critical reflection', in S. White, J. Fook and F. Gardner (eds) *Critical Reflection in Health and Social Care*, 16–31, Maidenhead: Open University Press.

Fook, J. and Askeland, G. (2007) 'Challenges of critical reflection: "Nothing ventured, nothing gained"', *Social Work Education*, 26(5): 520–33.

Fook, J. and Gardner, F. (2007) *Practising Critical Reflection; A Resource Handbook*, Maidenhead: Open University Press.

Fook, J. and Napier, L. (eds) (2000) *Breaking Through in Practice, Theorising Critical Moments in Social Work*, London: Whiting and Birch.

Fook, J., Ryan, M. and Hawkins, L. (2000) *Professional Expertise: Practice, Theory and Education for Working in Uncertainty*, London: Whiting and Birch.

Fook, J., White, S. and Gardner, F. (2006) 'Critical reflection: A review of contemporary literature and understandings', in S. White, J. Fook and F. Gardner (eds) *Critical Reflection in Health and Social Care*, 40–53, Maidenhead: Open University Press.

Ford, P., Johnston, B., Brumfit, C., Mitchell, R. and Myles, F. (2005) 'Practice Learning and the development of students as critical practitioners – Some Findings from research', *Social Work Education,* 24(4): 391–407.

Forester, J. (1999) *The Deliberative Practitioner: Encouraging Participatory Planning Processes*: Cambridge, MA: MIT Press.

Forman, R. (2004) *Grassroots Spirituality*, Exeter: Imprint Academic.

Foucault, M. (1973) *The Birth of the Clinic*, London: Routledge.

——(1979) *The History of Sexuality Volume 1*, trans. R. Hurley, London: Allen Lane.

——(1980) *Power/Knowledge: Selected Interviews and Other Writings*, New York: Pantheon.

——(1981) *The History of Sexuality: 1 The Will to Knowledge*, London: Penguin.

——(1991) *Discipline and Punishment: The Birth of the Clinic*, trans. A. Sheridan, London: Penguin.

Foundation Programme (2008) *Training and assessment.* www.foundationprogramme.nhs.uk/pages/home/training-and-assessment. [Accessed 30th December 2008.]

Freeth, D., Hammick, M., Koppel, I., Reeves, S. and Barr, H. (2002) *A Critical Review of Evaluations of Interprofessional Education*, London: Learning, Teaching and Support Network, Centre for Health Sciences and Practice.

Freire, P. (1972) *Pedagogy of the Oppressed*, Harmondsworth: Penguin.

Freshwater, D. (2005) 'Clinical Supervision in the Context of Custodial Care', in C. Johns and D. Freshwater (eds) *Transforming Nursing Through Reflective Practice*, Oxford: Blackwell.

Froggett, L. (2002) *Love, Hate and Welfare*, Bristol: The Policy Press.

Frost, N. (2003) 'A problematic relationship? Evidence and practice in the workplace', *Social Work and Social Sciences Review*, 10(1): 38–50.

Frost, N. (2005) *Professionalism, Partnership and Joined-Up Thinking*, Totnes: Research in Practice, www.rip.org.uk.

Fuller, A., and Unwin, L. (2002) 'Developing pedagogies for the workplace', in K. Evans, P. Hodkinson and L. Unwin (eds) *Working to Learn: Transforming Workplace Learning*, 95–111, London: Kogan-Page.

Furlong, J. (1995) *Mentoring Student Teachers*, London: Routledge.

——(2000) 'Intuition and the crisis in teacher professionalism', in T. Atkinson and G. Claxton (eds), op. cit. 15–31.

——(2005) 'New Labour and teacher education: The end of an era', *Oxford Review of Education* 31(1): 119–134.

Gear, J., McIntosh, A. and Squires, G. (1994) *Informal Learning in the Professions*, Report of a research project funded by the Higher Education Funding Council for England, Hull: University of Hull.

Gee, J.P. (2005) 'Semiotic social spaces and affinity spaces: From the 'age of mythology' to today's schools', in D. Barton and K. Tusting (eds) *Beyond Communities of Practice: Language, Power and Social Context*, 214–32, Cambridge: Cambridge University Press.

General Medical Council. (2008) *Consent: Patients and Doctors Making Decisions Together*, London: General Medical Council.

Gergen, K.J. (1994) *Realities and Relationships: Soundings in Social Construction*, Cambridge, MA: Harvard University Press.

Gewirtz, S., Ball, S. and Brown, R. (1995) *Markets, Choice and Equity in Education*, Buckingham: Open University Press.

Ghaye, T. (2004) 'Editorial: reflection for spiritual practice?', *Reflective Practice*, 5(3): 291–95.

——(2005) *Developing the Reflective Healthcare Team*, Oxford: Blackwell Publishing.

Gibbons, M., Limoges, C., Nowotny, H., Schwartzman, S., Scott, P. and Trow, M. (1994) *The New Production of Knowledge: The Dynamics of Science and Research in Contemporary Societies*, London: Sage.

Gibbs, G. (1988) *Learning by Doing: A Guide to Teaching and Learning Methods*, Oxford: Further Education Unit, Oxford Polytechnic.

Giddens, A. (1991) *Modernity and Self-identity*, Cambridge: Polity.

——(1999) *Globalisation*, BBC Reith lecture, www.bbc.org.uk.

Gilbert, T. (2001) 'Reflective practice and clinical supervision: Meticulous rituals of the confessional', *Journal of Advanced Nursing*, 36(2): 199–205.

Gillespie, R., Florin, D. and Gillam, S. (2002) *Changing Relationships: Findings of the Patient Involvement Project*, London: The King's Fund.

Gitlin, A. and Smyth, J. (1989) *Teacher Evaluation: Educational Alternatives*, Bristol: Falmer Press.

Glynn, M., Beresford, P., Bewley, C, Branfield, F., Butt, J., Croft, S., Dattani Pitt, K., Fleming, J., Flynn, R., Parmore, C., Postle, K. and Turner, M. (2008) *Person-centred Support: What Service Users and Practitioners Say*, York: Joseph Rowntree Foundation.

Godden, J. (1997) '"For the sake of mankind": Florence Nightingale's legacy and hours of work in Australian nursing 1868–1939', in A.M. Raffertey, J. Robinson, and R. Elkan, *Nursing History and the Politics of Welfare*, London: Routledge.

Goffman, E. (1971) *The Presentation of Self in Everyday Life*, London: Pelican Books.

Goldsmith, J. (1999) *British Medical Journal*, 318, 19 March, eletters, bmj.bmjjournals.com/cgi/eletters/318/7186/dc1. [No longer available online.]

Gould, I. (1996a) 'Social work education and the crisis of the professions', in N. Gould and I. Taylor (eds) *Reflective Learning for Social Work*, 1–10, London: Arena.

——(1996b) 'Using imagery in reflective learning', in N. Gould and I. Taylor (eds) *Reflective Learning for Social Work*, 63–78, London: Arena.

Gould, N. and Taylor, I. (eds) (1996) *Reflective Learning for Social Work*, Aldershot: Arena.

Greenwood, J. (1993) 'Reflective practice: A critique of Argyris and Schön', *Journal of Advanced Nursing*, 18(8): 1183–87.

Grimmett, P.P., Mackinnon, A.M, Erickson, G.L. and Riecken, T.J. (1990) 'Reflective practice in teacher education', in R.T. Clift, W.R. Houston and M.C. Pugach (eds) *Encouraging Reflective Practice in Education,* 20–38, New York: Teachers College Press.

Habermas, J. (1974) *Theory and practice*, London: Heinemann.

Hallam, J. (2000) *Nursing the Image: Media, Culture and Professional Identity*, Routledge: London.

Hargreaves, A. (1994) *Changing Teachers Changing Times: Teachers' Work and Culture in the Postmodern Age*, London: Cassell.

Hargreaves, J. (2004) 'So how do you feel about that?' Assessing reflective practice, *Nurse Education Today*, 24: 196–201.

Hargreaves, J. (2006) 'The Good Nurse: Discourse and Power in Nursing and Nurse Education 1945–55', unpublished thesis, Huddersfield: University of Huddersfield Library.

Harris, G., Dalton, E., Morris, P. (2008) *Continuing Professional Development and Continuing Patient Development: Challenges for Personal Development in Healthcare.* Paper presented at Professional Lifelong Learning: Critical Perspectives on CPD conference, University of Leeds. www.leeds.ac.uk/medicine/meu/lifelong08/papers/penny_morris.pdf. [Accessed January 2009.]

Hart, J.T. (1988) *A New Kind of Doctor: The General Practitioner's Part in the Health of the Community*, London: Merlin Press.

——, (2006) *The Political Economy Of Health Care: A Clinical Perspective*, Bristol: Policy Press.

Hart, M.V. (1990) 'Liberation through consciousness raising', in J. Mezirow and Associates (ed.), *Fostering Critical Reflection in Adulthood: A Guide to Transformative and Emancipatory Learning*, San Francisco, CA: Jossey-Bass.

Hasman, A., Coulter, A. and Asham, J. (2006) *Education for Partnership*. Oxford: Picker Institute.

Hayes, D. (2003) 'Emotional preparation for teaching: A case study about trainee teachers in England', *Teacher Development,* 7(3): 153–71.

Head, G. (2003) 'Effective collaboration: deep collaboration as an essential element of the learning process', *Journal of Educational Enquiry*, 4(2): 47–62.

Heath, H. and Freshwater, D. (2000) 'Clinical supervision as an emancipatory process: avoiding inappropriate intent', *Journal of Advanced Nursing,* 32(5): 1298–306.

Helman, C. (2006) *Suburban Shaman: Tales from Medicine's Front Line*, London: Hammersmith Press.

Helmstadter, C. (2002) 'Early nursing reform in 19th Century London: A Dr. driven phenomenon', *Medical History*, 46: 325–50.

Henkel, M. (1995) 'Conceptions of knowledge and social work education', in M. Yelloly and M. Henkel (eds) *Learning and Teaching in Social Work: Towards Reflective Practice,* London: Jessica Kingsley.

Heron, B. (2005) 'Self-reflection in critical social work practice: Subjectivity and the possibilities of resistance', *Reflective Practice*, 6(3): 341–51.

Heron, J. (1992) *Feeling and Personhood: Psychology in Another Key*, London: Sage.

——(1996) *Co-operative Inquiry: Research into the Human Condition*, London: Sage.

Heywood, J. (2000) *Assessment in Higher Education: Student Learning, Teaching, Programmes and Institutions*, London: Jessica Kingsley.

Hochschild, A.R. (1979) 'Emotion work, feeling rules and social structure', *The American Journal of Sociology*, 85(3): 551–75.

Hull, C. and Redfern, L. (1996) *Profiles and Portfolios*, Basingstoke: Macmillan.

HM Government (2007a) *Mental Health Act*, London: The Stationery Office.

HM Government (2007b) *Strong and Prosperous Communities: The Local Government White Paper; Making it Happen: The Implementation Plan*, London: The Stationery Office.

Hodge, M. (2004) Quoted in *Guardian Society*, 19 July.

Hollway, W. and Jefferson, T. (2000) *Doing Qualitative Research Differently*, London: Sage.

Holmes, C. (2002) 'Academics and practitioners: Nurses as intellectuals', *Nursing Inquiry*, 9 (2): 73–83.

Horder Committee (1943) *Nursing Reconstruction Committee Report*, London: Royal College of Nursing.

Horwath, J. and Shardlow, S. (2003) *Making Links across Specialisms: Understanding Modern Social Work Practice*, Lyme Regis: Russell House.

Horwath, J. and Thurlow, C. (2004) 'Preparing students for evidence-based child and family field social work: An experiential learning approach', *Social Work Education*, 23(1): 7–24.

Hoy, D.C. (1986) *Foucault: A Critical Reader*, Oxford: Blackwell.

Hudson Jones, A. (ed.) (1988) *Images of Nursing*, Philadelphia, PA: University of Pennsylvania Press.

Hugman, R. (1998) *Social Welfare and Social Value: The Role of Caring Professions*, London: Macmillan.

Hunt, C. (1996) 'Review of Becoming a Critically Reflective Teacher: Stephen Brookfield', *Studies in the Education of Adults*, 28(2): 300–302.

——(2001a) 'Shifting shadows: Metaphors and maps for facilitating reflective practice', *Reflective Practice*, 2(3): 275–87.

——(2001b) 'Climbing out of the void: Moving from chaos to concepts in the presentation of a thesis', *Teaching in Higher Education*, 6(3): 351–67.

——(2005) 'Reflective practice', in J.P. Wilson (ed.) (1999; 2nd edn 2005) *Human Resource Development: Learning and Training for Individuals and Organizations*, 234–51, London: Kogan Page.

Hunt, C. and West, L. (2006) 'Learning in a border country: Using psychodynamic ideas in teaching and research', *Studies in the Education of Adults*, 38(2): 160–77.

Hutchings, M. (2007) 'Teach First: 'A cut above the rest'', Paper to a Learning to Teach in Post Devolution UK conference, Roehampton, March.

Hyrkas, K. (2006) 'Clinical supervision: How do we utilise and cultivate the knowledge that we have gained so far?', *Journal of Nursing Management*, 14(8): 573–76.

Issit, M. (2000) 'Critical professional and reflective practice', in J. Batsleer and B. Humphries (eds) *Welfare, Exclusion and Political Agency*, London: Routledge.

Ixer, G. (1999) 'There's no such thing as reflection', *British Journal of Social Work*, 29(4): 513–27.

Jackson, P. (1998) *John Dewey and the Lessons of Art*, New Haven and London: Yale University Press.

Jackson, S. (2006) 'Learning to live: The relationship between lifelong learning and lifelong illness', *International Journal of Lifelong Education*, 25(1): 51–73.

James, N. (1989) 'Emotional labour: Skill and work in the social regulation of feelings', *Sociological Review*, 37(1): 15–42.

Jarvis, P. (1992) 'Reflective practice and nursing', *Nurse Education Today*, 12: 174–81.

Jarzabkowski, P. and Bone, Z. (1998) 'A "how-to" guide and checklist for peer appraisal of teaching', in *Innovations in Education and Training International*, 35(1): 177–81.

Johns, C. (1994) 'Nuances of reflection', *Journal of Clinical Nursing*, 3: 71–75.

——(2004) *Becoming a Reflective Practitioner*, Oxford: Blackwell.

——(2005) 'Expanding the gates of perception', in C. Johns and D. Freshwater (eds) *Transforming Nursing through Reflective Practice*, Oxford: Blackwell.

Jones, A.M. and Hendry, C. (1992) *The Learning Organization: A Review of Literature and Current Practice*, London: Human Resource Development Partnership.

Kalisch, P.A. and Kalisch, B.J. (1987) *The Changing Image of the Nurse*, Menlo Park: Addison-Wesley.

Katz, A.M., Conant, L., Inui, T., Baron, D. and Bor, D. (2000) 'A council of elders: Creating a multi-voiced dialogue in a community of care', *Social Science and Medicine*, 50(6): 851–60.

Kember, D. (2001) *Reflective Teaching and Learning in the Health Professions*, London: Blackwell.

Kennedy, A., Reeves, D., Bower, P., Lee, V., Middleton, E., et al. (2007) 'The effectiveness and cost effectiveness of a national lay-led self care support programme for patients with long-term conditions: a pragmatic randomised controlled trial', *Journal of Epidemiology and Community Health*, 61(3): 254–61.

Kelleher, D. (1994) 'Self help groups and their relationship to medicine', in J. Gabe, D. Kelleher and G. Williams (eds) *Challenging Medicine*, 104–18, London: Routledge.

Kemmis, S. (1985) 'Action research and the politics of reflection', in D. Boud, R. Keogh and D. Walker (eds) *Reflection Turning Experience into Learning*, 139–64, London: Kogan Page.

Kilminster, S., Roberts, T. and Morris, P. (2007) 'Incorporating patients' assessments into objective structured clinical examinations', *Education for Health*, 7: 6. www.educationforhealth.net.

Kitchener, K.S. and King, P.M. (1990) 'The reflective judgement model: Transforming assumptions about knowing', in Jack Mezirow (ed.) *Fostering Critical Reflection in Adulthood: A Guide to Transformative and Emancipatory Learning*, 159–76, San Francisco, CA: Jossey-Bass.

Knights, S., Meyer, L. and Sampson, J. (2007) 'Enhancing learning in the academic workplace through reflective team teaching', *Journal of Organisational Transformation and Social Change*, 4(3): 237–47.

Knights, S. and Sampson, J. (1994) 'Team Teaching as a Vehicle for Action Research', Paper presented and published in the proceedings of World Congress Three on Action Learning, Action Research and Process Management, July 1994, Bath, England, Bath: University of Bath, 115–18.

——(1995) 'Reflection in the context of team teaching', *Studies in Continuing Education*, 17(1&2).

Knowles, M.S. (1980) *The Modern Practice of Adult Education: From Pedagogy to Androgogy*, 2nd edn, New York: Cambridge Books.

Kolb, D.A. (1984) *Experiential Learning*, Englewood Cliffs, NJ: Prentice-Hall.

Kolb, D.A. and Fry, R. (1975) 'Towards an applied theory of experiential learning', in C.L. Cooper (ed.) *Theories of Group Processes*, Chichester: John Wiley.

Kondrat, M.E. (1999) 'Who is the "self" in self-aware? Professional self-awareness from a critical theory perspective', *Social Service Review*, 34(4): 451–77.

Kretzmann, J., McKnight, J. (1993) *Building Communities from the Inside Out*, Chicago: ACTA.

Langer, S.K. (1979) *Feeling and Form*, London: Routledge and Kegan Paul.

Laszlo, E. (ed.) (2003) *The Consciousness Revolution*, Las Vegas, NV: Elf Rock Productions.

Launer, J. (2002) *Narrative-Based Primary Care*, Oxford: Radcliffe Medical Press.

Lave, J. (1990) 'The culture of acquisition and the practice of understanding', in J.W. Stigler, R.A. Shweder and G. Herdt (eds) *Cultural Psychology*, 259–86, Cambridge: Cambridge University Press.

——(1993) 'The practice of learning', in S. Chaiklin and J. Lave (eds) *Understanding Practice: Perspectives on Activity and Context*, 3–32, Cambridge: Cambridge University Press.

Leadbeater, C. (1999) *Living on Thin Air: The New Economy*, Harmondsworth: Penguin.

Levinas, E. (1981) *Otherwise than Being or Beyond Essence*, Pittsburg, PA: Duquesne University Press.

Levenson, R., Dewar, S., Shepherd, S. (2008) *Understanding Doctors: Harnessing Professionalism*, London: Kings Fund.

Littlewood, J. (1991) 'Care and ambiguity', in P. Holden and J. Littlewood (eds) *Anthropology and Nursing*, London: Routledge.

LSE (2006) *The Depression Report. A New Deal for Depression and Anxiety Disorders*, Report by the Centre for Economic Performance Mental Health Policy Group, chaired by Lord Layard, London: LSE.

Lupton, D. (1997) 'Consumerism, reflexivity and the medical encounter', *Social Science and Medicine*, 45(3): 373–81.

Lymbery, M. (2000) 'The retreat from professionalism: from social worker to care manager', in N. Malin (ed.) *Professionalism, Boundaries and the Workplace*, London: Routledge.

——(2006) 'United we stand? Partnership working in health and social care', *British Journal of Social Work*, 36(7): 1119–34.

Maben, J., Latter, S. and Clark, J.M., 2006 'The theory-practice gap: Impact of professional-bureaucratic work conflict on newly-qualified nurses', *Journal of Advanced Nursing*, 55(4): 465–77.

Macdonald, J. (1981) 'Theory-practice and the hermeneutic circle', *Journal of Curriculum Theorising*, 3(2): 130–38.

Macleod, M.L.P. (1996) *Practising Nursing: Becoming Experienced*, New York: Churchill Livingstone.

Maggs, C. (1980) 'Recruitment to Four Provincial Hospitals 1881–1921', in C. Davies (ed.) *Rewriting Nursing History*, London: Croom Helm.

——(1985) *Nursing History: The State of the Art*, London: Croom Helm.

Malderez, A., Hobson, A., Tracey, L., Kerr, K. and Pell, G. (2005) 'Core themes in the experience of becoming a student teacher: Identity, relationships, relevance and emotion', Paper presented at the European Conference on Educational Research, University College, Dublin, September 2005.

Malllinson, S., Popay, J. and Kowarzik, U. (2006) 'Collaborative work in public health? Reflections on the experience of Public Health networks', *Critical Public Health*, 16(3): 259–65.

Manton, J. (1971) *Sister Dora: The Life of Dorothy Patterson*, London: Methuen.

Marsick, V.J. and Watkins, K.E. (1990) *Informal and Incidental Learning in the Workplace*, London: Routledge.

Martin, G. and Double, J. (1998) 'Developing Higher Education Teaching Skills Through Peer Observation and Collaborative Reflection', in *Innovations in Education and Training International*, 35(2): 161–69.

Marton, F. and Booth, S. (1997) *Learning and Awareness*, Mahwah, NJ: Lawrence Erlbaum Associates.

Ments, M.V. (1990) *Active Talk: The Effective Use of Discussion in Learning*, London: Kogan Page.

Merighi, J., Ryan, M., Renouf, N. and Healy, B. (2005) 'Re-assessing a theory of professional expertise: A cross-national investigation of expert mental health social workers', *British Journal of Social Work*, 35(5): 709–25.

Merrill, B. and West, L. (2008) *Using Biographical Methods in Social Research*, London: Sage.

Meyer, J.H.F. and Land, R. (2005) 'Threshold concepts and troublesome knowledge: (2) Epistemological considerations and a conceptual framework for teaching and learning', *Higher Education*, 49: 373–88.

Mezirow, J. (1981) 'A critical theory of adult learning and education', *Adult Education*, 32(1): 3–24.

——(1990) *Fostering Critical Reflection in Adulthood: A Guide to Transformative and Emancipatory Learning*, San Francisco, CA: Jossey-Bass.

——(1991) *Transformative Dimensions of Adult Learning*, San Francisco, CA: Jossey-Bass.

——(1994) 'Understanding transformation theory', *Adult Education Quarterly*, 44: 222–32.

——(1997) 'Transformative learning: Theory and practice', *New Directions for Adult Continuing Education*, 74: 5–12.

——(1998) 'On critical reflection', *Adult Education Quarterly*, 48(3): 185–98.

Mezirow, J. (ed.) (2000) *Learning as Transformation: Critical Perspectives on a Theory in Progress*, San Francisco, CA: Jossey Bass.

Mezirow, J. and Associates (1990) *Fostering Critical Reflection in Adulthood: A Guide to Transformative and Emancipatory Learning*, San Francisco, CA: Jossey-Bass.

Mishler, E.G. (1984) *The Discourse of Medicine: Dialectics of Medical Interviews*, Norwood, NJ: Ablex.

Moon, J. (1999) *Reflection in Learning and Professional Development*, London: Kogan Page.

——(2006) *Learning Journals*, Abingdon: Routledge.

——(2008) *Critical Thinking: An Exploration of Theory and Practice*, Abingdon: Routledge.

Morris, P. (1992) 'The development and evaluation of health education and information-giving skills for medical students and doctors', in *Health Promotion: The Role of the Professional in the Community*, Health Promotion Research Trust, Cambridge.

——(1992) 'Citizens in Health Care', in R. Hambleton and M. Taylor (eds) *People in Cities*, Bristol: SAUS.

Morris, P. and Trafford, P. (2004) 'Learning from patients', in J. Burton and N. Jackson (eds) *Work Based Learning in Primary Care*, Oxford: Radcliffe.

Morris, P., Burton, K., Reiss, M, and Burton, J. (2001) 'The difficult consultation. An action learning project about mental health issues in the consultation', *Education for General Practice*, 12: 19–26.

Morris, P., Dalton, E., Griffiths, J. and Stanley, M. (1998) 'Preparing for Patients: Preparing Tomorrow's Doctors', *Patient Education and Counseling*, 34: S5–S41.

Muir Gray, J.A. (2002) *The Resourceful Patient*. www.resourcefulpatient.org.

Mumford, A. (1995) 'Four approaches to learning from experience', *Industrial and Commercial Training*, 27(8) 12–19.

Munro, E. (2002) *Effective Child Protection*, London: Sage.

Murphy, E., Dingwall, R., Greatbatch, D., Parker, S. and Watson, P. (1998) 'Qualitative research methods in health technology assessment: A review of the literature', *Health Technology Assessment*, 2(16): 1–276.

Napier, L. and Fook, J. (2000) *Breakthroughs in Practice: Theorising Critical Moments in Social Work*, London: Whiting & Birsch.

National Association of Head Teachers (2008) 'School leaders workload continues to increase'. www.naht.org.uk/welcome/resources/key-topics/workload/school-leaders-workload-continues-to-increase/?locale=en. [Accessed 23 February 2009.]

National College for School Leadership (2004a) *NPQICL Volume One*, Nottingham: NCSL.

——(2004b) *NPQICL Volume Four*, Nottingham: NCSL.

National Consumer Council (2008) *Deliberative Public Engagement – Nine Principles*, London: NCC.

National Primary Care Research and Development Centre (2007) *National Evaluation of the Expert Patients Programme*, London: NPCRDC.

Neighbour, R. (1987) *The Inner Consultation: How to Develop an Effective and Intuitive Consulting Style*, Oxford: Radcliffe.

Newman, M. (2006) *Teaching Defiance*, San Francisco, CA: Josey-Bass.

Newton, J.M., Jolly, B.C, Billett, S., Cross, W.M. and Kelly, C. (2007) 'Engaging in learning in nursing practice', Royal College of Nursing, UK 1st International Nurse Education conference, Brighton, UK, 5–7 July.

Newton, J.M. and McKenna, L. (2007) 'The transitional journey through the graduate year: A focus group study', *International Journal of Nursing Studies* 44(7): 1231–37.

Nicholson, H. (1999) 'Aesthetic values, drama education and the politics of difference', *Aesthetic Learning*, 23(2): 75–91.

Nightingale, F. in V. Skretkowicz (1992) *Florence Nightingale's Notes on Nursing*, London: Scutari Press.

Nolan, M. R., Brown, J., Davies, S., Nolan, J. and Keady, J. (2006) 'The senses framework: Improving care for older people through a relationship-centred approach', Getting Research into Practice (GRiP) Report no. 2, Sheffield: University of Sheffield.

Noddings, N. (1964) *Caring: A Feminine Approach to Ethics and Moral Education*, Berkeley, CA: University of California Press.

Nursing and Midwifery Council (2008) *The Prep Handbook*. www.nmc-uk.org/aFrameDisplay. aspx?DocumentID=4340. [Accessed 30 December 2008.]

Nussbaum, M. (1997) *Cultivating Humanity: A Classical Defense of Reform in Liberal Education*, Cambridge, MA: Harvard University Press.

Obholzer, A. and Roberts, V.Z. (1994) *The Unconscious at Work*, London and New York: Routledge.

Olesen, H.S. (2001) 'Professional identity as learning process in life histories', *Journal of Workplace Learning*, 13(7/8): 290–97.

O'Neill, F. (2002) *Developing a Strategic Approach to User and Carer Involvement in Pre-registration Nursing and Midwifery Education in Leeds*, Leeds: University of Leeds.

Page, S. and Meerabeau, L. (2004) 'Hierarchies of evidence and hierarchies of education: reflections on a multiprofessional education initiative', *Learning in Health and Social Care* 3(3): 118–218.

Parsons T., Fox, R. (1985) 'Illness and the role of the physician: A sociological perspective', *American Journal of Orthopsychiatry*, 21: 452–60.

Parton, N. (2003) 'Rethinking professional practice: The contribution of social constructionism and the feminist "ethics of care"', *British Journal of Social Work*, 33(1): 1–16.

Parton, N. (2006) *Safeguarding Children*, Basingstoke: Palgrave.

Patient's Voice Conferences 'Where's the Patient Voice in Health Professional Education?' Vancouver, 2005. www.health-disciplines.ubc.ca/DHCC. [Accessed 4 December 2008.]

——Patient and Community Voices in Professional Learning. Cambridge, 2006. www.leeds. ac.uk/medicine/meu/voices06/index.html. [Accessed 4 December 2008.]

——Authenticity to Action. Cumbria, 2007. www.uclan.ac.uk/healthconf. [Accessed 4 December 2008.]

Parton, N. and O'Byrne, P. (2000) *Constructive Social Work*, Basingstoke: Palgrave.

Payne, M. (2002) *Social Work Theories and Reflective Practice*, London: Palgrave.

Peavey, F. (1994) 'Strategic Questioning', in T. Green and P. Woodrow (eds) *Insight and Action*, Philadelphia, PA: New Society.

Pendleton, D., Schofield, T., Tate, P. and Havelock, P. (1984) *The Consultation: An Approach to Learning and Teaching*, Oxford: Oxford University Press.

Phillips, V. and Bond, C. (2004) 'Undergraduates' experiences of critical thinking', *Higher Education Research and Development*, 23(3): 277–94.

Picker Institute (2007) *Doctor and Patient: Implementing 'Good Medical Practice'*. www.pickereuro pe.org/Filestore/Downloads/PCP_event_outcomes.doc.

Plummer, K. (2001) *Documents of Life 2*, London: Sage.

Poell, R.F., Chivers, G.E., Van der Krogt, F.J. and Wildermeersch, D.A. (2000) 'Learning network theory: Organizing the dynamic relation between learning and work', *Management Learning*, 31(1): 25–49.

Polanyi, N. (1967) *The Taat Dimension*, New York: Doubleday.

Pollock, K. (2006) *Concordance in Medical Consultations: A Critical Review*, Oxford: Radcliffe.

Postgraduate Medical Education and Training Board (2008) *Patients' Role in Healthcare: The Future Relationship between Patient and Doctor*. www.pmetb.org.uk/fileadmin/user/Content_an d_Outcomes/Working_group_reports/Patients_Role_in_Healthcare_working_group_repor t20080620_v1.pdf.

Power, M. (1997) *The Audit Society: Rituals of Verification*, Oxford: Oxford University Press.

Progoff, I. (1992) *At a Journal Workshop*, New York: Putnam.

Prosser, M. and Trigwell, K. (1999) *Understanding Learning and Teaching: The Experience in Higher Education*, Buckingham: Open University Press.

Rabinow, P. (ed.) (1984) *The Foucault Reader*, London: Penguin.

Raffertey, A.M. (1996) *The Politics of Nursing Knowledge*, London: Routledge.

Raffertey, A.M., Robinson, J. and Elkan, R. (1997) *Nursing History and the Politics of Welfare*, London: Routledge.

Rai, L. (2006) 'Owning (up to) reflective writing in social work education', *Social Work Education*, 25(8): 785–97.

Randle, J. (2003a) 'Bullying in the nursing profession', *Journal of Advanced Nursing*, 43(4): 395–401.

Randle, J. (2003b) 'Changes in self esteem during a three year Pre-Registration Diploma in Higher Education (Nursing) Programme', *Learning in Health and Social Care*, 2(1): 51–60.

Reber, A.S. (1993) *Implicit Learning and Tacit Knowledge; An Essay on the Cognitive Unconscious*, London: Oxford University Press.

Reder, P. and Duncan, S. (2004) 'Making the most of the Victoria Climbié inquiry report', *Child Abuse Review*, 13(2): 95–114.

Redfern, M. (2001) *The Report of the Royal Liverpool Children's Inquiry*, London: The Stationery Office.

Redmond, B. (2006) *Reflection in Action*, Aldershot: Ashgate.

Rees, D. and Johnson, R. (2007) 'All together now? Staff views and experiences of a pre-qualifying interprofessional curriculum', *Journal of Interprofessional Care*, 21(5): 543–55.

Reid, H. (ed.) (2008) *Constructing a Way Forward: Innovation in Theory and Practice for Career Guidance*, Occasional paper, Canterbury: Centre for Career and Personal Development.

Reynolds, M. (1999) 'Reflection and critical reflection in management learning', *Management Learning*, 29(2): 183–200.

Reynolds, M. and Vince, R. (eds) (2004) *Organizing reflection*, Aldershot and Burlington, VA: Ashgate.

Richards, N., Coulter, A. (2007) *Is the NHS Becoming more Patient-Centred? Trends from the National Surveys of NHS Patients in England 2002–7*, Oxford: Picker Institute Europe.

Rivett, G. (2006) *From the Cradle to the Grave; 50 Years of the NHS*, London: Kings Fund. www.nhshistory.net. [Accessed I January 2009.]

Rogoff, B. (1990) *Apprenticeship in Thinking: Cognitive Development in Social Context*, New York: Oxford University Press.

Rogoff, B. (2003) *The Cultural Nature of Human Development*, Oxford: Oxford University Press.

Rogoff, B. and Lave, J. (eds) (1984) *Everyday Cognition: Its Development in Social Context*, Cambridge, MA: Harvard University Press.

Rolls, S., Davis, E. and Coupland, K. (2002) 'Improving serious mental illness through interprofessional education', *Journal of Psychiatric and Mental Health Nursing*. 9: 317–24.

Roper, M. (2003) 'Analysing the analysed: Transference and counter-transference in the oral history encounter', *Oral History*, Autumn, 20–32.

Royal College of General Practitioners (2008a) *Good Medical Practice for General Practitioners*. www.rcgp.org.uk. [Accessed December 2008.]

——(2008b) *Revalidation for General Practitioners Consultation*. www.rcgp.org.uk/news – events/ college_viewpoint/current_consultations/revalidation.aspx. [Accessed 20 December 2008.]

Royal College of Nursing (2004) *Transcultural Healthcare Practice*. www.rcn.org.uk/resources/ transcultural/clinicalsupervision/index.php. [Accessed 4 February 2008.]

Royal Pharmaceutical Society of Great Britain (2008) *Consultation on CPD Professional Standards and Guidance and the Handling of CPD Cases*. www.rpsgb.org/pdfs/cpdconsultationdoc. pdf. [Accessed 4 December 2008.]

Ruch, G. (2005a) 'Reflective practice in contemporary child care social work: The role of containment', *British Journal of Social Work*, 37: 659–80.

——(2005b) 'Relationship based practice and reflective practice: Holistic approaches to contemporary child care social work', *Child and Family Social Work*, 10: 111–23.

Ruskin, J. (1895) *Sesame and Lilies*, London: George Allen.

Ryan, M., Dowden, C., Healy, B. and Renouf, N. (2005) 'Watching the experts: findings from an Australian study of expertise in mental health work', *Journal of Social Work*, 5(3): 279–98.

Salinsky, J. and Sackin, P. (2000) *What are you Feeling Doctor?* Oxford: Radcliffe.

Salter, B. (2004) *The New Politics of Medicine*, London: Palgrave Macmillan.

Salzberger-Wittenberg, I., Williams, G. and Osborne, E. (1999) *The Emotional Experience of Learning and Teaching*, London: Karnac.

Sampson, J. and Cohen, R. (2001) 'Designing peer learning', in D. Boud, R. Cohen and J. Sampson (eds), 221–34, *Peer Learning in Higher Education*, London: Kogan Page.

Savage, J. (1987) *Nurses, Gender and Sexuality*, London: Heinemann Nursing.

Sawicki, J. (1991) *Disciplining Foucault: Feminism Power and the Body*, New York: Routledge.

Schatzki, T.R. (2001) 'Introduction: Practice theory', in T. Schatzki, K. Knorr Cetina and E. von Savigny (eds) *The Practice Turn in Contemporary Theory*, 1–14, London: Routledge, London.

Scholte, J.A. (2000) *Globalization: A Critical Introduction*, Basingstoke: Palgrave.

Schön, D. (1963) *Displacement of Concepts*, London: Tavistock Publications.

——(1983) *The Reflective Practitioner: How Professionals Think in Action*, London: Temple Smith.

——(1987) *Educating the Reflective Practitioner*, San Francisco, CA: Jossey-Bass.

Schwandt, T. (2005) 'On modelling our understanding of the practice fields', *Pedagogy, Culture & Society*, 13(3): 313–32.

Scott Peck, M. (1978) *The Road Less Travelled*. London: Arrow Books.

Scribner, S. (1985) 'Vygostky's use of history', in J.V. Wertsch (ed.) *Culture, Communication And Cognition: Vygotskian Perspectives*, 119–45, Cambridge: Cambridge University Press.

Senge, P.M., A. Kleiner, Roberts, C., Ross, R. and Smith, B. (1994) *The Fifth Discipline Fieldbook: Strategies and Tools for Building a Learning Organisation*, New York: Doubleday.

Sennett, R. (1998) *The Corrosion of Character*, New York: W.W. Norton.

Sfard, A. (1988) 'On Two Metaphors for Learning and the Dangers of Choosing just One', *Educational Researcher*, 27(2): 4–13.

Sheehan, D., Wilkinson, T. and Billett, S. (2005) 'Junior doctors participation and learning in clinical environments', *Academic Medicine*, 80: 302–8.

Sheppard, M. (1995) 'Social work, social science and practice wisdom', *British Journal of Social Work*, 25(3): 265–93.

Shields, S. (2005) 'The politics of emotion in everyday life: "Appropriate" emotion and claims on identity', *Review of General Psychology*, 9(1): 3–15.

Silverman, J., Kurtz, S. and Draper, J. (1998) *Skills for Communicating with Patients*. Oxford: Radcliffe.

Sinclair, S. (1997) *Making Doctors*, Oxford: Berg.

Skelton, J.R. (2005) 'Everything you were afraid to ask about communication skills', *British Journal of General Practice*, 55: 40–46.

Skills for Health. (2006) *Quality Assuring Healthcare Education in England: Service User and Learner Involvement, Event Report*. www.skillsforhealth.org.

Smith, A.C. and Kleinman, S. (1989) 'Managing emotions in medical school: Students' contacts with the loving and the dead', *Social Psychology Quarterly*, 52(1): 56–69.

Smith, J. (2002) *Death Disguised: The First Report of the Shipman Inquiry,* London: HMSO.

Smith, P. (1992) *The Emotional Labour of Nurses*, Basingstoke: Macmillan.

Smith, R. (2001) 'Why are doctors so unhappy?', *British Medical Journal*, 322: 1073–74, May.

Smith, S. and Karban, K. (2006) 'Tutor experiences of developing an interprofessional learning (IPL) programme in higher education: Recognising a parallel process', unpublished paper.

Smith, S. and Roberts, P. (2005) 'An investigation of occupational therapy and physiotherapy roles in a community setting', *International Journal of Therapy and Rehabilitation*, 12(1): 21–29.

Stanley, L. (1992) *The Auto/biographical I*, Manchester: Manchester University Press.

Starns, P. (2000) *The march of the matrons*, Peterborough: DSM.

States, B. (1985) *Great Reckonings in Little Rooms: On the Phenomenology of Theatre*, Berkeley, CA: University of California Press.

Steinberg, D. (2005) *Complexity in Healthcare and the Language of the Consultation*, Oxford: Radcliffe.

Stenhouse, L. (1980). 'The study of samples and the study of cases', *British Educational Research Journal*, 6(1): 1–6.

Stephenson, J. (1995) 'Significant Others: Primary trainee view of practice in schools', *Educational Studies*, 21: 309–18.

Stepney, P. (2006) 'Mission impossible? Critical practice in social work', *British Journal of Social Work* 36(8): 1289–307.

Sternburg, R.J. (2003) *Wisdom, Intelligence and Creativity Synthesized*, Cambridge: Cambridge University Press.

Stoekle, J. (ed) (1987) *Encounters between Patients and Doctors: An Anthology*, Cambridge, MA: MIT Press.

Streubert, H.J. and Carpenter, D.R. (1999) *Qualitative Research in Nursing*, Philadelphia, PA: Lippincott.

Sullivan, W. (1995) *Work and Integrity: The Crisis and Promise of Professionalism in America*, New York: Harper Business.

Summers, A. (1988) *Angels and citizens, British Women as Military nurses 1854–1914*, London: Routledge and Kogan Page.

Swanson, K.M. (1991) 'Empirical development of a middle range theory of caring', *Nursing Research*, 40(3): 161–66.

Sweet, J. (2003) 'Curriculum', in J. Sweet, S. Huttly, and I. Taylor (eds) *Effective Learning and Teaching in Medical, Dental and Veterinary Education,* 51–70, London: Kogan Page.

Tate, S. (2004) 'Using critical reflection as a teaching tool', in S. Tate, and M. Sills *The development of Critical Reflection In the Health Professions,* Occasional paper no. 4. www.health-academy.ac.uk/publications/occasional.paper.

Taylor, C. (2003) 'Narrating Practice: Reflective accounts and the textual construction of reality', *Journal of Advanced Nursing*, 42(3): 244–51.

——(2006) 'Narrating significant experience: Reflective accounts and the production of (self) knowledge', *British Journal of Social Work*, 36(2): 189–206.

Taylor, C. and White, S. (2000) *Practising Reflexivity in Health and Welfare*, Buckingham: Open University Press.

——(2001) 'Knowledge, truth and reflexivity: The problem of judgement in social work', *Journal of Social Work*, 1(1): 37–59.

Taylor, K., Marienau, C. and Fiddler, M. (2000) *Developing Adult Learners*, San Francisco, CA: Josey-Bass.

Tew, J., Gell, C. and Foster, S. (2004) *Learning from Experience: Involving Service Users and Carers in Mental Health Education and Training*, London: Mental Health in Higher Education.

Thistlethwaite, J. and Morris, P. (2006) *The Patient–Doctor Consultation in Primary Care: Theory and Practice*, London: Royal College of General Practitioners.

Tilly, L. and Scott, J. (1987) *Women, Work and Family*, New York: Routledge.

Todres, L. (2007) *Embodied Enquiry*, Basingstoke: Palgrave Macmillan.

Tovey, M. and Lawler, D. (2008) *Training in Australia*, 3rd edn, Sydney: Pearson Education.

Towle, A. and Godolphin, W. (1999) 'Framework for teaching and learning informed shared decision making', *British Medical Journal*, 319: 766–69.

Trent Strategic Health Authority (2005) *Principles for Practice: Involving Service Users and Carers in Health Care Education and Training*, Nottingham: TSHA.

Tuckett, D., Boulton, M., Olsen, C. and Williams, A. (1985) *Meetings between Experts: An Approach to Sharing Ideas in Medical Consultations*, London: Tavistock.

Tsang, N.M. (2007) 'Reflection as dialogue', *British Journal of Social Work*, 37: 681–94.

Usher, R. and Bryant, I. (1989) *Adult Education as Theory, Practice and Research*, London: Routledge.

Usher, R., Bryant, I. and Johnson, R. (1997) *Adult Education and the Post-modern Challenge: Learning beyond the Limits*, London: Routledge.

Valsiner, J. (2000) *Culture and Human Development*, London: Sage.

Value for People (2007) *Public Service Co-Production*. www.valueforpeople.co.uk/co_production. [Accessed 24 February 2009.]

Van Lehn, V. (1989) 'Towards a theory of impasse-driven learning', in H. Mandl and A. Lesgold (eds) *Learning Issues for Intelligent Tutoring Systems*, 19–41, New York: Springer-Verlag.

Van Manen, M. (1977) 'Linking ways of knowing with ways of being practical', *Curriculum Inquiry*, 6(3): 205–28.

Van Ness, P. (1996) *Spirituality and the Secular Quest*, New York: Crossroad.

Vince, R. (2001) 'Power and emotion in organizational learning', *Human Relations*, 54(10): 1325–51.

Wanless, D. (2002) *Securing our Future Health: Taking a Long Term View*, London: HM Treasury.

Waterson, J. and Morris, K. (2005) 'Training in "social" work: Exploring issues of involving users in teaching on social work degree programmes', *Social Work Education*, 24(6): 653–75.

Weinstein, J., Whittington, C. and Leiba, T. (eds) (2003) *Collaboration in Social Work Practice*, London: Jessica Kingsley.

Weinstein, K. (1999) *Action Learning: A Practical Guide*, Aldershot: Gower.

Wellington, B. and Austin, P. (1996) 'Orientations to reflective practice', *Educational Research*, 38(3): 307–16.

Wenger, E. (1998) *Communities of Practice*, Cambridge: Cambridge University Press.

Wenger, E., McDermott, R. and Snyder, W. (2002) *Cultivating Communities of Practice,* Boston: Harvard Business School.

West, L. (2001) *Doctors on the Edge,* London: FABooks.

——(2007) 'An auto/biographical imagination: The radical challenge of families and their learning', in L. West, P. Alheit, A. Anderson and B. Merrill (eds) *Using Biographical and Life History Methods in the Study of Adult and Lifelong Learning: European Perspectives,* Hamburg: Peter Lang/ESREA.

West, L. and Carlson, A. (2006) 'Claiming and Sustaining Space: Sure Start and the auto/biographical imagination', *Auto/biography,* 14(4): 359–80.

West, L. and Carlson, A. (2007) *Claiming Space: An in-depth Study of a Local Sure Start Project.* Canterbury: CCCU.

White, S. (1997) 'Beyond retroduction? Hermeneutics, reflexivity and social work', *British Journal of Social Work,* 27(5): 739–53.

White, S. and Featherstone, B. (2005) 'Communicating misunderstandings: Multi-agency work as social work practice', *Child and Family Social Work,* 10(3): 207–16.

Whitehouse, C., Marks, B., Morris, P. (1984) 'The role of actors in teaching medical communication', *Medical Education,* 18: 139–46.

Wilks, T. (2005) 'Social work and narrative ethics', *British Journal of Social Work,* 35(8): 1249–64.

Williams, K. (1978) 'Ideologies of nursing: Their meanings and interpretation', in R. Dingwall and J. McIntosh (eds) *Readings in the Sociology of Nursing,* Edinburgh: Churchill Livingstone.

Williamson, L. (2001) 'Entering into the spirit of nursing: Holistic healers past an present', *International History of Nursing Journal,* 6(1): 18–26.

Willis, P. (2004) 'Mentorship, transformative learning and nurture: Adult education challenges in research supervision', in C. Hunt (ed.) *Whose story now? (Re)generating research in adult learning and teaching,* 319–26, Sheffield: University of Sheffield/SCUTREA.

Wilson, J.P. (2008) 'Reflecting-on-the-future: A chronological consideration of reflective practice', *Reflective Practice* 9(2): 177–84.

Winnicott, D. (1971) *Playing and Reality,* London: Routledge.

Woerkom, M., Van Nijhof, W.J. and Loek, F.M.N. (2002) 'Critical reflective working behaviour: A survey research', *Journal of European Industrial Training,* 26(8/9): 375–83.

World Health Organisation (2005) *Preparing the Workforce for the 21st Century.* Geneva, World Health Organisation.

Woodman-Smith, C. (1950) *Florence Nightingale,* London: Constable and Company.

Wright Mills, C. (1959 and 1970) *The Sociological Imagination,* Harmondsworth: Penguin.

Wykurz, G. and Kelly, D. (2002) 'Developing the role of patients as teachers: Literature review', *British Medical Journal,* 325: 818–21.

Yelloly, M. and Henkel, M. (eds) (1995) *Learning and Teaching in Social Work: Towards Reflective Practice,* London: Jessica Kingsley.

Zohar, D. and Marshall, I. (2000) SQ: *Spiritual Intelligence: The Ultimate Intelligence,* London: Bloomsbury.

Zuboff, S. (1988) *In the Age of the Smart Machine,* New York: Basic Books.

Index

LaVergne, TN USA
23 July 2010
190540LV00002B/21/P